LA'S EARLY MODERNS

Art / Architecture / Photography

Victoria Dailey — Natalie Shivers — Michael Dawson
Introduction by William Deverell

Balcony Press — Los Angeles

Published in the United States of America, 2003

No part of this book may be reproduced in any manner without written permission
except in the case of brief quotations embodied in critical articles and reviews.
For information address Balcony Press, 512 E. Wilson Suite 213, Glendale, California 91206.

LA's Early Moderns © 2003 William Deverell, Michael Dawson, Victoria Dailey, Natalie Shivers

Cover image: Knud Merrild. *Untitled Abstraction*. Construction: oil on wood, 1936.
First page: Prints on view at Zeitlin's bookshop, c.1936.

Designed by Distinc
Printed by Pace + Navigator, California

Library of Congress Catalog Card Number: 2002103808
ISBN 1-890449-16-4

Contents

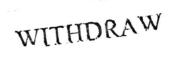

Introduction
by William Deverell

"Can there be any doubt but what Los Angeles is to be the world's greatest city. . . greatest in all of the annals of history? Can there be any doubt . . . that she has touched the imagination of general public opinion as no other city in history has touched the millions?"
–*Why Los Angeles will become the World's Greatest City*, 1923 [1]

Los Angeles has a rich and vibrant modernist past, stretching back to the earliest years of the twentieth century. That would seem natural, at least at first glance. After all, Los Angeles came of age as a metropolis in the first half of the twentieth century–exactly those heady decades of modernism's birth and exuberant adolescence. More to the point, rising Los Angeles was incessantly advertised and boosted precisely as "the city of the future." A moniker like that might suggest an urban environment receptive to modernist goals. Real estate promotions, banquet addresses, Chamber of Commerce testimonials–pamphlet after pamphlet and speech after speech–shouted out the promise of Los Angeles as the locale, the very model, of the urban future. The city would host the future, boosters promised, and the world would watch and learn from the Southern California example.

Yet we would be mistaken to assume that Los Angeles modernists and Los Angeles boosters had a common cause. Looking for modernism sprouting amidst the flowery language of Los Angeles boosterism is looking in precisely the wrong place. The very future boosted by the hyperactive promoters of early twentieth-century Los Angeles did not represent anything like the break with tradition we commonly associate with modernist aesthetics. To the Los Angeles booster the future looked better, certainly, than the present, but it didn't look fundamentally different. Those doing all the shouting about Los Angeles' future in the first half of the twentieth century were shouting about today as much as they were about tomorrow.

Ironically, all those exclamations about the future had a reactionary purpose to them. Boosters had no interest in refashioning Los Angeles in any profound –or even mundane–sense. Champions of Los Angeles as the city of the future worked themselves up into breathless enthusiasm in part to maintain their positions of power, authority, and privilege. The extolled future Los Angeles, in the collective mind's eye of its boosters, worked well for the prominent establishment figures and institutions of the present–exactly those groups and individuals well positioned and oiled enough to do the boosting.

But there were also the Los Angeles modernists whose vision of the future looked different, whose work sprung from the conviction that the future must be different. In the following essays, we meet people whose commitment to modernism made them virtual anti-boosters. The two groups shared a faith in Los Angeles as the city of the future, but any commonality immediately falls away when respective ideas about the future are compared. Nor did the modernists do much shouting. That collection of men and women pulling Los Angeles towards a different future–the extended family of artists, photographers, and architects described here–went about their work more quietly.

Modernism and Los Angeles, as these essays reveal, came together much earlier than we might have thought. Victoria Dailey, Natalie Shivers, and Michael Dawson push the take-off moments of regional modernism backward at least a full generation before the great influx of exiles seeking refuge from fascism and the Holocaust. We know that the contributions of those refugee musicians, artists, playwrights, novelists, architects, painters, and others were of inestimable artistic importance, but as these three essays attest, those refugees arrived in a Los Angeles in which critical modernist steps had

7

already been taken by a handful of pioneers. Dailey, Dawson, and Shivers teach us to view these pioneers as the early modernist fabric of Los Angeles. One of the thrills of reading these three essays is to see how intertwined these lives were, and how the "modernist project" of painters, photographers, and architects was itself furthered by ties of personal loyalty and mutual respect.

These are essays rich, and rightly so, in biographical detail. And yet we glimpse a metropolitan backdrop to the modernist picture painted here. Early twentieth-century Los Angeles is busily piecing together the infrastructure necessary to support the era's outlandish demographic growth and physical expansion. By the beginning of the twentieth century, Los Angeles had coaxed the federal government into carving a harbor at San Pedro. Within a decade, city leaders convinced fellow Angelenos that building (and paying for) an aqueduct 250 miles northeast to the Owens River would abate, for a time at least, the thirst borne of enthusiastic growth.

Engineer William Mulholland's success at convincing Angelenos to buy aqueduct bonds had everything to do with both implicit and explicit images of hearth and home. Aqueduct boosterism marketed a fully watered Los Angeles as Everyman's California Dream. With enough water, Los Angeles would be the very model of the prosperous metropolis. All workers would be able to afford single-family homes. Good jobs would be plentiful. The city and region would continue its planned decentralization, factories and industrial concerns would spread through the basin and suburbs would be connected by the spokes of transit lines. It was a rosy future, a quaint and pretty future.

Mulholland's plans to get water from the Sierra Nevada had once looked like fancy, if not fantasy. But by 1913, he'd done it. Civic pride swelled that same year with the opening of the Los Angeles Museum of History, Science, and Art, an institution sprung to life by a state, county, and city partnership and anointed in its infancy by aqueduct water splashed on its roses. An art exhibit added to the fanfare, and Angelenos who had cheered Mulholland flocked to their new museum, every bit the cultural counterpart to the coming of age that new water symbolized. What kind of museum, and what kind of museumgoer, would arise in "the city of the future?"

Stereotype suggests that we know those Angelenos who went to that 1913 show. The booster exhortation to "come west and see the future" had already been shouted from the rooftops for decades. Although the message spread round the globe, it was the Midwest that answered the call with Biblical devotion. Los Angeles has long been a diverse place, but there is no doubt a Midwestern cast to the place from the turn of the century forward, one that seems at odds with modernist ambitions.

Dailey offers perspective on this in her essay "Naturally Modern." In New York, as she points out, crowds gathered in 1913 to see the famed Armory Show. Art patrons and the curious public stood before Marcel Duchamp's *Nude Descending a Staircase* and wondered if the abstraction might be too far removed from conventional depiction; the subject matter was not a concern. Out west, Angelenos winced at Childe Hassam's painting of a nude. Angelenos cared little about technique and more about morality. In Los Angeles, nudes were the problem, not the manner in which they were represented.

Pre-World War I years in Los Angeles were flush times for important artists, artists doing far more than filling tourist demands for quaint scenes on planks of orangewood, or building conventional houses, or making sentimental photographs. The regional modernist story begins right alongside the triumph of the aqueduct and the auspicious Los Angeles Museum. It is hardly surprising that it is their work, amid a few important traditionalist offerings, that has lasted.

Divided, as the other two essays, into biographical portraits, Dailey's piece is a terrific introduction to the modernist personalities that so changed the artistic landscape of Los Angeles. As her essay makes clear, we would do well to think of the early Los Angeles modernists, regardless of medium, as a school, held together as much by social relations as shared artistic vision. The two strains were, in fact, overlapping. Long evenings over wine and food and free-ranging talk in local bookshops reinforced community and art at the same time. The picture is a compelling and attractive one—lives soldered together by shared aesthetic sensibilities, by love, by comradeship and solidarity sprung from artistic experimentation.

Certain figures stand out, and still seem to stand these eighty years later. Bookseller/gallery owner Jake Zeitlin, impresario Merle Armitage, patron Galka Scheyer, painter Paul deLongpre: each lived and worked at the center of vibrant, miniature colonies they created and sustained. They created a structure of artistic production, patronage, and camaraderie that those refugee modernists coming to Los Angeles in the war and post-war eras would inherit.

All three authors make good arguments about a "take-off" moment in Los Angeles modernism that occurred just as the twentieth century got underway. Like modernist transitions everywhere, this represented a change in direction, rather than a movement arising from nothingness. Regional impulses in photography, architecture, and art pre-dated the rise of Los Angeles modernism. Each of the three essays sketch precursor themes and practitioners well and explicitly trace the temporal and aesthetic boundaries within which modernist sensibilities first arose in Los Angeles.

It is not timing that is of importance here but actual perceptions of time. For if we pause to ponder those artists whose work does not fit beneath the modernist rubric (or who have pre-modernist examples in their portfolios), it is not terribly difficult to see a pattern emerge regarding visions of the regional past. Pre-modernists expected a certain kind of Los Angeles past to be their muse, and they did not have to look very hard to find it.

That past is sentimental, hazy, sun-dappled. It is rife with ethnic stereotype. It is a Los Angeles often described as "sleepy." That vision of somnolence occupied the attention of Los Angeles writers, photographers, and painters, and sleepy became the watchword descriptor of town, region, and people. The adjective stood in for all manner of other descriptions: pre-capitalist, pre-modern, lazy, primitive, Catholic. "I first visited Los Angeles in 1867," wrote inveterate booster Benjamin Truman. "Crooked, ungraded, unpaved streets; low, lean, rickety, adobe houses, with flat asphaltum roofs, and here and there an indolent native, hugging the inside of a blanket, or burying his head in a gigantic watermelon, were the, then, most notable features of his quondam Mexican town."[2] Angeleno Andrew Copp noted in his 1920s autobiography that the "half Mexican" population of 1870s Los Angeles were "reported to walk in their sleep most of the twenty-four hours."[3]

But of course the problem in all these visions of the region was not sleepiness. The unspoken problem was what "sleepiness" stood in for-non-white. Pre-modernist photographer and painters embraced this vision of the Los Angeles past. This past offered them quaint subject matter for their art; this past presented itself in sentimental repose. Perhaps less consciously, this past also allowed boosters to claim that their Los Angeles, the Los Angeles of the late 19th and early 20th centuries, had finally arrived. For painters, the

Will Connell. *Portrait of Jake Zeitlin.*
Photograph, c.1928. (Private Collection)

Will Connell. *Portrait of Merle Armitage.*
Photograph, c.1930. (Private Collection)

attractions were often of the "eucalyptus school" variety—artists carefully fit twilight mission scenes into landscape views. For photographers, ethnic Los Angeles exerted an irresistible pull: amateur and professional camera operators alike focused on the street corners and alleys of Chinatown or Sonoratown, offering images of racial and ethnic types every bit as inflexible and fixed as any booster pamphleteer. Such a vision, in which the ethnic past and the ethnic present co-existed, hit a cultural nerve among the region's residents and tourists alike. It was comforting, and it sold.

The modernists broke with this pattern. As Dailey writes, modernists found the regional past nothing but a "worn-out relic." That aesthetic break was perhaps most subtle in regional photographic circles. Again the critical moment is the point at which Sierra Nevada aqueduct water assured the metropolitan future of greater Los Angeles. Within a year, the Camera Pictorialists of Los Angeles came together over their shared interest in pictorialism's impressionistic qualities. As a move towards fine art photography, pictorialism represented a very real break with the photographic past. Yet the genre's aesthetic principles, which could easily slide towards hazy sentimentalism in both thought and technique, rendered it susceptible to nostalgia and the "sleepy school." As pictorialism evolved into fine art photography—a transition in which Southern California artists play crucial roles—modernism made a cleaner break with the past.

Michael Dawson's rich survey takes us through such key stages in the region's "fire of photographic enthusiasm" from the late 19th century forward. These practitioners are an eclectic group, some of whom we might wish had not answered the call of the motion picture industry. What contributions might they otherwise have made to fine art photography? Just as his fellow essayists have done, Dawson concentrates on careful genealogical research. Here we meet many of the now-obscure photographers of the first half of the twentieth century: Herve Friend, Louis Fleckenstein, Fred Archer.

Then there's Edward Weston, the prime modernist photographer on the west coast, if not the nation. Dawson makes a pyramid of his essay, with Weston placed at the top. What comes before him is foundational, and what comes after is a decrescendo. This makes sense, for Edward Weston was far ahead of the curve, and his reputation as one of the first and best of the American modernists can only grow over time. Like Thoreau, Weston was a wanderer and a walker, ever cognizant of nature. Los Angeles at this point is still Walden, an environment not yet victimized by the landscape degradation to which we have long since become inured. Again like Thoreau, Weston grew in his work. His artistic genius is in part the result of the dynamism of his practice and technique—a vitality clearly absent from the work of most of his contemporaries.

Modernists accepted at least one tenet of the booster vision—that Southern California would show the world how to re-think health and physicality. Southern California modernism, with Weston again as the de facto leader, fairly drips with exuberant physical display, even sensuality, as a particular manifestation of health consciousness. In this ironic way, key notes of the booster call—Southern California's climate and healthfulness—were re-shaped to modernist designs.

It was not only the painters and the photographers who overturned quaint perspectives on place and past. Architects battled booster claims on aesthetics as well. Southern California architecture embraced a vision of the regional past every bit as contrived and controlled as that found in any booster literature. Take the era's obsession with Mission Revival architecture, for instance.

When viewed from the angle suggested by Shivers, Mission Revival is but little more than Anglo re-casting of an adobe past: appropriative and, at heart,
deeply traditional. 1910s and 20s sloganeering about Mission-style architecture championed a debt to European tradition. But that reach back to Old
World inspiration deliberately ignored the modernist excitement of European
architecture at that very moment.

Shivers also employs an implicit geometry in her discussion of modernist
architecture. Richard Neutra sits at the pyramidal summit, supported by Irving
Gill and Rudolph Schindler. As Shivers describes the setting, modernist architecture in the first decades of the twentieth century sprung from wishful
progressive social change. Low-cost modernist housing designs, which reach
an aesthetic and political apex in the Case Study Houses of later years, are on
the landscape in these early years. They did not always succeed. Gill's model
industrial town plan for Torrance, which he planned with the sons of Frederick
Law Olmsted, failed. But modernist successes such as Gill's Dodge House, in
which he "elevated concrete to the dignity of stone" or Frank Lloyd Wright's
Hollyhock House, clearly represent breakthrough moments regionally and the-
matically. There's nothing "revival" about them.[4]

The second generation of regional modernists such as Gregory Ain, Lloyd
Wright, and Albert Frey carried on in much the same way as the pioneering
generation before them. They, too, kept reformist social aims in mind as they
planned. Shivers points out that Lloyd Wright had a hand in the design of
several famed public housing projects in the city, a fact that should serve as
reminder of what public housing once meant to engaged reformers in Los
Angeles and elsewhere.

These modernist pioneers of Los Angeles art and architecture made statements in their work and legacies, but they were every bit as much a
community as they were individual satellites of expression. It isn't just that they
knew one another, though that is abundantly clear. Galka Scheyer, Walter and
Louise Arensberg, Jake Zeitlin, Merle Armitage, Harriet and Sam Freeman,
and a few dozen others: This was a circle. But the larger point is that this
circle transcended the loose bonds of acquaintance. These people gathered
in solidarity, met as friends and lovers, and shared the excitement of making
important breaks with tradition. In modest but lasting ways, they changed
modernism forever. This collective story remains largely hidden from view, but
that has at last begun to change. This secret Los Angeles, filled with optimism
about a different kind of "city of the future," deserves a wider telling.

William Deverell is Associate Professor of History at the California Institute of Technology. He is
co-editor of *Metropolis in the Making: Los Angeles in the 1920s* and co-author of Eden by Design:
The 1930 Olmsted-Bartholomew Plan for the Los Angeles Region, both published by the University
of California Press.

Footnotes

[1] Sherley Hunter, *Why Los Angeles will become the World's Greatest City* (Los Angeles: H. J. Mallen and Co., 1923), p. 29.

[2] Benjamin Truman, *Semi-Tropical California: Its Climate, Healthfulness, Productiveness, and Scenery* (San Francisco: A.L. Bancroft, 1874): 27.

[3] Andrew James Copp, *Autobiography of Andrew James Copp* (Sierra Madre, CA: Sierra Madre Press, 1927), 46. Similarly, the booster pamphlet "Greater Los Angeles Illustrated" recalled the Los Angeles of the mid-nineteenth century as "untouched by any spirit of progress, culture or art. ... [witness to] the lethargic going to and fro of a somnolent collection of human beings unconscious of the beauties and glories of the encompassing woods and hills, and the exquisite penciling of landscape, sea and sky." "Greater Los Angeles Illustrated," compiled by The Pictorial American (Los Angeles, ca. 1906): 39.

[4] For more on, especially, Gill and the modernist consistency of his work from the earliest years of the twentieth century forward, see Thomas S. Hines, *Irving Gill and the Architecture of Reform* (New York: Monacelli Press, 2000). An insightful overview of regional built forms, one that also enshrines Gill as a breakthrough figure, is William Alexander McClung's *Landscapes of Desire: Anglo Mythologies of Los Angeles* (Berkeley: University of California Press, 2000), see esp. 110-112; "concrete to the dignity of stone" quote from McClung, 112.

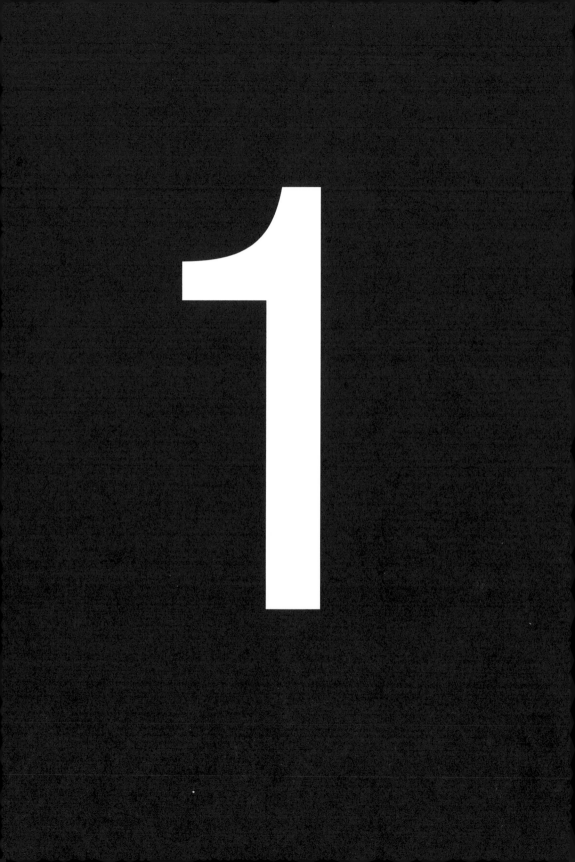

Art

NATURALLY MODERN

by Victoria Dailey

Contents:

Foreword

Foreword

I have been involved with and thinking about the art of Southern California created before World War II for some twenty years, and it has often been a lonely pursuit. Very few people have shared my interest, and I have often received blank stares from otherwise knowledgable art collectors when I mention my interest. Usually I receive a response on the order of "Oh, you mean artists like David Hockney and Ed Ruscha?" "No," I tell them, "while I love the work of Hockney and Rusha, they are not the ones I am referring to. In fact, there is a whole history of modern art in Los Angeles that precedes World War II, and there are several artists I find worthwhile including Knud Merrild, Henrietta Shore, Peter Krasnow, Elise and Paul Landacre." More blank stares. If my interlocutor seems intrigued, I begin to give a little lecture on the history of art in Los Angeles. Lately however, I have noticed a greater interest in Los Angeles' past, and a recognition that indeed, a Los Angeles art world existed before the 1960s. Rather than give informal lectures to those I encounter at random, I decided to write a book about the subject so that anyone interested, not just those I meet personally, could have access to information I have been gathering over the years.

After carefully studying the period, I winnowed down to five the number of artists to include in my book. I did not want the book to be an encyclopedic overview of the period, but rather, an in-depth study of five artists who, as emblems of their era, could give a reader a good idea of what modernism in Los Angeles was all about. This meant excluding such artists as Ben Berlin, whose career and output were slight; Lorser Feitelson and Helen Lundeberg, who have received attention elsewhere; Warren Newcombe and Richard Day, whose main careers were as set designers, and Grace Clements, whose influence came about more through her teaching and writing rather than her artwork. While I do discuss Stanton McDonald Wright, I did not include him as one of the five because his main achievement as an artist was the work he did mainly in Paris before he returned to Los Angeles after World War I. The five artists I chose all had careers as artists, and all were original and innovative. Their work may be viewed within the context not just of Los Angeles, but within American art in general. I also wanted to give attention to artists who were not exclusively painters, and chose Krasnow for the decade he spent as a sculptor and Landacre, who worked only as a printmaker.

I also wanted to provide information on the milieu in which the artists lived and worked, and to give credit to the enormous contributions made by bookseller Jake Zeitlin and impresario Merle Armitage. They provided an arena in which modern artists could flourish, and without their help and support, many artists would have had a difficult, if not impossible, time as modernists in Los Angeles.

As the 21st century begins, it seems fitting to look back and bring to light those who may have been overlooked during the last fifty years. I hope that in the coming years, these artists will receive the attention and acclaim they deserve, and trust that they will be incorporated into the fabric of American art history. I hope that when their names are mentioned, they will be greeted with nods, and that blank stares will be a thing of the past.

"We would hold great parties… we would broil lobsters, and have great songfests, and dance, and talk, and shout."

−Jake Zeitlin, recalling the 1930's parties held by Los Angeles writers, artists and bohemians.

1

The Eucalyptus School

"Climate, cinema, citrus, construction, plus Chambers of Commerce produced this modern Cinderella." –Merle Armitage

Los Angeles faced a crisis at the beginning of the twentieth century. It was running out of water. In this land of little rain, the city had grown like an exotic weed, unstoppable and unexpected, and if more water could not be found, the growth of this unusual city would be stunted. A trickle in summer and a torrent in winter, the Los Angeles River had been the city's main water supply, but it could not sustain a population greater than several hundred thousand. In 1900, there were 100,000 Angelenos and in 1910, the population swelled to 300,000. The city desperately needed water, and in a scheme of gigantic proportions, the city's thirst was quenched. Water diverted from the Owens River over two hundred miles to the northeast could sustain a population of two million, and a proposal to build an aqueduct was enthusiastically endorsed by Los Angeles voters in 1905.[1] Design and planning commenced immediately under the direction of the city's chief water engineer, William Mulholland, and construction of the largest water transportation system in the Western Hemisphere began in 1908. On November 5, 1913, a gala event was held to celebrate the completion of the aqueduct at its terminus in the San Fernando Valley. After the laudatory speeches and tributes by various city officials, and after the drum rolls, music and gun salutes, the giant spigot was turned to release the first gallons of aqueduct water. As the water began to rush through the canal, over thirty thousand cheering celebrants heard Mulholland declare with characteristic bluntness: "There it is. Take it."

As part of the great aqueduct celebration, Exposition Park and the newly built Los Angeles County Museum of History, Science and Art opened the next day.[2] While Angelenos had enthusiastically endorsed the aqueduct, art was another matter. Everett C. Maxwell, art critic for the Los Angeles Graphic and the museum's first art curator, was well aware of the difficulties he faced in interesting the public in the new venue. His speech might well have been: "There it is. Take it. Please." It had been a struggle of more than twenty years to found and build a museum in the rapidly growing city where most citizens cared more for amusement than art.[3] It would be difficult to bring people indoors to look at paintings when the pleasures of mountain, beach or garden enticed.

Angelenos celebrate the opening of the
Museum of History, Science and Art
in Exposition Park, November 6, 1913.
(Private collection)

Squabbles within the art community were also threatening the museum. In his column written just days after the museum's opening, Maxwell commented "an art gallery must be a co-operative proposition if it is to be a real force. The public, the artist and the press must all lay aside petty feeling and narrow-minded intrigue and put their shoulders to the wheel and push."[4] Maxwell was certainly referring to the recent controversy surrounding the museum's opening exhibition in which some members of the community objected to one painting among a group of 27 pictures by prominent American artists, a nude by American Impressionist Childe Hassam. The inclusion of the nude caused a great deal of consternation to some of the local women who had participated in fund-raising for the museum, and they did not want their efforts culminating in a display of female flesh. Headlines in one local paper satirized the problem: "Art Censors May Fight Display of Fine Work. Word 'Nude' Gives Committee Chills, Fever," while the headline in the Los Angeles Times ran: "Childe Hassam, Value $2000, Loaned for Public Gallery, Causes Apprehension." Mrs. William H. Housh, chairman of the museum's art committee,[5] museum board member and wife of the principal of Los Angeles High School, had to ponder the issues: Would children be permitted in the gallery? Would ministers declare the new museum a corrupter of morals? Mrs. Housh summed up the problem when she spoke before fellow members of the Ruskin Art Club, a prominent women's group dedicated to the study of art: "Some have said they hoped this would be the only public gallery of the country where nudes would never be exhibited, but the art committee does not take that position."[6] Mrs. Housh and the art committee prevailed, the exhibition took place and Los Angeles would have a museum where nudes could be exhibited. Although there had been a similar controversy on the East Coast that same year over a painting of a nude, it was not nudity that caused New Yorkers to react with hostility to Marcel Duchamp's *Nude Descending a Staircase*, on exhibit at the tradition-shattering Armory Show. It was just the opposite—it was the modern way in which she was depicted. In New York in 1913, a nude could descend a staircase, as long as she looked like a nude woman, but in Los Angeles, the very fact that she was nude was objectionable. New Yorkers worried over style. Angelenos fretted over content, and their objections to such subject matter hardly abated with

time. Although Los Angeles became home to numerous faddists, cultists, and counter-culturists, it was also a bastion of sober, conservative-minded traditionalists, and its artists were divided along similar lines.

Those who advocated traditional art, the artists whose landscapes were sold mainly to tourists, found modern, abstract work unskillful and ugly. The modernists, or "purists," regarded the work of the "tourists" as hackneyed, old-fashioned and dull. The tourist vs. purist debate became a major issue in Los Angeles art, and the battle between traditional and new was part of another looming issue to which Maxwell must have been referring in his article, the recent tiff brought about by William Wendt, the leading California landscape artist of the day and the chief exponent of the tourist group. When the museum opened, the California Art Club, with Wendt as its president, objected to the rule that in order to exhibit, artists had to submit pictures individually to a jury. The club, founded in 1909, was made up of artists who worked in the prevalent *plein air* style and represented the status quo. With a jury judging their work, club members risked losing their preeminence, especially if a jury was composed of modern-leaning artists. Wendt adamantly believed that the club should submit work as a group, unscrutinized by a jury. Furthermore, he stated that "our organization should have been given charge of opening the art exhibit of the museum…"[7] Although the painters in the debut exhibition were mostly traditional (including California artists Elmer Wachtel, Granville Redmond, Gardner Symons, Paul de Longpré and Franz Bischoff), there were several modern artists, including George Bellows, Helena Dunlap, Maurice Prendergast and Irving Couse. Wendt did not want to cede control of the Los Angeles art community, and he deeply resented any usurpation of his power. The Los Angeles Graphic reported that there was "widespread comment upon the fact that the California Art Club, comprising the majority of recognized artists in Southern California, is, as such, unrepresented in the newly-opened Los Angeles County Museum… [This] brought to light yesterday [the] severely-strained relations between the club and the committee in charge of the art exhibits in the great museum… As a result, the club has declined to recognize the Museum of Art."[8] Rather than compromise, the California Art Club held its own exhibition downtown at Blanchard Hall in a move reminiscent of the Impressionists' Salon des

Refusés of 1874. In this dramatic showdown, Wendt was positioning for the continued power of the club, and when thwarted, he simply refused to recognize the fledgling museum. With this daring move, Wendt and his colleagues proved that the museum would have a difficult, if not impossible time mounting exhibitions of work by local artists, and the museum would lose the support of those it needed most. The museum soon solved the problem by abandoning the jury system in favor of what were called "loan exhibitions": letters would be sent to individual artists requesting that they "loan" pictures for specific exhibitions. This was satisfactory to the club, and although the controversy ended, it underscored the power of the California Art Club over the local art scene.

After its controversy-plagued start, the museum undertook an energetic program of exhibiting work by local, national and international artists, showing work by traditional and modern artists. Some of the traditional exhibitions during 1914–15 were *American Watercolors* and *Paintings by George Inness*, while some of the modern exhibitions were *Paintings by Robert Henri* and *Watercolors by Donna Shuster*. Curator Maxwell also began a schedule of exhibiting California artists in solo shows that lasted for two weeks. In December, 1914, there was an exhibition of Francis McComas followed by one devoted to Henrietta Shore; in January, 1915 husband and wife Elmer and Marian Kavanaugh Wachtel shared the spotlight; in February, 1915, there were exhibitions by Wendt and Jean Mannheim. A year later, the *First Annual Exhibition of Paintings by Contemporary Artists* was displayed in the spring of 1916. Being a juried show, it marked a reversal in museum policy, and demonstrated the reconciliation between the museum and the California Art Club. A prize was awarded for the best canvas, which was purchased by the museum for its permanent collection. The five-person jury was composed of none other than William Wendt, along with Guy Rose, Alice Klauber, Robert Harshe and Antony Anderson.[9] Other groups also began to hold their annual exhibitions at the museum, including the Print Makers of Los Angeles, the Arts and Crafts Salon, the Camera Pictorialists, the California Water Color Society and the Painters and Sculptors of Southern California. The Los Angeles art community was an active one, and the museum brought cohesion to the local art scene. It also represented authority and approbation, becoming the focal point for the art community, a place

Paul de Longpre's home in Hollywood, c.1901.

Paul de Longpre at home, c.1902. (Private collection)

The artist's Mission Revival-Moorish style home was a major tourist attraction.

Paul de Longpre. *Yellow Roses and Bees.*
Watercolor, 1904. 12 3/4 x 18 inches.
Courtesy William A. Karges Fine Art.

where artists could meet one another and view recent work, and where the public could see and learn about contemporary art.

Although Los Angeles had no museum before 1913, attempts to organize an art museum had begun as early as 1887, when artist J.H. Von Keith remarked that "at present our lovely city has no public collection of paintings or natural history specimens worthy of a name. But a year ago I organized a society for this very purpose… but the chief members are for the time absorbed in reaping the great pecuniary benefits of the real estate boom while our artists are languishing for support and encouragement."[10] By the 1890s, the city had a growing and educated citizenry, and the museum movement gained momentum, spurred on by the series of art exhibitions held at the Chamber of Commerce during 1894–95. Among those who exhibited were J. Bond Francisco, J.G. Borglum, Fannie Duvall and Elmer Wachtel.

Around the turn of the century, as Von Keith described, many artists did languish in Los Angeles. Yet some began to succeed when they realized they could profitably sell souvenirs of California to visitors. Local artists, who were painting landscapes in a style derived from French Impressionism, soon found customers in the well-heeled tourists from the East and Midwest. The grand hotels that had been built throughout the Southland catered to their guests' every wish, and provided not only elegant accommodations, but also arranged concerts, tours, and recreational activities. They also housed souvenir shops where local crafts were on display, including woodcarving, shell work, and photographic views. Artists, noticing that tourists were buying such items in quantity, realized they could sell their paintings as well, although tourists were renowned for their disinclination to spend more than a few dollars for a souvenir. "Many of the Eastern visitors carry Kodaks with them so that they do not care to buy anything in art for more than two dollars…"[11]

By the turn of the century, numerous hotels boasted art galleries, including the Los Angeles Biltmore, the Ambassador, the Beverly Hills Hotel, and the Vista del Arroyo in Pasadena. Artists also sold work directly to collectors, and several buildings housed artists' studios. The Blanchard Building in downtown Los Angeles opened in 1899 with ground floor commercial space, artists' studios on the upper floors and an exhibition hall featuring a changing exhibit each month. The Blanchard Building was also home to the Ruskin Art

William Wendt. *Late Afternoon*.
Oil on canvas, 1923. 25 x 30 inches.
(Courtesy William A. Karges Fine Art)

Club, founded in 1888, which was dedicated to the study of art.[12] Among those to exhibit at the Blanchard Building in 1899 was Paul de Longpré, a French artist who had arrived in Los Angeles in March of that year after having spent nearly ten years in New York.

De Longpré, more than any other artist, fostered the notion of the artist-as-tourist-attraction, setting the stage for the next generation of Southern California artists to appeal to tourists. Like Monet at Giverny, de Longpré created a garden that served both as inspiration and attraction. Already an artist with a national reputation, de Longpré became even more popular in Los Angeles; his beautiful watercolors of flowers (roses were his specialty) were so sought after that he turned his home into a tourist attraction. Wagonloads of visitors would arrive at de Longpré's exotic, palatial house and luxuriant garden and come away with one of his originals. If this proved too expensive, there were high quality reproductions available. Known as "The King of the Flower Painters," de Longpré built his Mission Revival-Moorish style villa in Hollywood in 1900, and the estate was soon pictured in a slew of postcards and pamphlets and touted as one of the leading tourist destinations.

Unlike de Longpré, most other artists ventured out into the countryside for inspiration. Unspoiled, wild and fragrant, the mountains and valleys of Southern California offered an entirely new subject for artists. Several groups of artists coalesced in and around the areas that had earlier been established as health and pleasure resorts, including the beach village of Laguna, the seaside resort of Santa Barbara and the canyons and arroyos of Pasadena, while many artists lived in Los Angeles, conveniently central to all the remote locations.

Most of these landscape artists valued simplicity and preferred the natural pleasures of the outdoors rather than the artificial environment of the expanding city. They were emblematic of the Arts and Crafts aesthetic of the time, preferring to record the beauties of nature unspoiled by man. In this, they continued the American 19th century landscape tradition and were its last practitioners. The sun-drenched coastline, the hillsides covered with sycamores, oaks and chaparral and the wildflowers carpeting the valleys all offered vistas of remarkable beauty. A brisk trade in California views afforded many artists a good living, and by the early 1900s, Impressionism became the style preferred by California artists and their patrons. It would be the mainstay of the Los Angeles art market for nearly half a century. Although the bright colors and saturated palettes at first struck many observers as unusual, and perhaps a bit too modern, this initial reaction soon gave way to acceptance and support, so much so that artists became numerous and their work began to seem repetitive. The majesty of nature, so central to 19th century painting, was interpreted and redeveloped in California, the last remaining American outdoor paradise. While the East had lost much of its natural beauty to industrialization, California remained untouched and nature was still imparting her wonders to those artists in search of communion with her.

Arthur Millier, long time art critic for the Los Angeles Times, described the local scene as follows:

"...the homogeneity of the Southern California landscape school, which can at times seem rather tame and obvious [can be traced] to the fact that... William Wendt and others, once they had discovered the new country, settled down to acquaint themselves with it more intimately than had the earlier painters, choosing small, rather than grand, subjects and seeking for truth of appearance."[13]

Impresario Merle Armitage was more acerbic in his description of the local landscape artists. Soon after his arrival in the early 1920s, he observed that

"Southern California was infested with a whole group of academic and semi amateur painters, many of whom sold their works surprisingly well. They painted the brilliant scene in pallid colors, making use of the fuzziness of the many eucalyptus trees, and the absence of sharp esthetic content was the common denominator that identified their works. ...I dubbed this group the 'Eucalyptus School,' a name still current and valid."[14]

2

Beyond Doubt Or Peradventure

Los Angles was a city unlike any other in America, and it followed no known pattern. Los Angeles was a novelty and became a place for the new, the untried, and the offbeat. Its attractions were nature-based and carefree, not heavy with the burdens of history, culture or society. While Mrs. Astor might be giving a ball in New York for her four hundred carefully selected guests, the businessmen of Los Angeles were making plans for the annual Los Angeles Flower Festival and Fiesta, a street celebration open to all. Los Angeles didn't follow the rules. The city had grown wildly since 1885, when the Santa Fe Railroad opened its first direct route from Chicago, and Los Angeles became the most advertised city in the world. The advertising worked. The city, confident, determined, and with a touch of arrogance, proudly announced after it had secured the water it needed: "That which Los Angeles has not and wills not, is not." [15]

When Los Angeles' will to build a museum was realized in 1913, plans were already underway for a grand celebration to mark the opening of the Panama Canal, a waterway which would bring California into direct contact with world markets. With its recently completed deep-water harbor at San Pedro, Los Angeles had become the major port on the West Coast, while San Francisco and San Diego were hosts to the canal festivities during 1915–16, and in both venues, art exhibitions were held. The Panama-Pacific International Exhibition in San Francisco contained the largest international art exhibition ever held in the United States with 8,000 works of art. There was an entire room assigned to Edvard Munch, a room for the Italian Futurists, and a section for the Impressionists, including Monet, Renoir, Pissarro and Sisley. Modern American artists who exhibited at the PPIE included Bellows, Frieseke, Glackens, Henri, Sloan and numerous others. California artists were also well represented at the fair; among them were Wendt, Dixon, McComas, Braun, Hobart, and Mathews. Some of the American artists who exhibited in San Francisco also sent work to the San Diego venue, the Panama California Exposition, where works by Luks, Sharp, Prendergast, Glackens, Pene du Bois, Sloan, Hassam, Henri, Lawson and Bellows were shown and offered for sale in a small exhibition in the Fine Arts Building.

The exhibits, in San Francisco and San Diego, together with the publication of a monumental volume, *Art in California*, gave credibility to the West Coast as an art center for the first time. No longer a provincial outpost, California was linked to the world and California art began to be accepted as a distinct entity within American art. As one reviewer noted in 1916, "Art in California is entering a new era in incalculable significance. The state has been definitely detached from provincialism by the strong tide of new life created by the Exposition and *[Art in California]* proves beyond doubt or peradventure the exceptional worth and surprising variety of the art created by Californians."[16]

The opening of the Panama Canal, on August 15, 1914 made California more accessible to the world, changing the pastoral, outdoor way of life that had been distinctively Californian. What had initially attracted people to California was soon to be altered, if not destroyed. The natural beauty of the state would be eroded by the very immigrants who were enchanted by it. California would undergo change, and its art world was not immune to new ideas and trends. A growing state with an unparalleled climate proved irresistible to thousands. People were pouring in, and a new culture was in the making.

3

The Futility Of Painting Facts

"At approximately the beginning of this [20th] century many artists came to the conclusion that the future of art lay in abstract development. The literal representation of objects was believed to be a completely exhausted field. The men of the renaissance had solved the problem of space; the impressionists were masters of the rendition of light on the surface of things… The more adventurous and original artists, having become impressed with the futility of painting facts, were moved by a powerful compulsion to abandon the imitation of surfaces, or photographic appearance." –Merle Armitage

In Western art, the abandonment of imitation and the release from narrative became known as modernism, and it arrived in Los Angeles around 1913 along with those other portends of the future, the Panama Canal, the aqueduct and the art museum. Modernism had developed, mainly in France, when artists realized that the invention of photography in 1839 had freed art from duplicating objective reality. The artist's task changed, and art changed. Art was no longer the medium for conveying collective cultural values; it became an arena in which individuals expressed their private visions, and when photography took over the task of duplicating reality, the course of art changed.[17]

With the waning power of monarchy and clergy, artists were no longer called upon to paint the political and religious images that had been demanded of them for the past five hundred years, nor were they required to paint idealized portraits of aristocratic subjects; they became free to paint in an entirely new way. Abandoning history, time and place, artists became modern, and art began to look strange, unrecognizable and indecipherable. Because the resulting painted images were not necessarily based in the observable world, the public became confused. Whereas an average viewer might look at a painting by Rembrandt and visually understand it, he could only look bewilderingly at a Manet, which looked unfinished, or at a Picasso, which was unintelligible. The context of art changed, and images were no longer readily identifiable by a bewildered public. Just as photography had released art from verisimilitude in mid-century, motion pictures released it from narrative by the century's end. When the job of story telling was appropriated by cinema, art began to deal with abstract issues; art became not a story about something else, but about itself. It took the public

Stanton Macdonald Wright. *Synchromy, Cubist Head*. Oil on canvas, 1916. 36 x 28 inches. (Steve Martin Collection)

a long while to adjust to this new role for art, and many people never did.

Modernism underwent many mutations, and each new art movement was based on a new source, many of which had origins in science. Science was changing and challenging basic assumptions in Western culture and its effect on art was profound. Discoveries in physics, chemistry, medicine, and biology would all reverberate in art. Photography, the culmination of the study of optics, was the first link in this chain and further research into the nature of vision and perception was expressed in one of the earliest of the new movements, Symbolism. Taking fantasies and myths as subject matter, Symbolists interpreted the past as poetry rather than as history, and posed questions about the interpretation of the past. In their search for poetic experience and their inquiry into the nature of perception, many Symbolists induced hallucinatory experiences through the use of such psychoactive drugs as opium and hashish, incorporating into their work the dreamy and sometimes terrifying images that resulted. Art began to scare the public, and artists began to enjoy confusing the bourgeoisie upon whom the art market now depended. Symbolism's subsequent offshoot, Surrealism, went a step further, taking dreams and the unconscious as subject matter in response to the discoveries of Freud, whose *Interpretation of Dreams* appeared in 1899. Artists began to mine the unconscious. Deep emotional states, sex, or just weird thoughts became new territory for expression.

Impressionism originated in the study of optics, colors and perception, and was largely based on the research of M. E. Chevreul, who published his monumental work *De La Loi du Contraste Simultane des Couleurs* in the seminal year 1839.[17A] Taking the issue of perception even further, Cubism, by depicting objects from more than one point of view, paralleled Einstein's relativity theory, first published in 1905. Time and space no longer appeared linear, and artists reacted to a newly defined universe. Motion pictures also began to influence the static art of painting when artists, after seeing reverse action in film, began to disassemble and rearrange objects from everyday life. Ultimately, modernism reached its conceptual end when all theories and sources collapsed with Dada, which declared that art was whatever the artist decided was art, precipitating post-modernism.

Just as photography altered the way artists responded to the world, another force changed the way artists rendered it: Japanese art. Its impact in the West was immense. When Japan re-entered the world market in 1854 after two hundred years of self-imposed isolation (the Japanese imposed a ban on foreign trade in 1640), the Japanese prints that circulated in Europe, mainly in Paris, were a revelation to artists drilled in the rules of perspective and anatomy. Japanese prints, with their bright colors, bold decoration, flattened perspective and strong diagonals, had a huge effect on all the arts. Japanese art became the rage, as artists, among them Van Gogh, Monet and Whistler, collected Japanese prints and porcelain, while other artists founded Japanese art clubs. Japanese art was simple and profound at the same time, and cut through the cluttered sensibilities of late 19th century European art and decoration. Japanese art proved that observation need not be literal and that reality was flexible, and thereby prepared Western art for abstraction. The study of Japanese art also led Western artists to discover other exotic sources, among them, African, Mexican and pre-Columbian art. The combination of photography, scientific discoveries and exotic art, especially Japanese, changed the course of Western art and created modernism, the umbrella term for all of the non-traditional art movements that appeared throughout the West.

By the 1910s, artists were primed for innovation. Finding the past a worn-out relic, artists sought to express what was becoming known as "modern." After World War I especially, old patterns of manners and morals were changing; those born in the 1880s and 1890s had a vision different from that of their parents. Inspired by science and non-Western art and fed up with copying Old Masters, art students sought new ways to represent the world. For them, the idea mattered, not its outward manifestations. They sought the world within the world, and with Japanese art as inspiration, artists pared down and simplified their images. Artists began to redefine the world in spare, taut versions based not on narrative, not on the old idea of beginning-middle-end, but on multi-dimensional viewpoints derived from Einsteinian physics. Art, like science, became theoretical, speculative, difficult to understand. Art no longer showed the world as it appeared, and confusion ensued.

The public no longer recognized art, and artists no longer painted for the general public. The older generation of artists, those outdoor enthusiasts who advocated the physical experience of nature, was looked upon as old-fashioned by intellectual, manifesto-oriented young artists seeking to transform art. Their elders had looked to nature as inspiration and subject; these new artists looked to the forces within nature. A tree was no longer a biological thing but a metaphor for the sum of its parts: life force, color, shape. Since the invention of photography, a person was no longer the observable sitter in a painted portrait: he was the conglomeration of his attitudes, moods and physicality. Artists defended their new vision with fervor, and faced immense struggles with a bewildered and hostile public. In the United States, the message of modernism was being spread from coast to coast, at the Armory Show in New York and at the Panama-Pacific International Exhibition in San Francisco. In the forty years from 1875 to 1915, art had changed dramatically. But not everyone rode the crest of the new wave. Some artists preferred the old, traditional ways, others stayed within the confines of the first wave of modernism and painted in a style derived from Impressionism, while some explored the edges of artistic possibility. By 1915, one could choose one's own brand of modernism.

In the United States, the modern had always been welcome, and modernism, in a political sense, had been imbedded as one of the country's founding principles. Defying history, the United States became the first country to declare as one of its founding principles the right to pursue happiness. Pleasure had certainly been sought, but happiness was not a goal a common man could pursue in any previous society. The pursuit of happiness was a remarkable new right, and it did not take long for Americans to embrace it. They became the standard-bearers of progress and technology in order to pursue happiness, and Americans either invented or fully developed most of the hallmarks of modernism: the telegraph, electricity, railroads, the skyscraper, jazz, the assembly line, the automobile, the airplane, the telephone, cocktails, movies, radio, television, air-conditioning, refrigeration, swimming pools, blue jeans, psychoanalysis, physical fitness—nearly everything that made life modern.

4

Unwelcome Stranger

In Los Angeles, where the American pursuit of happiness was never in jeopardy, and just when California landscape art was at its height, a group of artists dissented from this cultural vision and insisted on looking at things from a new perspective, as artists throughout the Western world were doing. Elizabeth Bingham, art critic for Saturday Night, wrote in 1924 that "in Los Angeles, we treat modern art as an intruder, a stranger, unwelcome within the gates."[18] Few members of the public discerned the integrity of the new art, but eventually, the modernists would succeed, in theory if not in practice. It was the same with the allied arts of architecture, music and typography. A few radicals came to define a new movement, but they were rarely popular in their own time and found little in the way of work or commissions. The first modern buildings in Los Angeles, Irving Gill's Dodge House, 1916 and Frank Lloyd Wright's Hollyhock House, 1917–20, had little impact on most Angelenos, who ignored these departures from tradition. Los Angeles architects Rudolph Schindler and Richard Neutra stand out as innovative, clearly modern architects, but they were responsible for only a small number of buildings. Most homeowners preferred the comforts of the familiar, the Spanish, the Colonial, the Tudor. Few patrons had the ability to peer through their own illusions and aspirations, and could not accept the dream of modernism.

It was the same with art patrons. Very few could find value in the new modern art, yet there were some. New Yorkers Walter and Louise Arensberg brought a major collection of modern art to Los Angeles when they settled permanently in 1927, and they held a salon attended by members of the modernist community.[19] Ruth Maitland, a friend of the Arensbergs, also supported and acquired works by local modern artists. The director Josef von Sternberg assembled a major collection of European modern art, which was exhibited at the Los Angeles Museum in 1935, and he acquired work by several Los Angeles artists as well.[20] Various art dealers supported local artists working in a modernist vein, and several curators promoted the new art and held museum shows to which these artists contributed. But many of the modern artists had to earn their living teaching or working as set designers in Hollywood, while some relied on a spouse to bring in a small income. It was difficult to make a living selling pictures, and these artists did not appeal to the tourist market, as did the traditional artists. The prevailing aesthetic, landscape-based, conservative and repetitive, was rejected by the modernists, and they in turn, were usually rejected by the public.

California landscape artists had little need for intellectual art theories; they just wanted to go on painting landscapes for a ready market. Los Angeles in 1913, still known mainly as a health resort, was not at the forefront of art theory. Yet the climate and natural beauty of Los Angeles attracted not only landscape artists, but others, some of whom were interested in the new ideas filtering in from New York and Europe. The first modernist group in Los Angeles was formed in 1916, the Los Angeles Modern Art Society. Its members included Henrietta Shore, Meta and Bert Cressey, Helena Dunlap, Edgar Kellar and Karl Yens. With the exception of Shore, these artists do not stand out today as particularly modern, but at the time, their loosely painted, brightly colored canvases were in contrast to the prevailing trends.

Mabel Urmy Seares, a Los Angeles art critic, wrote perceptively on the problem modern artists faced in Southern California in a 1917 article:

"No one has yet painted the Pacific Coast country as it first appears to the Eastern tourist… The misty land of the north coast, and the enchanting stretch of alternating fog and sunshine from Humboldt to Ventura have long been represented in the tonal school of painting… But not until the advent of broken color, brilliant contrasts and direct painting from nature in its modern high key has the tourist's own little section of the southern part of the State found true interpretation… In the little artificial towns with their miles of concrete walks and bordering palm trees, the red-tiled roofs and gleaming plastered walls give to the modern painter inspiration in striking contrasts…"[21]

This first showing of Los Angeles' modern artists was greeted enthusiastically in the press. Mary Dubois, critic for the Los Angeles Graphic, wrote that "the insincere, the mawkish, the imitative, the atrophied in art might just as well consider themselves in the debris now, for they will eventually be but a heap of shattered wood and splinters… Watch out! Los Angeles is still, we must confess it, to be put on the art map and, if I mistake not, these artists are the ones who will do it." It was not just the art that struck the visitor as modern; the entire exhibit was designed to reveal something new. The artists had made special chairs "in keeping with the spirit of modernity. They are painted in creamy white, with effective touches of black, relieved by painted flowers of many hues… It differs from the usual exhibition… The sunshine pouring through the windows, the furniture of bold and striking design, the high-keyed canvases in their simple white frames, the prevailing air of modernity is contrasted with the usual dim, dank exhibition interior."[22]

This exhibition marked a departure from traditional shows, and by the 1920s, the Los Angeles Museum was holding large exhibitions of modern art. In February 1920, it hosted an exhibition of painting by American modernists which included work by Demuth, Dove, Hartley, Man Ray, Sheeler and Stella, some of the country's pioneering modernists. The appearance of such work in Los Angeles was unprecedented, and helped to bring together local artists experimenting with new ideas. The catalogue preface, written by Stanton Macdonald Wright, expressed the aims and ideals of the modernists: "We modern artists are just what our name implies; we are alive with you today—we are not animated corpses—we speak your language, the language of the hum and stir of moving things, of energy and intensity, of the aspirations of the twentieth century."[23]

Soon after, in 1923, the Group of Independent Artists was organized, which proclaimed in its manifesto that "The group maintains that artistic manifestations such as Cubism, Dynamism and Expressionism, are sincere intellectual efforts to obtain a clearer aesthetic vision… The apparent preference, in the past, for dead form, is not so much a preference… as a habit… The public will at last have an opportunity to comprehend the New Form and an incentive will thus be provided for a more fluent expression on the part of the artist."[24] As if in support of the Group of Independent Artists, a significant exhibition of contemporary French art was held at the museum in the spring of 1923, where work by Bonnard, Cézanne, Gauguin, Matisse, Monet, Pissarro, Redon, Renoir, Vuillard and others could be seen for nearly two months. Los Angeles was slowly expanding its artistic tastes, and although the landscape artists still dominated, a small but resolute group of modern artists was making itself known.

One artist in particular had even left Los Angeles to study in Paris where he became a sensation, inventing a new form of art to go along with Cubism and Futurism: Synchromism. Stanton Macdonald Wright proposed a way to look at art,

Henriette Shore, *Tree.* Pencil on paper,
c. 1930. 12 x 10 3/4 inches.
(Private collection)

through color, and color alone. His color theory was based on his intuition that all colors are simultaneous, and for a short time, the world took notice of him. His "synchromist" paintings were a kind of Cubism filtered through color theory, and he relied on this early acclaim for the rest of his life, although his later works came nowhere near this level of achievement. Edward Weston found his work to be "no more than Saturday Evening Post figures seasoned with splashes of unrelated prismatic color."[25] But in the Teens, he was very advanced, very modern, when young artists only wanted to be modern. He declared "To copy nature implicitly implies many kinds of ignorance. It shows that one considers nature and art to the be same thing; it exposes the greatest misunderstanding of the precepts of the masters who postulated the continual study of nature."[26]

Born in Virginia in 1890, Wright moved to Santa Monica in 1900 with his family, and he later took courses at the Los Angeles Art Students' League. He went to live and study in Europe in 1907, returning to Los Angeles in 1919. He became director of the Art Students' League of Los Angeles in 1922, and also taught at Chouinard, the art school founded by Nelbert Chouinard in 1921. Active in the art community, Wright became one of the founding members of the Modern Art Workers in 1925 along with Henrietta Shore, and he experimented with color film, designed theater sets, made mosaics and created murals in the 1930s for the WPA. "S. Macdonald Wright, one of the leading artists and experts on color in America, has perfected what he feels is an absolute synchronization of color and music. The discovery came while he was working upon a theory for colored motion pictures..."[27] Wright was among a small group of artists who were experimenting with form, color and representation, all of whom challenged most of the rules they had been taught. Wright's early recognition in Paris made him a modernist of some note, and the fact that he settled in Los Angeles was unusual. He helped give legitimacy and authority to the new movement in a city where landscape art reigned supreme, and his support was valuable to his fellow artists working against the grain.

These artists demanded a more personal expression than their parents and grandparents, yet they were old-fashioned in that they still believed in the sanctity of art. They felt, as did their predecessors, that through art, they could transform and be transformed. They wanted to reveal the unity of the universe, the cosmic underpinnings of all things, through form, color and abstraction. Whereas the generation before them had seen God in nature, painting majestic scenes such as Yosemite, the Sierra, or the Grand Canyon, the modernists contemplated nature in a different way. Rather than paint an entire scene from the observable world, a modernist might reveal nature in a single leaf, a single color, a single line.

It has been supposed that modernism was a complete break with the past, but only in its outward manifestations was it different, for it still had the same messianic desire to teach the truth, to reveal the essence of nature and to heal through art. While some of the modernists in New York and the East Coast had became enamored of the machine and its manifestations—bridges, skyscrapers, factories—the California modernists, living in a place where nature was still so apparent, continued to explore the natural world with a new vision. Likewise, architecture in Los Angeles did not develop as monumentally as it did in New York, where skyscrapers became urban mountains and bridges resembled towering cathedrals. The bridge paintings of Stella, the skyscrapers of O'Keeffe, the factories of Sheeler had no counterparts in Los Angeles. Because of earthquakes, building codes forbade the construction of skyscrapers until the mid-20th century, and so, unlike New York, the Los Angeles skyline kept a low profile. The tone of the city was dominated by climate, by nature. Its architecture attempted to fit into nature, not contrast to it or dominate it. Modernism in Los Angeles celebrated nature, not machine, and thus took a significant turn from American modernism in general.

Along with Stanton Macdonald Wright, other young artists found their way to Southern California, including Henrietta Shore, a Canadian; Knud Merrild, a Dane; Peter Krasnow, a Ukrainian; Elise Seeds, from Philadelphia; and Paul Landacre, from Ohio. All of these artists, born in the 1880s and 90s, had come of age as new, radical ideas were forming about science, art and politics. Shore and Merrild both took nature as their source. Shore revealed the power in natural forms, the strength, grace and balance of natural things, while Merrild actually used the forces of nature in his work. One of the earliest artists to make assemblages, Merrild's constructions took advantage of the play of natural sunlight, and his poured paintings were expressive of the forces of gravity and random action. Peter Krasnow made intricate, monumental sculpture and Paul Landacre created a graphic vision of the California landscape in his wood engravings. Elise Seeds, known simply as Elise, was among the first artists in Los Angeles to practice complete abstraction and in her elegant, often lyrical compositions can be detected both traces of nature and purely geometric forms.

Apart from their advocacy of modern art, these artists were active physically and their physicality informs their work. Emphasis on the body and its well-being would become a California contribution to modern culture. Elise had studied dance with Isadora Duncan and had been a professional dancer before coming to Los Angeles. Shore studied modern dance, probably with Ruth St. Denis, in order to understand movement more clearly. Merrild had been a championship swimmer in his native Denmark, and before an illness left him partially handicapped, Landacre was a promising middle-distance runner. Sculpting and woodcarving were intensely physical acts pursued by Krasnow, and his art is a reflection of his physicality. Their interest in the physical realm was not just an intellectual pursuit; it had a physical basis, and a strong physical presence is evident in the work of each of these artists.

Other Los Angeles artists also used the modernist vocabulary to create images: Lorser Feitelson and his wife Helen Lundeberg sought truth in the juxtaposition of everyday objects in their brand of Surrealism, which they called Post Surrealism. Their belief in the conscious mind contrasted with the Surrealists who drew inspiration from the unconscious. In this baffling reversal, Feitelson and Lundeberg sought to use logic as the basis for their art, and seemed rather unsophisticated and naive when compared to the spicy, chic output of their European counterparts including Dali, Ernst, and the expatriate Man Ray. Feitelson lectured frequently on art and supported the aims of the modernists, but was not an active member of the social circles that played so important a part in the development of many artists' ideas and lives. Another artist whose work deserves mention is Agnes Pelton, who worked in the isolation of the desert community of Cathedral City, where she created powerful abstractions reflecting her interest in spirituality. Alfredo Ramos Martinez, born in Mexico, moved to Los Angeles in 1929, bringing with him a distinctive style derived from Rivera and the Mexican Muralists. His work is a direct link between Mexican art and that of Southern California.

Later, in the mid-1930s, many artists in Los Angeles were employed by the Public Works of Art Project, creating murals, sculptures and other works of art for public buildings. The project had as its goal the representation of the American Scene, and its hidden emphasis on American, rather than foreign influences, created an anti-modernist subtext to much of the rhetoric. As a result, many artists, especially those working in abstraction, felt restricted by the PWAP, as described by Jackson Pollack in 1944: "The idea of an isolated American painting, so popular in this country during the thirties, seems absurd to me, just as the idea of creating a purely American mathematics or physics would seem absurd... An American is an American and his painting would naturally be qualified by that fact, whether he wills it or not."[28] Because taxpayers funded the project, it was implied that the art had to appeal to, and be understood by, the public. "For the first time the public collector is taking the place of the private collector, and the artists are aware that in addition to painting to express themselves, they must also speak a language which is directed to the people and comprehensible to them."[29]

Because the public was generally hostile to abstract art, artists were discouraged from using it in federal projects. Olin Dows, Chief of the Treasury Relief Art Project, said in a letter to one artist: "Abstractions are impossible for us to use under this Project. I would suggest that you do no more abstractions like the one you sent in. Won't you, instead, do some more landscapes?"[30] Because they often needed money and were eager to work, artists complied with the guidelines of the PWAP, and modernists created many mural projects in California. Among them was Henrietta Shore, who completed a series of four murals for the Santa Cruz Post Office as well as two other murals in Monterey. Elise installed a mural in the Oceanside Post Office, and Stanton Macdonald Wright made murals for several buildings, including the Long Beach Civic Auditorium, Santa Monica City Hall and Santa Monica High School. For the most part, however, the aims of the WPA and the modernists were not parallel.

Because the Los Angeles art community was small, and because they had so few allies, modern artists knew one another. Although their mediums might have been different, the Los Angeles modernists were often friends, frequently influencing one another. Shore and the photographer Edward Weston were close friends; it was Shore who first suggested to Weston that he photograph shells and vegetables. In turn, he suggested that she visit Mexico, which she did in 1928. Upon her return, she took up lithography to record her impressions of Mexico, resulting in a substantial output of technical skill and beauty. In this way, the arts were integrated, and artists exchanged ideas freely. Franz Geritz, a painter turned printmaker, made portraits of many of his friends, including Weston and the architect Lloyd Wright. This latter image was included in a Geritz show at the Pasadena Art Institute in 1926 and was described as "one of the most notable wood-block portraits in the current exhibition."[31] He also made wood-cuts of the visiting stars of the opera and ballet, including Muratore and Pavlova, who were in Los Angeles because of Merle Armitage, the music director around whom most of Los Angeles art came to revolve.[32]

Impresario, collector, manager, publisher, writer, epicure and booster, Armitage had more single influence on the arts in Los Angeles than anyone else. During the 1930s, he was married to actress-turned-artist Elise, and his friend, the photographer Will Connell often photographed members of the Armitage group. One of Connell's portraits of Geritz includes a mask of Geritz made by another fellow artist and friend, Grace Marion Brown. A woman of many talents, Brown designed some of the books written by her friends, and her unusual masks and costume designs were exhibited at the museum in 1926. Connell also photographed his friend, the bookseller Jake Zeitlin, who, along with Armitage, became a central figure in the development of Los Angeles modernism.

The various art circles socialized and interacted. Among the frequent guests of the Arensbergs were Merrild, Elise, Armitage, Peter Krasnow, Beatrice Wood, Zeitlin and Weston. Merle Armitage not only promoted but was friendly with various artists, most of whom came to events at his Silver Lake home, and there was a circle of writers, artists and designers who met at Zeitlin's bookshop, while George Gershwin was host to a group of writers, musicians, actors and artists at his Beverly Hills home.

While the art world remained small, with very few collectors, the rare book world boasted major patrons, including Henry Huntington, William Andrews Clark and Estelle Doheny. Collecting rare books was a sign of cultural authority and prestige, while modern art was on the fringes of the cultural landscape. As a result, through these mag-

isterial book collectors, Southern California came to have some of the best libraries in the world. Occasionally, the rare book world intermingled with the modern art world. Alice Millard, one of the foremost rare book dealers, commissioned a home by Frank Lloyd Wright, La Miniatura, in Pasadena and she had books and catalogues printed by the premier Southern California book designer, Ward Ritchie. Ritchie was a good friend of many artists, including Paul Landacre, and he was a close friend of Jake Zeitlin. Zeitlin, who was a supporter of many artists—he gave Landacre his first exhibition and did the same for Edward Weston—sold books to Mrs. Doheny, and he was often an intermediary between the rare book world and the modernists.

Franz Geritz. *L'Orientale. (Portrait of Grace Marion Brown.)* Etching, 1923. 7 x 5 1/2 inches. (Private collection)

5

Galka Scheyer

Moving easily within these various circles was Galka Scheyer, a German émigre who devoted her intense energies to promoting the work of four artists known as The Blue Four: Kandinsky, Klee, Jawlensky, and Feininger.[33] They were little known in America in 1924, even in New York. Finding a more receptive audience for their work in the West, Scheyer moved to San Francisco in 1925, and organized the first exhibition of the Blue Four at the Oakland Art Gallery in early 1926. This exhibition of more than 70 works traveled to the Los Angeles Museum, where it opened in October. Museum director William Alanson Bryan wrote in the catalogue that "in presenting the Blue Four Exhibition to the public the Los Angeles Museum has the hope of broadening the outlook and increasing the understanding of modern art, which is not easily appreciated due to its very abstract nature." Scheyer did all she could to promote understanding of the artists' work, and gave a lecture at the museum, "Art, Life and The Blue Four." The significance of the exhibition was well understood by local critics, who gave the show excellent and at times, perceptive notices. "[The works] continue to astonish the majority and delight a few of the visiting public."[34] The reviewer goes on to cite an article by Anna Priscilla Risher in the magazine Laguna Life: "…It reminded me of crawling things—of worms or things mouldering in the ground. Ugh! It was awful." This was the opinion of many local, conservative artists, and the critics had to present to an often hostile public reasons for accepting the new art. "Perhaps there is something vital here for you, give it a chance. And you painters, are you sure you know all about the laws of art? Are not some of you like barren trees, awaiting new fertilization to bear fruit? Perhaps there is pollen here."[35] Another critic counseled the public "to accept the advice of Mme. Scheyer… and approach a picture as you would a queen—wait until it speaks to you."[36]

Scheyer, meanwhile, had become a teacher at an exclusive private school for girls, the Anna Head School in Berkeley, and continued her efforts to bring the work of the Blue Four to Californians. She also went to Mexico, where she became friends with the leading Mexican artists, Rivera, Tamayo and Mérida. Rivera arranged for a showing of the Blue Four at the Bibliotheca Nacional in Mexico City in 1931. Scheyer relocated to Los Angeles around 1930, moving into Rudolph Schindler's house on King's Road. Finding her experience there unsatisfactory, she commissioned

Richard Neutra to design a house for her in Santa Monica that was completed in 1934. She continued to promote the Blue Four, and sold work to collectors Walter Arensberg, Ruth Maitland and Joseph von Sternberg. In 1936, she arranged for the Stendahl Galleries to hold a Kandinsky exhibition and, relying on her friendship with Rivera, persuaded him to write remarks for the catalogue. Although a decade had passed since Kandinsky's debut in Los Angeles, hostility to his work still surfaced, yet most reviewers were supportive. Yet most reviewers were supportive. Arthur Millier, critic for the Los Angeles Times, wrote that the exhibit "is an event of first importance… I believe Kandinsky is one of the giant artists of our time." [37]

These exhibits were attended by the modern art community in Los Angeles, and Kandinsky's influence can certainly be seen in Elise's work, especially in her abstract lithographs. Scheyer was unflagging in her support of her artists, and Jake Zeitlin recalled that "[Scheyer] was trying very hard to get people to buy their paintings and drawings, and she would come to me and say, 'Jake, why don't you come up and buy one of those paintings." Although Zeitlin, to his regret, did not buy anything from her, he remembered "the only man who really supported her in those days was Walter Arensberg." [38] Scheyer had a strong personality, and often rubbed people the wrong way. "She never asked people to do things—she told them," recalled Zeitlin, adding that Scheyer "lived not too well, but she lived off of acting as [the Blue Four's] agent, selling their things, making a commission off of them, but kept pushing these things at people whether they wanted them or not." [39]

As a German émigré, Scheyer had close ties to the Austrian/German community, especially to Rudolph Schindler, who became a good friend and who introduced her to members of the art community, including Edward Weston, who recorded in his diary in 1930 that "Galka repelled me at the very start of our acquaintance but now I find myself wishing she would drop in once more before leaving. She is a dynamo of energy. She would wear me out in a few days but insight of unusual clarity, and an ability to express herself in words, brilliantly, forcefully, to hit the nail cleanly, buoys me up for the time. She is an ideal 'go-between' for the artist and his public." [40]

While the Blue Four were fortunate in having Scheyer as their agent, several Los Angeles artists had the good fortune to know Jake Zeitlin and Merle Armitage, who promoted their work with energy, loyalty and perception.

6

From Z to A:
Jake Zeitlin and Merle Armitage

Arriving in Los Angeles from Texas in 1925, Jake Zeitlin was a literary-minded young man in search of a bibliographic future. He had considered going to Chicago, but a friend in his hometown of Fort Worth knew some people out west and suggested Los Angeles, and Zeitlin was intrigued. He hitch-hiked his way out and found a job driving a fertilizer truck for E.L. Doheny's oil company. It would have been impossible to predict then, his overalls covered in fertilizer, that years later, Zeitlin would sell rare books to Mrs. Doheny. Although Zeitlin gained an immediate knowledge of the city's puzzling geography, it was bibliophily he was after, and he soon found a job in the book section of the May Company, a popular department store. Realizing that Bullock's, another large store, offered better books, he took a job there, and began to meet members of the local book world. One of the first of those was Phil Townsend Hanna, just beginning his career as editor of the magazine Touring Topics, and through Hanna, Zeitlin met the photographer Will Connell and the designer Grace Marion Brown. Through these connections, a small literary group began with Zeitlin at its center. Zeitlin had also just published a book of poems with an introduction by Carl Sandburg, whom he had met in Texas. This gave Zeitlin some notoriety, and Carey McWilliams, then a young writer for the weekly magazine Saturday Night, came out to interview the promising poet, and another literary friendship began. Through Will Connell, Zeitlin also met Merle Armitage, who was the manager of the Los Angeles Opera Company, and Lloyd Wright, son of the world-renowned architect and an architect himself. He also met Arthur Millier, who had become art critic for The Los Angeles Times in 1926, and Kem Weber, the architect/designer. Zeitlin quit his job and began selling books directly to the customers he had made at Bullock's, and in April 1928, he opened his first shop, a hole-in-the-wall on Hope Street near Sixth, where most of the city's bookshops were then located.[41] His shop, which was designed by Lloyd Wright, quickly became a meeting place for literary and artistic Los Angeles. Ward Ritchie reminisced: "Somehow, Zeitlin attracted creative people. His shop was a magnet to them. His own enthusiasm, his innovative mind and his drive to start things resulted in many cooperative ventures with his friends."[42]

Inspired by the Weyhe bookshop in New York, where print dealer Carl Zigrosser was showing the work of young American printmakers, Zeitlin decid-

Will Connell. *Portrait of Merle Armitage and Jake Zeitlin.* Photograph, c.1930. (Private collection)

ed to mount a few print exhibitions. Zigrosser agreed to send out prints that Zeitlin mounted on the one wall of his tiny shop reserved for art. Within a short time, he organized his first show of the work of a local artist, Peter Krasnow, and no longer relied on imports from New York; Zeitlin's second show was Edward Weston's photographs, and he soon gave Paul Landacre his first show of wood engravings. These small exhibits were reviewed in the Times by Millier (who was an occasional etcher), and as Zeitlin was the only dealer doing such print and photography exhibits, he became known as a champion of modern graphic artists. As he recalled: "Well, my wall was about 6 feet x 8 feet, but it was the only wall in which these things were being shown, and through some peculiar stroke of luck, I managed to get publicity for it." [43]

Zeitlin then moved to larger quarters in 1929 around the corner at 705 1/2 West Sixth Street, again using Lloyd Wright as designer. Although the shop was architecturally sound, it had a noticeable peculiarity: the light bulbs were impossible to reach because the lighting fixtures were installed behind the bookshelves. It was therefore impossible to change the bulbs when they blew out, and as a result, the shop became dimmer and dimmer; finally lamps had to be set out on the floor. A catalogue of fine press books issued at the time includes an announcement that "Our Print Gallery is Exhibiting Constantly the works of new and interesting moderns. We shall be pleased to show… prints by the following artists: [among others] Rockwell Kent, Paul Landacre, Arthur Millier, Franz Geritz, Henrietta Shore… and photographs by Will Connell and Edward Weston." [44] In 1930 an advertisement for the gallery stated: "We maintain a continuous exhibition, changed twice monthly, of the work of modern artists," and went on to mention "lithographs, wood-blocks, or metal prints" by Landacre, Millier, Juan Clemente Orozco, Shore, and Richard Day and photographs by Connell, Edward Weston and Brett Weston. [45] Zeitlin also sold the occasional painting, as when he offered for sale two works from the collection of his friend Merle Armitage, who had begun to collect art in 1912. In 1918, his interest shifted solely to prints, and to finance his print collection, he would sell off paintings. [46] Zeitlin's bookshop became a meeting place for literary and artistic people and developed not only as place to buy books and prints, but also as a sort of clubhouse of modernism. "After a while, the bookshop

Jake Zeitlin's bookshop at 705 1/2 West 6th Street. He was located here from 1929 until 1934.

became more than the expression of myself; it became the expression of the wishes and the dreams of a great many other people… It was something different, I think, from any other book-shop, certainly in this community, and I don't think there's been any other quite like it." [47]

Zeitlin also began to publish books, and in 1929, he set up a vanity press for little-known authors. One of his first works was a small book by Armitage, *The Aristocracy of Art*, and it was the first modern book printed in Los Angeles. Grace Marion Brown, an artist, and Grant Dahlstrom, a typographer, designed it, and this little book generated much more than its small size would indicate. Its large, bold type, stylized ornaments, black covers and overall layout indicated a break with the past and a new sense of display. Armitage was so pleased with the way in which his ideas were presented that he began to think seriously about book design. Several participants on the book project had definite ideas about art and politics. Having found working together congenial, they founded a magazine, Opinion, which had its headquarters in Zeitlin's shop. Designed by Brown, its contributors included Walter Arensberg, Will Connell, Phil Townsend Hanna, Carey McWilliams and Lloyd Wright. Opinion lasted only for a year, publishing a total of six issues, but all of its contributors continued to be in the forefront of artistic and literary life in Los Angeles. As Zeitlin described it, the magazine was the "outgrowth of the social activities, really—the getting together of a number of different kinds of people who used to circulate around my shop, have parties, and eat and drink together… these people managed to enjoy the kind of free-wheeling exchange of ideas and ribaldry and storytelling and joking that went on in the group." [48]

Zeitlin soon called his press The Primavera Press, taking the name from the original Spanish name of Spring Street, Callé de Primavera. The press soon evolved into a private press mainly for the publication of local history when Zeitlin's friends Phil Hanna, Carey McWilliams, Ward Ritchie and Lawrence Clark Powell became partners in the corporation in 1933. Although Zeitlin and Hanna had published a bibliography of the rarest books on California history in 1932 under the title *Libros Californianos, or Five Feet of California Books*, the first joint effort of all the partners was *A Gil Blas in California*, 1933. Carey McWilliams wrote an announcement summarizing the goals of the press. "The Primavera Press

Interior of Zeitlin's bookshop at 614 West 6th Street designed by Lloyd Wright.

Cartography by Paul Landacre

BOOKS AND GREEN GROWING THINGS

Paul Landacre. Map designed for an
annoucement of Zeitlin's move to 624
Carondelet Street, 1938. Wood engraving.
(Private collection)

intends to devote much of its attention to the
reprinting of rare classics of California which have
become lost or inaccessible through the high
prices they fetch in the original editions… It
intends to make its productions outstanding examples of the best tradition in modern book
design…"[49]

Books published by the Primavera Press often
had content taken from the past, but it had a for-
ward-looking approach to style. Zeitlin employed
Ward Ritchie as typographer and designer, and
often had Paul Landacre supply the illustrations.
The past, reinterpreted in these books through
modern design, appealed to a new audience.

The press continued to publish books until
1936. The last book published by the press, 5,000
copies of the play *Everyman*, was sponsored by
the California Festival Association, which intended
to sell the book during performances of the play at
the Hollywood Bowl. But the play was a flop and
the books did not sell. As a result, the association
could not pay the Primavera Press for the printing,
and the corporation was formally dissolved. "And
that was the end of Primavera—the end of
spring."[50]

Zeitlin's main business, bookselling, was pros-
pering, and in December 1934, he moved up the
street to larger quarters at 614 West Sixth Street.
Once again, Lloyd Wright designed the shop, considered the most attractive of the three, as well as
Zeitlin's grasshopper logo. Zeitlin expanded his art
exhibition schedule and his shop remained a nexus
for modernists. Because there were few galleries
willing to exhibit modern works, Zeitlin took up the
cause of the artists who had a difficult time reaching the public. The few galleries that existed "were
so far up on the scale that they didn't want to be
bothering with the small, local artists, the begin-
ners in the field."[51]

Among the few large galleries showing modernist works were the Biltmore Gallery, Dalzell
Hatfield and Stendahl Gallery, but there were also
three small galleries in Hollywood—Harry Braxton,
Howard Putzel and Stanley Rose. But it was a
bookshop that had the most success as a gallery
for modern works largely because most of the
modernists were also printmakers. Their prints
were easily exhibited in Zeitlin's shop, and since
prints were typically printed in editions of 50 or so,
one image could be sold to more than one client.
As prints were also less expensive than paintings,
they fit more easily into the budgets of Depression-
era customers. Shore, Krasnow, Elise and

Landacre all showed their prints at Zeitlin's shop.

By 1938, rents had risen on Sixth Street, and Zeitlin wanted to find a location west of downtown. A carriage house on the old Earl estate at 624 Carondelet at Wilshire Boulevard provided the new location. The opening of the new shop attracted a large crowd, and the party, catered by a friend, Helen Evans Brown, was a gastronomic triumph. Brown went on to author several cookbooks, and was another of those who got her start through Jake Zeitlin.

Zeitlin was at the center of various social and artistic circles and he had a hand in organizing and encouraging creative endeavors. "Jake Zeitlin was a catalyst. He gathered artists and authors as well as printers and book collectors into his humble den. He had a small gallery, not more than ten feet of space in which he had shows of great importance... [This] initiated an intellectual ferment previously foreign to staid and culturally backward Los Angeles."[52] In 1931, he helped found The Rounce & Coffin Club, a group of printers and artists devoted to fine printing. The original members were printers Gregg Anderson, Ward Ritchie and Grant Dahlstrom, and a short time later Paul Landacre was admitted along with printer Saul Marks. As Lawrence Clark Powell humorously reminisced, "The origins of The Rounce & Coffin Club are already shrouded in mystery. Only one fact is irrefutable: it was founded by an itinerant book peddler and a band of starveling printers—Zeitlin, abetted by Gregg Anderson, Grant Dahlstrom, and Ward Ritchie— back in the bitter Autumn of 1931."[53] As Zeitlin defined The Rounce & Coffin, "it wasn't exclusive... it was very disorderly and... it never took itself very seriously. It had no regular meeting places or times..."[54] Nevertheless, the club provided a medium through which its members could communicate their ideas about design, printing and publishing, and its members helped give Los Angeles the reputation as a city where fine books were published.

A lack of formality characterized the modernists in Los Angeles. They moved fluidly in and out of social groups, they enjoyed one another's company, they had a good time. One meeting of The Rounce & Coffin Club in 1932 was held at Ward Ritchie's print shop in South Pasadena, ostensibly to print a memorial keepsake for Arthur Ellis, a lawyer and book collector, who had just died. Ritchie's menu of spaghetti and red wine was

Henrietta Shore, *Canadian Weed*.
Lithograph, c. 1928. 11 x 8 1/2 inches.
(Private collection)

Franz Geritz. *Lloyd Wright, Architect.*
Color linocut, 1928. 8 x 6 inches.
(Private collection)

Henrietta Shore. *Portrait of Merle
Armitage.* Pencil drawing, c.1933.
17 x 13 1/2 inches. (Private collection)

eagerly consumed by his guests, and as Zeitlin recalled: "There must have been six of us [Zeitlin, Ritchie, Landacre, Marks, Dahlstrom, and Gloria Stuart] and Ritchie's ample ration of spaghetti left only room for gargantuan libations of the most insidious red ink that ever was trod from the grape... The evening ended in a shambles of spaghetti, red wine, pied type, and printer's ink with no keepsake to our credit but the memory of a magnificent and glorious catastrophe which Ritchie had to clean up the following morning."[55] Ritchie often was host to various gatherings, and his hillside home on Griffith Park Boulevard became known as "Ritchie's Roadhouse," where another group known informally as "The Club" congregated. Among its members were artists Paul Landacre, Gordon Newell, Lee Blair, Fletcher Martin, Barse Miller, Tom Craig, and Alexander Brooks; John Cage, the composer; Theodore Criley, an architect; Zeitlin; Armitage; Tee Hee, a Disney artist; Leigh Harline, a Disney composer; Grant Dahlstrom; brothers Maxon and Roger Smith, lawyers; and Delmer Daves, a motion picture writer/director.

The interconnectedness of these people in various professions is key to understanding the modernists and how they were able to continue with their work. Delmer Daves and Jake Zeitlin were instrumental in providing money for Paul Landacre so that the artist could work without having to seek outside employment. They formed the Paul Landacre Association, a group of twelve members who each contributed $100 a year for which they each received a new Landacre print each month. This arrangement lasted for three years and its members included Estelle Doheny, Kay Francis, Carl Zigrosser and Mrs. Samuel Goldwyn. Zeitlin employed Landacre's wife Margaret as a secretary in the late '20s, insuring that the couple had at least a modest income, and Daves, the most affluent member of the group, paid for the repairs to the Landacre's modest home.

Another group in which Zeitlin participated met on Sunday mornings and consisted of Zeitlin, his wife Josephine, their friends Mildred and Preston Tuttle, and the Landacres. They met for breakfast after which they would read a Shakespeare play. After a few meetings, the group decided to print something, and as they gathered occasionally at Grant Dahlstrom's house, access to type and a printing press was simple. The first book printed by the group was The Amphisbaena, The Crocodile, and Other Poems by A.E. Houseman, issued in an edition of 100 copies with small illustrations by Landacre. Their second and last production was an article by Harold Ickes, also with Landacre illustrations, but because printing was so labor intensive, the group ended its publishing endeavors. "It got to be work," Zeitlin recalled. "As long as it was fun and we did it more or less as a recreation, it was all right. But when it got to be something that we felt under compulsion about and didn't have the urge to get out there and pull at the hand press for several hours on a Sunday afternoon... we just dropped it which is the way it should be."[56]

Zeitlin continued to be a force in the intellectual life of Los Angeles until his death in 1987, developing an expertise in books on the history of science. He curtailed his activity in the contemporary art world, especially after moving to his La Cienega Boulevard shop in 1948, but in the '20s and '30s, Zeitlin had been at the center of all that was modern in Los Angeles.

The other great organizing personality in the Los Angeles art world of the '20s and '30s was Merle Armitage who, having been named Elmer, realized that the anagram Merle would provide him with a name more suited to his talents and personality. Always quick to seize an opportunity, Armitage wasted neither time nor talent. Born in Iowa in 1893, he became a civil engineer in Texas, where his eyesight was damaged by exposure to the sun and the detailed nature of the work. Recovering his eyesight, he returned to Detroit, where his family was then living, and began to draw again, devoting his time to stage sets rather than engineering projects. He was introduced to the New York theater producer and concert manager Charles L. Wagner, who liked the young man's work, and Wagner soon asked him to manage a music festival in Wisconsin. Although Armitage did not know what a "music festival" was, in his usual fashion, he accepted and thus began his career as a music and opera impresario. He managed Wagner's concerts throughout the East Coast for three years, whereupon Wagner made him a full partner. By the mid-teens Armitage was in charge of the cross-country tours made by Diaghilev's Ballet Russe and the Russian Grand Opera Company, and managed tours of Metropolitan Opera singers as well. Arriving in Los Angeles in 1923 to organize an opera season, he mounted productions of Turandot, Carmen, La Bohème, Tosca, Falstaff and The Marriage of Figaro and soon after founded the

Gallery space at Zeitlin's bookshop,
c. 1936. The print storage cabinet
was designed by Lloyd Wright.

Will Connell. *Portrait of Franz Geritz.*
Photograph, c.1928. 10 x 8 inches.
(Private collection)

Connell included Grace Marion Brown's
mask of Geritz in this unusual portrait.

Los Angeles Grand Opera Association, where he
remained as general manager until 1930. "Fresh-
flower-bedecked and blue-skied Los Angeles
seemed friendly, peaceful, awash with opportunities, and a wonderful place to work."[57] Armitage
made the decision to stay in Los Angeles and he
was soon at the center of its cultural life, becoming a West Coast counterpart to Alfred Steiglitz.

Armitage's professional interest in music led
him to the George Gershwin circle that gathered
at the composer's home in Beverly Hills. His interest in art led him to the group of artists that met at
the home of the Arensbergs in the Hollywood
Hills, and his interest in books led him to the
Zeitlin circle. Armitage has been universally
described as energetic and dynamic. "He was
continually delving into and promoting a variety of
activities… I have never known a man with such
drive and energy."[58] "He was a spectacular personality. He had style about him; he dressed as an
impresario should."[59] He was also interested in
women, and was married at least five times,
including once to the artist Elise.

His friendship with Jake Zeitlin led to an
impromptu trip to the mountains with Arthur Millier
in 1927 in Armitage's elegant car. "Merle sported
a Packard roadster, which was just about the peak
of smartness."[60] The trio traveled up the east side
of the Sierra, crossed over the mountains at Truck-
ee and descended into Sacramento, where
Maynard Dixon was painting murals on the walls of
the State Library, and it was there that Zeitlin and
Armitage became acquainted with the noted
artist.[61] They proceeded to San Francisco and the
Gold Rush country. Returning home, they stopped
in Carmel where they visited Robinson Jeffers.
This freewheeling attitude, mixing literary and artistic pursuits with fun, was typical of Zeitlin,
Armitage and their friends. They did not have to
travel far to enjoy themselves. Members of the
group, including Zeitlin, Armitage, Edward Weston, Ramiel McGehee and Tone Price, often went
down to a swimming club in Palos Verdes where
they held summer parties. "We would hold great
parties there at night… we would broil lobsters,
and have great songfests, and dance, and talk,
and shout."[62] Armitage's interest in cuisine would
lead him to write several cook books. Others in his
set were also interested in food and wine, including
Phil Townsend Hanna, who had founded the Los
Angeles branch of the Wine and Food Society.

An advocate of modernism, Armitage was
appalled by the art being produced by local land-

Grace Marion Brown. Cover design for *Opinion*, May, 1930.

Although only six issues were published, *Opinion* had a lasting effect on its contributors, who were at the forefront of modernism in Los Angeles. (Private collection)

Title page to *Armitage's Aristocracy of Art*, 1929.

The ornament, resembling a succulent, was by Grace Marion Brown, and modern book design in Los Angeles originated with this work. (Private collection)

scape artists, whom he referred to as "painters myopically fascinated by eucalyptus trees."[63] Realizing that many of his friends were artists who had no way to reach a broader public, Armitage began organizing and designing a series of books to feature their work. The earliest of these was *The Work of Maier-Kreig* of 1932, but the first books to feature Armitage's emerging, distinctive style were *Warren Newcomb* and *Rockwell Kent*, published in the same year. The book on Newcomb, a California artist who also worked as a set designer, was selected as one of the Fifty Books of the Year by the American Institute of Graphic Arts, and helped establish Armitage as a designer of note. Armitage's next book, *The Art of Edward Weston*, 1932, is one of Armitage's most striking, and is one of the first books entirely devoted to an American photographer. It was also selected as one of the Fifty Books of the Year and has become a touchstone in the design of American art books. Weston's great friend, the artist Henrietta Shore, was the subject of Armitage's first book of 1933. With this publication, Armitage first used a design technique that would become his trademark—the use of relatively small type with wide "leading," or spacing between the lines. This technique gave Armitage's books a distinctive flair. Armitage changed the look of American books, and in so doing, became one of the leading modernists in Los Angeles. In an ironic twist, three of the best artists in Southern California were not painters, but were Armitage, a book designer; Landacre, a printmaker; and Weston, a photographer.

In 1934, Armitage married Elise Cavanna Seeds, artist and former actress, and published *The Works of Elise* the same year. The portrait of Elise in the book is by Beatrice Wood, the noted ceramic artist and a friend of the Armitages. Elise also created illustrations for many of Armitage's books, and although they were divorced in the early 1940s, they continued their artistic collaboration. Armitage designed and published books on art and artists throughout the 1930s, among them *Napolitano*, 1935; 2 *Statements by Picasso*, 1936; *Sculpture of Boris Lovet-Lorski*, 1937; and *So-Called Abstract Art*, 1939.

Knowledgeable about art, friendly with many artists and capable of organizing large events, Armitage was chosen as Regional Director of the Public Works of Art program for the WPA in Southern California in 1933–34. Under his supervision was a committee composed of artists including Hugo Ballin, Millard Sheets and

Clarence Hinkle; writers Mrs. Samuel Clover and Arthur Millier; movie director Cecil B. DeMille; art dealer Dalzell Hatfield, curator Reginald Poland and art patron Preston Harrison. The committee chose numerous artists to execute murals, sculpture and other projects for public buildings. Although supportive of the artists who worked under him, he disliked much of the rest of the art created under the WPA, calling it "so much paint, mere illustrations by hacks and students repeating over again endlessly problems which were solved by better men years ago."[64] Armitage's views on art were such that he could not tolerate art created by a committee, stating, "only mediocre artists run in packs. The creative artist is always the lone wolf."[65]

Armitage was also on the board of the influential magazine California Arts and Architecture from 1933 to 1938 and helped shape its policies. In one editorial from November 1938, Armitage urged that a modern opera house be built in Los Angeles rather than the French Renaissance design proposed by D. Joseph Coyne, Chairman of the Opera House Committee. Direct and to the point, Armitage's open letter to Coyne says of the proposal:

"It displays an unawareness of what is going on architecturally in America for us to build in Los Angeles… an Opera House of 'French Renaissance architecture, expressed in artificial stone' is an admission not only of imaginative poverty, but also a complete unawareness of the sound trends in American life… I will do everything in my power to fore-stall the building in Los Angeles of any opera house or art center which is not of a contemporary character."

Armitage also advocated the use of modern architecture for the construction of UCLA in the 1920s, and bitterly resented Board of Regent member Edward Dickson's overriding decision to use Florentine Renaissance as the architectural style for the campus. Armitage felt that "here was probably the one chance in the history of America where an entire university could be built, …unhampered by old buildings, a contemporary treatment—a uniquely functional, beautiful, and significant ensemble that would have won the admiration of the world." Instead, according to Armitage, Los Angeles got "A campus completely lacking in function as an educational institution, a style utterly alien to its time and place—a monstrosity!"[66] Armitage also blamed Dickson for UCLA's failure to secure the

Arensberg Collection, which went instead to the Philadelphia Museum of Art. Armitage's stature in the Los Angeles art community was such that in 1946, Paul Landacre proposed that Armitage become director of the Los Angeles Museum, a job which, had he taken it, would have changed the course of institutional collecting in the region.

Armitage left Los Angeles during World War II when he was commissioned a Major in the Army Air Force, and later, a Lieutenant Colonel. After the war, he designed titles for films, designed more books, and moved to Santa Fe, where he became involved with the Laboratory of Anthropology, publishing books on Native American topics. In 1947, Armitage accepted publisher Gardner Cowles offer to redesign Look magazine, and moved to New York, where he remained until 1954. He then returned to California, to a ranch he had purchased in the desert near Joshua Tree. Armitage continued writing and designing books until his death in 1975.

7

The Art Press

The Los Angeles art community received extensive and favorable coverage from its leading newspaper and magazines. The Los Angeles Times' chief art critic in the 1920s and '30s, Arthur Millier, was also an artist and therefore sympathetic to the concerns of his friends and contemporaries. His weekly reviews shed light on the new ideas then swirling throughout the art world. While he was a consistent, supportive writer on modernism, he also wrote favorably on California Impressionists and other traditional artists. Born in England, Millier immigrated in his teens to San Francisco where he was employed as an artist at the Schmidt Lithograph Company, the leading producer of orange crate labels on the West Coast. Later, moving to Los Angeles, he became art editor of the Times, taking over from another Englishman, Antony Anderson.

Aside from the daily papers, monthly magazines provided information and opinion about local artists and activities. Several, like Touring Topics and California Arts & Architecture, were influential and long-lived. Touring Topics, founded in 1909, changed its name to Westways in 1934 and remains in publication. California Arts & Architecture, a combination of three magazines formed in 1929, ran until 1966. A weekly magazine, Saturday Night, lasted from 1920 until 1939. Occasionally, an inspired artist or writer would undertake the publication of a little magazine, such as Ferdinand Earle's journal The West Wind, published in Hollywood in 1925–26. Its colorful covers reproduced some unusual artwork, including a painting by Xavier Cugat, and inside there were reproductions of paintings by local and international artists, along with articles by Dane Rudhyar (on art), Charles Wakefield Cadman (on jazz) and William Counselman (a short story). Other small magazines, like Opinion and Dune Forum, also had very limited runs but their existence testifies to the intellectual currents that were flowing in Southern California.

Touring Topics

As Los Angeles grew, and as the automobile became a significant part of California life, a magazine emerged to fill the needs of the motoring public, Touring Topics. Published by the Automobile Club of Southern California, the first issue appeared in February 1909, and the magazine grew to include articles relevant not just to driving but to all aspects of Western life. The magazine changed direction in 1927 when the literate and sophisticated Phil

Grace Marion Brown. Cover design
for *Touring Topics*, September, 1932.

_____

One of two covers designed by
Brown and among the most modern
ever published by the magazine.
(Private collection)

Henrietta Shore. *California Cacti*,
cover for *Touring Topics*, 1929.

_____

This is one of a series of ten covers
by California women artists.
(Private collection)

Townsend Hanna, who had been night editor of The
Los Angeles Times, assumed the job of editor. A
leading member of Los Angeles' community of bib-
liophiles, Hanna often published the work of friends
and colleagues in Touring Topics; the June, 1927
issue features a poem by Jake Zeitlin illustrated with
a Will Connell photograph.[67] Hanna often commissioned leading artists to design covers, and the
work of many Southern California artists became
known to a greater public through his efforts. Traditional artists including Maurice Braun, Alson Clark
and Hanson Puthuff designed a series of covers in
1928. The series was extended into 1929 with a
redesigned format featuring covers by ten modern
women artists including Henrietta Shore and Donna
Schuster. Commissioned to provide an entire year's
covers, Maynard Dixon supplied 12 designs in
1930 illustrating the history of transportation in California, and in 1931, Carl Oscar Borg designed 12
covers illustrating exploration in the Southwest. In
1932 Grace Marion Brown designed two of the
most modern covers (April and September) ever to
adorn the magazine, along with Alvin Lustig's cover
for May 1933.[68] In January 1934 the magazine
changed its name to Westways, the new name having been supplied by a reader through a contest
held late the previous year. A rotogravure section,
begun in 1922, featured work by artists and photographers, and Hanna reproduced the work of
both Shore and Weston in 1930. Among the many
literary contributors to the magazine were Zane
Grey, Carey McWilliams and Paul Jordan Smith, the
literary editor of the Los Angeles Times who wrote
several books on California history.[69]

As a young man, Hanna had contracted a form of
mountain fever that left him with a deformed spine,
which "had no apparent effect on his personality,"
according to Ward Ritchie. "He was the most
immaculately groomed of all the habitués of book-
sellers' row and the one with the greatest capacity
for enjoying every delicious crumb of life."[70] His politics were conservative, and he would later clash
with some of his liberal friends, including Zeitlin and
Armitage. But as an editor, he was fair and impartial,
providing his readers with a mix of information, eru-
dition and entertainment.

California Arts & Architecture

California Arts & Architecture emerged in 1929
when several publications, Pacific Coast Architect
and California Southland, merged with California
Homeowner. Harris Allen, an architect, was its first
editor. Working with Mabel Urmey Seares, the

managing editor, Allen immediately began coverage of Los Angeles art galleries. That same year saw the founding of the Southern California Art Dealers' Association.[71] With arts coverage now consolidated in the new magazine, galleries found it advantageous to join together in order to pool advertising and other resources. By the early 1930s, there were at least 30 active galleries in Southern California, most of whose exhibitions were listed in California Arts & Architecture's monthly calendar. The magazine covered not only modern work, but also featured articles on period architecture and furnishing and happily combined the old with the new. It also covered decoration and fashion.

While Touring Topics' readership was anyone with an automobile, California Arts & Architecture reached a smaller, more discerning audience of affluent homeowners. The advertisers in Touring Topics, mainly insurance companies and auto repair businesses, contrasted with California Arts & Architecture's advertisers, made up of interior decorators, furniture shops and purveyors of architectural products. Yet at times, the two journals seemed to be competing for the same audience. During 1928–34, both ran covers by California artists. Edward Weston was featured in Touring Topics in June 1930, and five months later California Arts & Architecture published an article on him in November. The March 1934 issue of Touring Topics included photos by Weston, while the August issue of California Arts & Architecture had a cover by his son, Brett. Both magazines published articles on travel, gardening and history, but as time went on, they diverged. Touring Topics stuck to literary and travel-oriented features, while California Arts & Architecture became the champion of modernism in all the arts. With architect Mark Daniels as its new editor in 1935, California Arts & Architecture underwent a redesign in 1936. The change in appearance was striking, and may have come about through Merle Armitage, a member of the magazine's editorial board from 1933 until 1938. The new, updated look certainly resembles his typographic style, and he would certainly have advocated a less cluttered, bolder design. The magazine makes no mention of the change, but the new design signaled the beginning of California Arts & Architecture's conversion from a luxury magazine aimed at a genteel reader to a journal advocating modernism.

The Los Angeles art scene was often lively and contentious, with traditional vs. modern art a topic

Harwell Hamilton Harris. Cover design for *California Arts and Architecture*, March, 1940.

With this issue, the first under editor John Entenza, the magazine presented a redesigned logo and signalled its allegiance to modernism. (Private collection)

Announcement for a debate on contemporary art between Merle Armitage and Paul Jordan Smith sponsored by the Society for Sanity in Art, 1939. (Private collection)

of frequent debates. An anti-modern group, The Society for Sanity in Art, had been founded in Chicago by Josephine Hancock Logan in the 1930s and local chapters sprang up across the country. On November 6, 1939, the Los Angeles branch sponsored a debate between Armitage and Paul Jordan Smith on the subject of contemporary art which was held at the Stendahl Galleries. It must have been a lively presentation, as the opponents were both strident partisans and articulate speakers. Local members of the Society for Sanity in Art included traditional artists Edgar Payne, James Swinnerton and Joe Duncan Gleason, all of whom Armitage had castigated as members of the "Eucalyptus School." Armitage, who collected the work of Picasso, Braque, The Blue Four, Miro, and numerous other modern artists, must have been irked by his opponent, Paul Jordan Smith, who detested modern art, and who had, in the late 1920s, submitted hoax abstract paintings to several art shows under the name "Pavel Jerdanovitch."

California Art & Architecture's San Francisco-based art writer, Edwyn A. Hunt, sided with Jordan Smith, and supported the aims of the Society for Sanity in Art. Writing in the November 1939 issue, he stated: "I personally believe that much of this modern art movement is due to the insincerity and business acumen of various people who can only earn a living by exploiting the bizarre and unusual. Human beings want novel things to look at, and exhibitionists, who are unable to paint a decent picture, try their hand at abstractions and monstrous distortions of real objects, until there has come to be a cult of so-called modernism." He went on to praise Logan, who "finally rose up in her wrath against such high-handed imbecility and started a wonderful movement called "Sanity in Art." Although California Arts & Architecture was usually supportive of modern artists and architects, it also had its conservative side, as expressed by Hunt. His words however, would be among the last in support of traditional art to appear in the pages of the magazine.

In 1940, California Arts & Architecture underwent a dramatic change under its new editor, John Entenza.[72] Under his direction, the magazine became a leading advocate for modernism, and probably in direct response to Hunt, published an article by Man Ray entitled "Art in Sanity" in the January, 1941 issue. Articles by Paul Frankl, Laslo Moholy-Nagy, Charles Eames and other practitioners of vanguard styles filled the pages of the newly streamlined magazine, with monthly coverage of art, books, and theatre. The change took place immediately upon Entenza's taking over and was evident in the March, 1940 issue, which featured a redesigned logo and cover illustration of a very modern house in sectional view by Harwell Hamilton Harris. Entenza wrote a monthly column entitled "Notes in Passing," and with a new format created by Alvin Lustig, California Arts & Architecture featured articles on modern artists, including Kmid Merrild and Peter Krasnow, in the 1940s. Entenza's main interest was architecture, and he went on to sponsor the influential Case Study House project, beginning in 1945, catapulting the magazine into the forefront of modern design theory.[73]

Saturday Night

Saturday Night presented coverage of the arts by Elizabeth Bingham in the 1920s, and in the '30s, the duties fell first to Madge Clover (wife of the publisher), and later to Harry Muir Kurtzworth. Reports on the arts were in keeping with the tone of Saturday Night, which featured society weddings and Los Angeles and Pasadena social events, but the magazine did publish columns on music, theatre and books. Its coverage of art was usually conservative although Bingham did try to understand and encourage modern artists, describing them as "original" and "virile," while Kurtzworth, an artist himself, vacillated between support of modernism and condemnation of it. In one review he had little good to say about the modern art at a 1936 show at the Los Angeles Museum: "As if to balance the sunshine of California, certain painters in this show seek to emphasize the dismal, dire, doleful, if not the disgusting, aspects of the modern age." He then damned Knud Merrild with faint praise, "In the field of sculpture, the painting by Knud Merrill [sic] should be given first place since it provides more places for gathering a patina of dust than a first class 'whatnot'..."[74] Yet in a column a few months later, Kurtzworth wrote that "the work of Merrild... will some day be appreciated by the multitudes."[75] Although he may have had inconsistent viewpoints, Kurtzworth was a consistent advocate of the arts in Los Angeles and was an early supporter of the view that American cinema was a distinct art form. With its art column on the inside front cover, Saturday Night gave the arts in Los Angeles a prominent spot throughout the 1930s.

8

Henrietta Shore

Born in Toronto on January 22, 1880, Henrietta Shore studied art from 1900 to 1913 in Toronto, in New York (under William Merritt Chase and Robert Henri), and in Europe. Perhaps at the urging of her brother Wilbur, who had already moved to Southern California, she visited the Pacific coast and decided to settle in Los Angeles in the seminal year 1913. She began to exhibit, attracting notice, and held her first exhibit at the new Los Angeles Museum in December, 1914. In 1915, she won an award at the Panama-California Exposition in San Diego, and in 1916, she helped found the Los Angeles Modern Art Society. Her second exhibition at the Los Angeles Museum took place in November 1917 and was well received. In his Los Angeles Times review, Antony Anderson remarked that "…Miss Shore has taken her unalterable stand among the ranks of the modernists… [Her pictures] have an astonishing vitality, an amazing carrying quality… I used to have serious disagreements with Miss Shore, but I am not at all sure that I have them any more."[76] Perhaps in search of a more cohesive community of modernists, Shore moved to New York in 1920 and remained there until 1923. This was a significant period for the artist, for it was there her style began to change and her interest in abstraction and simplification first surfaced. She became a founding member of the New York Society of Women Artists, and exhibited simultaneously with Georgia O'Keeffe, with whom she was often compared.[77] She must have seen work by Thomas Hart Benton and Arthur Dove as her style evolved from a robust naturalism, evocative of Robert Henri, to her own distinctive style of nature-based abstraction. By the time she returned to Los Angeles in 1923, Shore had established herself as one of the leading modernists whose images, which she referred to as "semi-abstractions," always had a basis in the natural world.

Upon her return to Los Angeles, Shore began to study modern dance in order to increase her feeling for rhythm. The noted pioneer of modern dance, Ruth St. Denis, along with her husband Ted Shawn, had opened the Denishawn School, facing Westlake Park, in 1915. St. Denis' goal was to make dance an expression of the senses, and her exotic repertoire, often based on eastern mysticism, departed radically from traditional western dance movement. The Denishawn curriculum included yoga, eurhythmics and folk dance at a time when instruction in such areas was unusual. The 400-seat theater at the school was the only

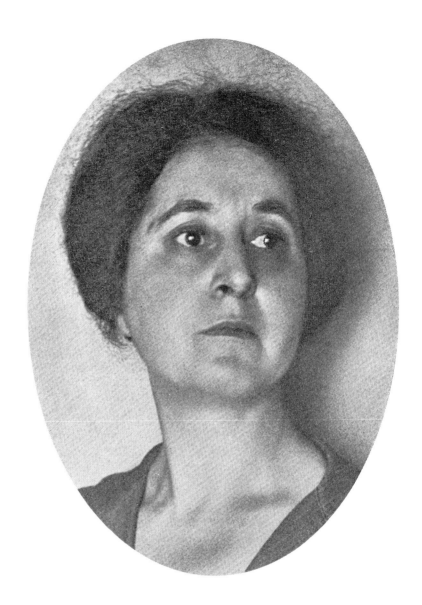

Edward Weston. *Portrait of Henrietta Shore*. As published in "A Private Collection of Paintings by Some of the Living Artists of Southern California," The Memorial Art Gallery, Rochester, New York. (Private collection)

one in America devoted exclusively to dance, and Denishawn's influence ran deep. Martha Graham became a student in 1916, and nearly all modern dance in America may be traced to roots at Denishawn. It seems likely, with her interest in modernism, that Shore would have studied at Denishawn. Certainly Shore's paintings began to take on a rhythmic flow, and her pictures often show two entities undulating in a balanced counterpoise. These images, whether leaves, trees or people, often seem to be locked in an eternal dance.

Shore also opened a restaurant/gallery, the Studio Inn, with her sister-in-law Annette. She continued painting, and prepared for her next exhibition at the Los Angeles Museum, an exhibition of thirty-five works in 1927. Early in that year, on Valentine's Day, a significant event in her life took place: she met Edward Weston. On February 14, 1927 the artist Peter Krasnow brought his friend Weston to Shore's studio. From this initial meeting a long and deep friendship would grow, each artist relying on the other's intuition and advice. Shore began a portrait of Weston, and during the sittings, they exchanged opinions. On April 30, Weston wrote: "Sat to Henrietta yesterday. We do have good times together! She is a jolly companion, keenly alive with word and thought, besides being a really good artist. I want to write about her work—yet to find words?—It would be a difficult subject, maybe beyond my ability." [78] Their friendship blossomed, with Weston referring affectionately to Shore as "Henry." He was extremely pleased to receive one of her paintings as a gift: "She gave me amazing news, that I am to have one of her paintings… This will be an event in my life!" [79] Their interaction affected them both profoundly. It was from Shore that Weston got the idea to photograph shells: "I think the Chambered Nautilus has one of the most exquisite forms, to say nothing of color and texture, in nature. I was awakened to shells by the painting of Henry. I never saw a Chambered Nautilus before. If I had, my response would have been immediate! If I merely copy Henry's expression, my work will not live… Henry's influence, or stimulation, I see not just in shell subject matter, it is in all my late work, in bananas and the nudes. I feel it not as an extraneous garnish but as a freshened tide swelling from within my self." [80] Weston's studies of gourds and vegetables also trace Shore as a source, as he records that "I have worked with two gourds recently: a truly marvelous one, black lacquer, belonging to Henry…" [81]

Henrietta Shore. *Water Carrier.*
Lithograph, c.1928. 6 x 8 inches.
(Private collection)

Weston also had a strong influence on Shore, for in August 1927, Shore, accompanied by her friend the artist Helena Dunlop, left for Mexico, undoubtely at Weston's urging. He had spent the years 1923–26 in Mexico, and must have felt it would benefit Shore to have a similar experience. While she was in Mexico, Shore and Weston had simultaneous exhibitions at the Los Angeles Museum of Art. Arthur Millier, in The Los Angeles Times, said: "I group [Shore and Weston] together for several reasons: each has a full one-man exhibit at the Los Angeles Museum; they are friends; they show a like progression in viewpoint and work… The thirty-four paintings by Henrietta Shore form one of the most satisfying exhibits of the year. Most interesting to me is the self-educational process by which, through a study of universal organic forms, typified in the 'semi-abstractions,' she has come to be intensely interested in the specific forms of individual objects."[82]

Weston borrowed many items from Shore's studio while she was away including shells, cacti, books and a painting.[83] She wrote to him often, remarking, "I like Mexico and I know why you love it."[84] She met the Mexican artists Orozco and Charlot and painted their portraits, and she was also introduced to Diego Rivera, whose work she did not find as interesting as the others. "I prefer his earlier work–the earliest. It is most unfortunate that I am unable to fully appreciate his work, I grant its excellence–but I am bored by it."[85]

Upon her return to Los Angeles in 1928, Shore executed a series of lithographs based on her Mexican sojourn. She had been introduced to the medium in Mexico, where artists were reviving the technique of drawing on stone, a medium that had been ignored during the recent heyday of the woodcut. She worked with Lynton Kistler, Los Angeles' leading lithographer, and produced a group of seventeen different images between 1928 and the early 1930s. She had a show at the Brick Row Gallery in Hollywood in March 1928, and exhibited a group of her lithographs at Jake Zeitlin's shop in September 1928. She was awarded a first prize at the 1928 exhibition of the San Francisco Society of Women Artists, where the "art critic of the San Francisco Examiner, Jehanne Bietry-Salinger, grasped instantly Shore's ultimate goal, the portrayal of universal movement and growth in nature."[86] Shore was also admired by Arthur Millier, who said that "Miss Shore was justly recognized; she is unquestionably one of the important living painters of this country, as strong as any on the West coast for a synthesis of intellectual, technical, and aesthetic qualities in her latest work."[87]

In 1933, Edward Weston had his chance to write about Shore's work when he collaborated with Merle Armitage on a monograph of their friend's work. Not only did Weston contribute an essay on Shore, the reproductions were taken from photographs by Weston. The attractive book also includes a portrait of Shore by Jean Charlot, and an appraisal of her work by Reginald Poland, Director of the Fine Arts Gallery, in San Diego. Weston wrote: "Returning from Mexico in 1926, after three years of intense life, in which pre-Hispanic monuments, the contemporary crafts, the bull-fight and the renaissance of fresco painting had given me fresh stimulus, I found art in California–with few exceptions–uninspired, lacking vitality. Then came a day when a friend took me to the home of Henrietta Shore… Ushered directly into a room hung with Shore's canvases I stopped short in my tracks silently amazed; here was something outstanding, a notable achievement. There was no question, the response was immediate; those deeply felt, finely executed paintings moved me at once… When she paints a flower she IS that flower, when she draws a rock she IS that rock… Shore realizes a technical perfection rarely seen in contemporary art…"[88]

Shore moved to Carmel in 1930 where she found the rocky contours of Point Lobos and the twisted cypress tress expressive of her interest in organic forms. Weston had moved to Carmel the previous year, and both artists continued their explorations of the natural world. Shore exhibited occasionally during the 1930s and she won a commission to create six murals for the post office in Santa Cruz in 1936; she also made murals for the Old Customs House, Monterey, and the Monterey Post Office. Her last exhibition was in 1939, in New York. The lack of a dealer to champion her paintings, combined with her reclusive personality, caused her work to disappear from view. Weston said Shore was "an artist of destiny… lost in Carmel."[89] To survive, she was forced to sell works she had collected, including a painting by Robert Henri and several Weston photographs. Her nephews in Canada helped with expenses, but by the late 1950s, Shore was in her seventies and struggling. As her friend Jehanne Bietry-Salinger recalled, "some so-called 'do-gooders' went to her studio, found it disorganized, and had Henrietta committed to an asylum."[90] She died there in 1963.

9
Knud Merrild

Knud Merrild, a Dane by birth, arrived in Los Angeles in 1923 determined to be a modern abstract artist. His goal was difficult, his destination unusual, but Merrild was a man of independence, vision and fortitude, and he succeeded in becoming the artist he had envisioned, one of very few in Southern California to truly understand the implications and methods of modern art. His work in various styles and mediums over a span of thirty-five years was unified by his deep-seated inner belief in the natural laws of change and chance. For Merrild, the profound task of an artist was to create works which could serve as reminders of basic, often mysterious, natural phenomena and which could function as tools for personal transformation. His works are meditations on his spiritual realizations.

Knud Merrild was born in Odum, Denmark in 1894, the son of a choirmaster. Leaving school in 1908, he apprenticed himself to a housepainter and in his spare time began to paint. From 1909 to 1912 he studied at the Art and Technical School in the small town of Stege, south of Copenhagen, and in 1912 moved to Copenhagen where he enrolled in the Arts and Crafts School, studying there until 1917. An exhibition of Cubist painting in 1913 in Copenhagen was a revelation to Merrild: he immediately determined to become a "modern artist." He exhibited for the first time in 1916 at the annual Danish Royal Academy's Fall Salon and he entered the Royal Academy of Art in 1917, studying there until 1918. Unhappy with the conservative outlook at the Academy, Merrild left and founded Anvendt Kunst, a group of artists and craftsmen dedicated to making objects of useful beauty; he organized annual exhibitions of their works at the Kunstindustri Museum until 1922.

Influenced by the Danish art critic George Brandes who said that the creative vortex of 20th century art would be in America, Merrild left Copenhagen for New York, arriving on August 14, 1921 with $25 and conviction to be an artist. He did not have long to wait, as he was immediately commissioned to create panels for an exhibition of decorative domestic objects at the Belmaison Galleries located in Wanamaker's department store. He also was employed making movie posters and through this work met a fellow Danish artist, Kai Gotzsche (b.1886). They became friends and decided to see the vast country that had so intrigued them. With Los Angeles as their destination, they set out in a beat-up Tin Lizzie in mid-1922. Curious about the art colonies in Santa Fe and Taos, they arrived in New Mexico with a letter

Man Ray. *Portrait of Knud Merrild*.
Photograph, 1944. (Courtesy Steve
Turner Gallery)

Knud Merrild. *Lou/El-36*. Gesso,
watercolor, pencil and wax on
paper, 1936. 11 1/4 x 9 3/4 inches.
(Courtesy Steve Turner Gallery)

of introduction to the artist Walter Ufer, who soon introduced the pair to the resident artists and writers, including D.H. Lawrence and his wife Frieda, then living in Taos as guests of Mabel Dodge. Merrild and Gotzsche (who became known by one and all as "The Danes") struck up a friendship with the Lawrences, and when The Danes were making plans to head west before the onset of winter, Lawrence generously invited them to stay the winter with him and his wife on a remote ranch 17 miles outside of Taos. They accepted the offer, and the months spent together were recalled in Merrild's book, *A Poet and Two Painters*, a major literary achievement and an important first-hand account of the writer. Merrild and Gotzsche continued to paint while in New Mexico and later showed their work, much of it with Indian themes, at the Santa Fe Museum of Art in 1923. Leaving New Mexico in the spring, Merrild and Gotzsche arrived in Los Angeles on May 11, 1923, armed with several letters of introduction from Lawrence. Gotzsche found work as a set decorator, but Merrild steadfastly refused to be employed by the movie studios, resenting being told what and how to paint. The world of motion pictures held no interest for Merrild: "I detested the atmosphere of the movies and if I couldn't get a creative position where I could inject some artistry, I would have nothing."[91] He instead relied on his old trade of housepainting and gradually received commissions for painting murals in private homes; it was this house painting and decorating business that would provide Merrild with much of his regular income throughout his life.

He began to exhibit locally, both at the Los Angeles Museum, and at other museums and galleries throughout the state. He had been a champion swimmer in Denmark, and his interest in athletics was maintained when he exhibited paintings with sports subjects at the 1924 Paris Olympics and at the 1932 Los Angeles Olympic Games. He continued exhibiting throughout the 1930s and '40s, gaining in stature and reputation, showing at, among many other places, the San Francisco Museum of Art, the Museum of Modern Art, the Brooklyn Museum of Art and the Whitney Museum. He won numerous awards, was the subject of many articles and his work entered major private and public collections. After the death of his mother in 1937, he returned to Denmark, spending a year abroad, traveling to France and England. He returned to Los Angeles in 1938 and continued to work, experiment and exhibit through-

out the 1940s. Merrild suffered a heart attack in 1952, and with his wife, Else, returned to Denmark where health care was more affordable. He died there in 1954.

Once in Los Angeles, Merrild's art went through several phases that can be loosely categorized as, decorative and Cubist-derived work of the 1920s; surrealist paintings, drawings, collages and constructions of the 1930s; and Flux paintings of the 1940s. His early decorative work comprised a variety of mediums, including ceramics, painted screens, and murals. He often used themes from Danish folk art including stylized flowers, deer, rabbits, and birds, and this decorative work was much in demand in Los Angeles. He supervised the decorations of the Cassandra apartment building, a luxury residence noted for its ultra modern decor, and he created murals for many private homes including that of actor Jean Hersholt. His paintings of this period are Cubist inspired, show Merrild's stylistic debt to Picasso, Braque and Gleizes, and may be considered the work of his youth, the work of an artist endeavoring to find his true voice. In content, these works range from sports subjects to social commentary, such as a 1923 work, *American Beauty, or The Movie Star*, a satiric portrait of a vain Hollywood starlet. Painted shortly after his arrival in Los Angeles, *American Beauty* is Merrild's response to the cultural environment of Hollywood he found so appalling.

Merrild soon evolved into his next phase, loosely connected to Surrealism, which comprises a large number of works and marks Merrild's development into a mature artist. Although undoubtedly aware of Breton's manifestos and other writing of the Surrealists, Merrild was not a strict Surrealist. He did not belong to any unified group and did not adhere to any codified dogma, yet his pictures of this time contain enigmatic biomorphic forms, references to sex, and images of space, clouds, water, stones and animals. Such imagery certainly falls within the framework of Surrealism, with its striving to represent states of mind, the force of the unconscious, and the power of signs.

In a variation of Surrealism, Merrild painted a group of still lives which relate to a branch of Surrealism that originated in Los Angeles called at first New Classicism and later, Post-Surrealism by its creators, Lorser Feitelson and Helen Lundeberg. Theirs was a surrealism of intellectual order rather than emotional chaos, and their works are more like diagrams than puzzles. Although a surrealist painting, like a Zen koan, cannot be grasped intellectually and must be understood intuitively, a Post-Surrealist painting, like a riddle with an answer, can be understood through the intellect. Where the Surrealists broke down the old intellectual order of reason and linear thinking, the Post-Surrealists tried to reinstate order and maintain it.

Merrild exhibited with the Post-Surrealists for a time (1934–36), but was really more of a guest than member since he did not work exclusively in that manner. In a show at the Stanley Rose Gallery in May 1935 entitled "Post-Surrealists and Other Moderns," Merrild, Feitelson and Lundeberg exhibited with such international contemporaries as Picasso, Derain, Dali, Léger, Gris and Arp. In his catalogue foreword, Jules Langsner explains some of the differences between Surrealism and Post-Surrealism: "PostSurrealism… affirms all that Surrealism negates: impeccable esthetic order rather than chaotic confusion, conscious rather than unconscious manipulation of materials, the exploration of the normal functionings of the mind rather than the individual idiosyncrasies of the dream…"[92] The key concepts of Post-Surrealism, as Langsner summarizes, are order over chaos and normal over idiosyncratic. While Merrild exhibited with the Post-Surrealists, he did not entirely share their views for his understanding of art was expansive: "It is all beautiful. Art is in all things. There is something in all ideas. There is beauty in creation, but also destruction."[93]

Soon after the show at the Stanley Rose Gallery in May, Merrild was given a one-man show in July, 1935, which opened the Hollywood Gallery of Modern Art, owned by Feitelson. Feitelson appreciated Merrild's work in that, although it expressed subjective content, it did so through clearly recognizable forms. Not all of Merrild's works were so easily defined, especially his wood constructions, several of which were in the show. Writing in the Los Angeles Times, Arthur Millier said: "Of all the artists who practice 'abstract' art in Southern California, Knud Merrild is the most convincingly impressive… [Merrild] is one of our best artists and his show offers an opportunity to study the abstract without the too frequently met complication of dubious 'self-expression' seeping through the work. Merrild pleases most when his work is most abstract. The favorite piece with most visitors is a little relief in white plaster of form that cast light shadows. It has no verbal 'meaning' whatsoever, yet it strikes everyone as beautiful…"[94] Millier also responded to the lack of chaos in Merrild's work.

But he may have misunderstood, in a sense, Merrild's preoccupation, which was not to repress or reject emotional content in favor of intellectual order, but to express the universal forces at work in which both emotion and intellect originate.

During the 1930s, Merrild developed an unusual medium in which to work that involved applying gesso to paper, painting or drawing on the resulting textured surface with watercolor or pencil, then coating the picture with wax. Gesso is commonly used to prime canvas and wood, and is applied to create a uniform, smooth surface on which to paint. Applying gesso to paper creates an ivory-like surface that Merrild manipulated to achieve the desired texture. The gesso and wax give the pictures a luminous quality, as if to suggest the patina built up over time on ancient objects. Merrild may have been inspired by the pre-Columbian works of art he saw in the Arensberg Collection, whose forms and surfaces reverberate in these works on paper.

His wood constructions of about this same period show Merrild's complete absorption and understanding of Cubism, and his ability to extend this understanding into three dimensions. His constructions, elegantly wrought and assembled, are Merrild's meditations on the most basic and yet most complicated concept: time and space. They bear such simple yet descriptive titles as *Aesthetic Function in Space* and *Perforation, (Space Organization)*. Built in three dimensions, these constructions often employ the use of daylight, their cutout shapes and forms changing as the light moves over them, at one time casting a shadow, at another, appearing flat. *Perforation (Space Organization),* 1933, is completely white, receiving its definition from sunlight passing over the cutout shapes which creates shadows of varying degree, changing the areas of dark and light as the day moves on. The use of an external force, in this case, light, in a work to create change is a complete and perfect example of Merrild's philosophy. It prefigures his use of another natural force, gravity, which he used in his Flux paintings. Many of the wood constructions incorporate the use of common objects like linoleum, wire, and mirrors, and in so doing, Merrild became California's first assemblage artist.

Aesthetic Function in Space (1928–33), his first assemblage, makes use of wood, corrugated paper and a silvered metal mirror. The mirror acts as an element of surprise when the viewer unexpectedly sees himself in the work, perhaps acting his part in an "aesthetic function." There are suggestions of a violin and an artist's palette (images which recur in Merrild's work) floating in a space of many dimensions and textures. Space is as important a component in Merrild's work and he subjects it to as much manipulation as he does form. Certainly the discovery of Pluto in 1930 would have added to Merrild's reflections on space and the cosmos. As Merrild explained: "In regarding space as a medium, I surround it by restricted areas of varied proportions; penetrate it at different angles and depths with shapes and planes, creating movement and rhythm, and in addition use various materials and colors in a related harmony to the whole." [95]

In the early 1940s, Merrild expanded his explorations into the meaning of a painting's surface, attempting to resolve its inherent message as both an image of something else and a self-contained object. He was also questioning the relationship of creator to object. These experiments and meditations resulted in Merrild's invention of "Flux," his method of pouring paint onto a moistened canvas while manipulating the motion of the canvas to create different shapes until a satisfactory result was achieved. In this bold gesture, Merrild had fused the elemental forces of gravity and movement in order to create an image, and had effectively eliminated the intermediate hand of the artist. Images became pure reflections of basic natural forces and the surface was united in form and content. The stripping away of preconceived reality begun by Cubism and elaborated by Surrealism had finally resulted in the elimination of all perspective, image, or controlled thought and had become a pure expression of motion, of Flux. It was a complete summation of Merrild's metaphysical belief in change and chance. As Merrild himself stated "To place oneself in the realm of Flux affords joy and liberation. Somewhere between life and knowledge or as D.H. Lawrence says, '—in the tension of opposites all things have their being." [96] Merrild's Flux paintings are pure expressions of his spiritual values, and his technique came to be used by other artists, especially Jackson Pollock, who employed a similar method but whose aims were different. In describing his invention, Merrild said: "Flux painting consists of applying liquid colors to a fluid surface by pouring, dripping, or other means. A natural consequence of the process is that orthodox tools are of little use, being replaced by gravitation. The point is

Knud Merrild. *Exhilaration.*
Mixed media collage on wood, 1935.
14 7/8 x 18 3/4 inches. (The Buck Collection, Laguna Hills, Calif.)

expelled at various distances, from zero to several feet above the surface—painting by remote control. The pattern created differs according to the velocity or gravitational force, and to the density or fluidity of the paint. The impact of the expelled paint with the fluid surface creates fissions or explosive eruptions, more or less violent, and the painting is set in motion in four dimensions. Mutations follow, lasting from seconds to several hours. When in motion, incessant mutations of color and form ensue, until arrested in a metaphor of its own Flux. Left alone, it becomes on automatic creation by natural law, a kinetic painting of the abstract…"[97]

Merrild worked slowly and methodically, destroying works that did not completely please him and carefully finishing those that did. His output was not large and he exhibited and retained only fully realized works. His work received critical praise from many quarters and he had as friends several important writers on art. Man Ray, who spent the 1940s in Los Angeles, made several photographic portraits of Merrild and said in a letter to him in 1943: "Having first seen your work and then spoken with you, I have been fascinated and convinced. The consistency running through all your works, their appeal to my mind and to my senses, has given me a feeling of satisfaction…"[98] He acquired Merrild's work for his own private collection. Henry Miller said of Merrild in 1945: "I regard him as one of the rare beings now alive and unfortunately all too little known." Miller showed great intuitive understanding of Merrild when he said: "In his youth a champion swimmer, Merrild is inclined to believe that it was his passion for water which inspired the discovery of a medium permitting such freedom of expression."[99] Miller owned works by Merrild, as did the Arensbergs, Lorser Feitelson, Jean Hersholt, Aldous Huxley, Ruth Maitland, Clifford Odets, Galka Scheyer and Hugh Walpole. His work appealed to literary figures, some of whom he met at the Arensbergs' home, a nexus for artistic and literary Los Angeles. It was this great and extensive collection to which Merrild had access, and for a long time it was the only place in Los Angeles where important works by Duchamp, Brancusi, Miro and other leading European artists could be seen. The Arensbergs collected pre-Colombian art as well, and the stimulating contact with both ancient and modern art must have had its effect on Merrild. In recalling the Arensbergs and their influence, Henry Hopkins stated:

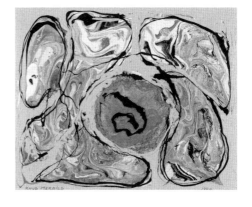

Knud Merrild. *Shawl of Petrified Fragrance.* Oil flux on paper mounted to masonite, 1944. 14 1/2 x 19 inches. (Courtesy Steve Turner Gallery)

"The collection, one of the most sophisticated ever assembled, brought together pre-Columbian objects and superior examples of twentieth-century European avant-garde art. The unusual blending of the primordial stone and clay images of Mexico and Central America with the extreme of European modernism in the Arensberg collection would affect us throughout our careers. There were no attractive impressionist pictures, so favored by American collectors at that time, but rather a group of magnificent Brancusi sculptures… an early primitive Calder mobile… as well as transitional Picassos trembling on the very edge of cubism. There was the best of Miro, Ernst, and Dali, as well as major paintings and several confounding objects by Marcel Duchamp. The only Californian that I remember to be in the collection was the enigmatic Knud Merrild, who would later become an underground hero for younger Los Angeles artists. Merrild produced strange little paintings of poured enamel which were either almost nonobjective or formed floral bouquets. Jackson Pollock may have seen these poured 'Flux' paintings during his high school days in Los Angeles. Merrild also created boxlike assemblages with constructivist and surrealist overtones." [100]

That Merrild would become a heroic figure to the next generation of Los Angeles artists is not surprising. His perseverance, his insight, his philosophical, mystical quest in combination with his unorthodox techniques and use of materials appealed to such artists as Wallace Berman, Ed Kienholz and George Herms. His importance is not only that of an innovator whose creative expressions are among the most significant of his time and place, but also as a major figure in the artistic evolution of Southern California. Through Merrild, the modernists of the 1920s, '30s and '40s were linked to the moderns of the 1950s and '60s. Apart from his significance to California, Merrild is a key figure in the evolution of American Surrealism, Abstract Expressionism and modern American sculpture. Courageous and creative, Merrild, whose own life was filled with change and chance, sought consistently to express these qualities in his art.

10

Peter Krasnow

Like most Angelenos at that time, Peter Krasnow was born elsewhere, in his case, in Ukraine in 1887. He studied art with his father, who was a house painter, and in 1907, upon hearing that art school was free in the United States, made his way first to Boston, then to Chicago, where he completed his studies at the Art Institute of Chicago in 1915. To pay his expenses, Krasnow held a job teaching art at the Hebrew Institute, where he met and soon married the organizer of the art program, Rose Bloom. Following a friend to New York in 1919, he held his first exhibition at the Whitney Studio Club. A chance remark about eucalyptus trees by a reviewer intrigued the artist and led to the Krasnows setting out for Los Angeles in 1922. They arrived in the fall at the Casa Verdugo, an old adobe landmark in Glendale on the tourist itinerary. "Here in the tropical gardens and surrounding landscape I found ample subject matter. It lasted but one season; the adobe was demolished," Krasnow recalled.[101] He nevertheless entered immediately into the local art scene. In December 1922, he exhibited his recent New York work in a four-man show at the Los Angeles Museum. It was at this exhibition where Krasnow met photographer Edward Weston, who became a lifelong friend.[102] In a letter to Krasnow written in 1955, Weston wrote: "Not many friendships last 30 or 40 years— or how many years has it been? I guess you are my oldest friend—I can't recall anyone older."[103] His work contrasted to the more staid work of his fellow exhibitors, and Krasnow, a Russian Jew, was viewed as an exotic. Headlines such as "Slav Painter Starts L.A. Art Row" and "Jewish Artist Depicts Life" described his Los Angeles art debut. The "row" referred to was the contrast between Krasnow's bold modernism and the work of his *plein air* co-exhibitors. In an interview with R.W. Borough, Krasnow said "I seek for variety of expression and believe in the fundamental principles of the old masters, which I endeavor to reconcile with the spirit of today."[104] Elizabeth Bingham, writing in Saturday Night, called Krasnow's show "a most stimulating event" and said that "No better examples could be offered for an intelligent study of modern art…"[105] Krasnow's arrival in Los Angeles had been an event of which the city took notice.

Edward Weston's wife Flora owned some lots in Tropico (now Glendale) and soon after their arrival, the Krasnows bought from her a small plot of land (with a $10 down payment) where Krasnow built his house and studio next door to the Westons.

Edward Weston. *Portrait of Peter Krasnow.* Photograph, 1923. (Courtesy Tobey C. Moss Gallery, Los Angeles. ©1981, Center for Creative Photography, Arizona Board of Regents)

Although Weston moved away in 1929, the Krasnows continued to live in this same house on Perlita Drive for the next 50 years. Krasnow would create all of his work here, and it was where the Krasnows cultivated "one of the most impressive, seemingly wild, succulent gardens in southern California."[106]

An interest in succulents and cacti gripped gardeners and artists in Los Angeles in the 1920s and 1930s. The popularity of Spanish-style homes led homeowners and landscape architects to plant gardens that would harmonize with the architecture. Succulents and cacti, many native to Mexico, soon became the plants of choice. In 1928, a Cactus and Succulent Society was formed, with headquarters at Clyde Browne's Abbey San Encino in Pasadena's Arroyo Seco.[107] Nearby, the Krasnow's garden may have been a source for images made by their friends Weston, Shore and Elise, who all found inspiration in the unusual shapes and textures of the succulents. So unlike the plants and flowers traditionally depicted in art, succulents appealed to the group of artists intent on experiencing nature anew. While Paul de Longpré painted roses, with their delicate, silky petals and pastel hues, the modernists departed from such traditional imagery and expressed nature's forms in a new way. The sturdy and sometimes grotesque-looking succulents, nearly always in shades of gray, revealed a more spare and serious side of nature than did luxurious roses.

In January 1923, Krasnow gave a talk at the MacDowell Club on "Modern Art," and in February, Stanton Macdonald Wright invited him to join the Group of Independent Artists of Los Angeles. The Group held its first exhibition that same year and produced a catalogue with an introduction by Macdonald Wright in which he pled the case for modern art. Krasnow's work of this period shows the modern influences of New York Ashcan painters and European Expressionists.

Remembering scenes and images from childhood, Krasnow began to explore Jewish themes in the mid-1920s, producing watercolors and paintings of Biblical characters and events, as well as a bronze sculpture of Adam and Eve. In 1926 he received a major commission from Temple Emanu-El in San Francisco to carve the panels for a large ceremonial chest designed by Los Angeles architect R.M. Schindler. Krasnow took Weston to see the chest in December, 1928, and Weston was moved by its power and beauty: "I take off my hat to you Peter, for a superb piece of work both in

Brett Weston. Silverpoint photograph, 1939 of a Peter Krasnow sculpture. (Courtesy Tobey C. Moss Gallery)

Peter Krasnow in his studio, c.1938.
(Courtesy Tobey C. Moss Gallery)

Peter Krasnow. *Temple Doors*, (Study).
Pencil, gilt and crayon on paper, 1940.
12 x 20 inches. (Courtesy Tobey C.
Moss Gallery)

Peter Krasnow. *Self-Portrait*.
Oil on canvas, 1928. 20 x 16 inches.
(Courtesy Tobey C. Moss Gallery)

conception and technical execution. Tears came to my eyes, which would not come hearing Al Jolson. No doubt some of the emotion was from a very personal angle: knowing Peter, his life struggle, and details of the story woven around this chest."[108]

The collaboration on this chest gives insight into the friendships between many of the artists in Southern California. Schindler and his wife Pauline were at the center of a social and artistic circle that included Weston, Armitage and the Arensbergs. Pauline Schindler had many interests, including typography, music and children's education. And she was a link to another circle, the Dunites, an eccentric group of writers, artists and spiritual seekers who made their home in the sand dunes at Oceano, just south of San Luis Obispo, during the 1930s.[109] Among the Dunites were Ella Young, poet of Celtic mythology, and Gavin Arthur, astrologer, poet and grandson of President Chester A. Arthur. Schindler wrote an article in Westways in 1934 describing the dunes and their residents, and it may have been through her that Weston first came to the dunes. There is also evidence that it was Galka Scheyer who first told Weston about the dunes. Furthermore, Weston had already met and photographed Ella Young in 1930, and he may also have come to the dunes at her invitation.[110] However he discovered them, Weston found in the dunes some of his greatest subject matter, resulting in his 1936 series of dune photographs. Weston provided photographs for the cover of the Dunites short-lived literary magazine, Dune Forum, which lasted from February to May 1934. Weston's son Brett also did cover art for the little journal. Schindler was an associate editor of the magazine, which published articles by her husband Rudolph Schindler (he was by then her ex-husband), Richard Neutra and John Cage, among others. The dunes provided an unusual retreat for those artists from Los Angeles who knew about them.[111]

At about this time Krasnow also took up lithography and created a number of images printed in small editions, among them portraits of his close friends including Weston and the writer and critic Sadakichi Hartmann. He also had his second exhibit at the Los Angeles Museum, in October 1928. In May 1930 the Stendahl Galleries held a major Krasnow exhibition that included woodcarvings, sculptures, paintings, drawings and lithographs. Arthur Millier reported "Krasnow's

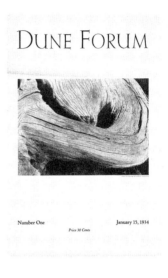

Brett Weston. Cover for Dune Forum, January, 1934. (Private collection)

semi-abstract paintings are among the best works of a modernist character produced in this region." [112]

In 1931, a comprehensive exhibition of his work at the Legion of Honor in San Francisco caused a change in the artist's direction. "A great urge to see more of the art world, to learn and to advance took possession of me that summer. I must go away. Where? France, then the art capital of the world." [113] The Krasnows lived in Paris and in the small village of Cazilliac in the Dordogne, and remained in France until 1934. During their stay, Krasnow and Weston corresponded, comparing notes on how difficult it was to be an artist during the Depression. Weston affectionately addressed the Krasnows as "Pedro and Rosita" and in one letter, reported that the collector and art patron Ruth Maitland had visited his studio and had admired one of Krasnow's lithographs. "I could have sold it if I had known the price… and sales are not to be sneezed at" wrote Weston. [114]

Upon returning to Los Angeles, Krasnow began to explore wood as a medium for sculpture. He recalled, "I canvassed the lumber yards, procured stumps, roots and entire trees, my chisel set. I began to work, probing and striving to produce work of pure sculptural character… Trees in my garden, leftover chunks in the lumber yards cast off for firewood—I combined grain and color and created huge demountables, corresponding and harmonizing, something completely inventive." [115] These demountables are among Krasnow's most original work, presenting his sense of abstraction in three-dimensions. Wood sculptures made up of slotted and pegged parts, the demountables could be assembled and reassembled in various configurations. Part organic, part abstract, these constructions are related to Weston's photographs of vegetables, shells and driftwood and to Henrietta Shore's paintings of flowers, leaves and trees. All three artists had as a goal the exploration and expression of the basic forms and rhythms of nature. From pieces of walnut or pear wood, Krasnow carved powerful tectonic forms expressive of the elemental powers in nature. Elegant yet sturdy, these sculptures of archetypal, primal forms are evocative of totems. Krasnow purposefully chose to work in wood, a medium he felt had been neglected by sculptors in favor of stone and metal. Part of his aim was to reveal the natural beauty of wood, the texture and feel of the grain, while maintaining "the 'treeness' in the finished work." [116] He worked in wood for ten years, then returned to painting after 1943.

By the late 1930s Krasnow had a sufficiently important reputation that Merle Armitage proposed doing a book on him. In a letter to Rose Krasnow, Armitage wrote that "It seems to me that Peter's work has reached a place and maturity where a book would be a very helpful and timely thing… I would like to do it—if it can be done without going broke—Certainly Peter is one of the most significant men in the west—and I know of no other man who handles wood with such skill…" [117] Unfortunately, the project did not come to pass, but Armitage clearly recognized Krasnow as one of the best artists in Southern California.

After he took up painting again in the 1940s, Krasnow evolved a semi-abstract style using intense, bright colors. Krasnow was a steadfast individualist, preferring to find his own way, resisting outside influences and steering clear of the local art scene. Scorning the marketplace, he did not have gallery representation, and preferred to sell directly to those collectors who sought him out. Several museums held retrospective exhibitions of his work before he died in 1979.

Peter Krasnow. *The Photographer. (Edward Weston).* Lithograph, 1928. 16 x 10 1/2 inches. Krasnow met Weston in 1922 and they became lifelong friends. (Private collection)

P Avashow 1928

Edward Weston. *Portrait of Elise*.
Photograph, 1936. 3 1/2 x 4 1/2 inches.
(Private collection. ©1981, Center for
Creative Photography, Arizona Board
of Regents)

11

Elise

Artist, actress, dancer, chef and vocalist, Elise Cavanna Seeds Armitage Welton (1905–1962), known simply as Elise, was another pioneer of abstraction and modernism in Los Angeles. She studied art in her native Philadelphia with Arthur B. Carles and Daniel Garber, and was active in artistic and literary circles in New York, counting among her friends e.e. cummings and Ernest Hemingway. She was a versatile, eccentric and striking woman. More than six feet tall and at one time sporting purple hair, she studied dance with Isadora Duncan and later became W.C. Fields' comic partner at the Ziegfeld Follies. At Fields' request, she came to Hollywood to act in his films, appearing notably as Field's patient in "The Dentist." Soon after her arrival she met and married Merle Armitage, who encouraged her artistic talents. Elise soon after gave up acting to devote herself exclusively to art.

In 1932, Elise began to experiment with lithography, collaborating with the premier Los Angeles printer Lynton Kistler, creating small editions of 15, 20 or 35. A contemporary review of an exhibition of her lithographs at Stendahl Galleries described "the cool precision of her lines and spots of tone, the images visualized, not through the eye, but through the mind's eye." She gained a reputation as a painter and had several exhibitions, both in Los Angeles and New York. She won the WPA commission to design the mural for the Oceanside post office in 1935, and her painting *Out of Space* was exhibited at the 1939 New York World's Fair. She illustrated many of her husband's publications, translated several others, and wrote her own cookbook. In 1934 Weyhe Gallery, New York, published the monograph on her work designed by Armitage that also included a portrait of Elise by her friend Beatrice Wood. She continued to paint throughout the 1940s, and began making sculptures from discarded aircraft parts she found at the aircraft factory in which she worked during World War II. Divorced from Armitage, she married James Welton, a music producer, in the 1940s. He featured Elise's distinctive voice on several spoken-word albums, most notably, the stories of Poe. In the early 1950s, she co-founded the art group Functionists West with Lorser Feitelson, Helen Lundeberg and Stephen Longstreet, whose goal was to break away from New York influences and reinterpret Southern California in modern forms.

Experimenting with total abstraction, Elise represents an unusual aspect of modern art in Los Angeles. While some of her work is based on natural forms, other work is non-objective, and she was one of only a few Los Angeles artists to work non-representationally. Paintings like *Red* and *Approach* are examples of such pure abstraction; they depict color and form without referring to specific objects in the physical world. In other work, although natural forms are nearly abstracted beyond recognition, they still seem to depict some of the inner workings of nature, on scales both large and small. Elise's works often have a graceful rhythm and balance, perhaps as a result of her background as a dancer. Shapes float lithely in space, their delicate equilibrium enhanced by the artist's choice of seldom-used colors. Like Merrild, Elise used abstraction to explore fundamental natural forms, and like Shore, she often portrayed the sensuous nature of flowers and plants. In the realm of abstraction, Elise had few peers in Los Angeles.

Elise was also witty, and her wry self-portraits reveal her strong comic bent. Versatile and sophisticated, Elise could illustrate Edward Bellamy's futuristic novel *Looking Backwards* in a spare, modern style, and also provide the pictures for David Hertz's *Valdemar*, a whimsical children's story about a dachshund who visits Paris.

Because of her premature death and lack of regular gallery affiliation, Elise's work was not shown widely and she has been overlooked, yet she is among the pioneers of modernism in Los Angeles and one of its ablest exponents.

Elise. *Red*. Oil on canvas, 1939. 26 x 26
inches. (Private collection, courtesy
Steve Turner Gallery)

Elise. *Hands and Pods*. Lithograph, c.1932.
9 1/2 x 12 inches. (Los County Museum
of Art, Gift of Merle Armitage)

Elise. *(Untitled, Abstract).* Oil on canvas,
1935. 30 x 25 inches. (The Buck Collection,
Laguna Hills, Calif.)

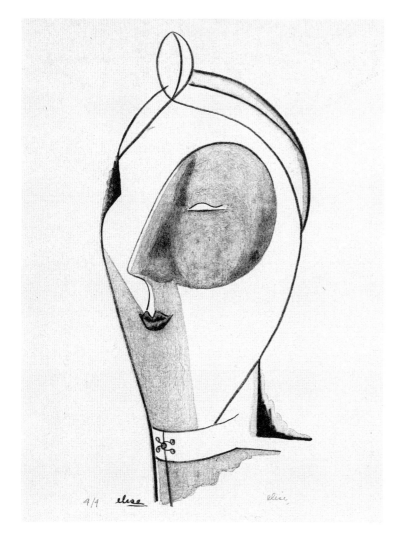

Elise. *Self-Portrait*. Lithograph, c.1930.
10 1/4 x 5 inches. (Private collection)

Elise. *Modern Dance*. Lithograph, 1935.
7 x 4 inches. (Private collection)

12

Paul Landacre

As a young man, Paul Landacre (1893–1963) was interested in horticulture and track. He had been an outstanding athlete in high school and intended to join the Ohio State University track team after he enrolled there in 1913. But in the spring of 1915, the promising runner contracted a severe sinus infection that required surgical intervention. A secondary infection resulted, and he was near death. Bedridden for six months, he eventually recovered, but the illness left him with several physical disabilities, including an inability to raise his arms above his head and a crippled right leg. In a cruel twist of fate, the former track star would have to walk with a cane for the rest of his life.

Because his father had moved to Southern California, Landacre went to visit him in Chula Vista in 1916 hoping to continue his recuperation. Still interested in horticulture and while enjoying the countryside near his father's home, Landacre began to sketch the local scenery. He submitted his work to an advertising agency in nearby San Diego, and, to his surprise, was hired as an illustrator, beginning what he thought would be a career as an advertising artist. To learn more technical skills, Landacre moved to Los Angeles and enrolled in the Otis Art Institute in 1923. Finding that wood engraving was a medium that appealed to him, he abandoned advertising and decided to pursue the difficult art of carving and printing woodblocks as a fine artist. He recalled:

> "I came to California and tried to make a living as a commercial artist as I had a natural ability–or inclination–to draw. I soon found there wasn't any art in commercial art; at least, there was no satisfaction in it. I don't know exactly why I took up wood engraving except that black and white seemed more interesting and colorful than color and after trying various mediums–etching, dry point, aquatint, lithography, etc., I settled on wood engraving as the medium that had to me a greater range than anything else. Its exacting technical requirements are a challenge–in fact, no one in this country or any other has faintly touched the possibilities inherent in the medium...."[118]

Paul Landacre at his press, c.1934.
(William Andrews Clark Memorial Library)

Landacre excelled at creating imaginative, simple, well-designed works. That he worked only in black and white is a testament to his abilities. While other artists used a full color palette to render their visions of hill, coast and arroyo, it is Landacre's images that remain in the mind's eye as among the most evocative and accurate of all the artistic views of California. His simple, sinuous lines, his ability to render sunlight and shadow and the palpable weight of his images are unrivaled by any of his contemporaries.

Landacre had met advertising copywriter Margaret McCreery in San Diego in 1922, and they were married in 1925. Margaret began working in a department store when the couple first settled in Los Angeles, but she took a job as Jake Zeitlin's secretary in 1928, whereupon the Landacres and Zeitlin became close friends. They were also neighbors, living in the same hillside area of Echo Park. With Margaret holding down a job, the couple had enough money for Landacre to pursue his career as an artist. Landacre transformed his interest in horticulture to an inspired interpretation of nature, and his athletic ability became the physical prowess needed to carve thick blocks of wood and operate heavy printing presses. With Margaret's unflagging help, he was able to meet the physical challenges presented to him.

In 1930, the Landacres were invited by friends and neighbors, Fay Fuqua (an old friend of Jake Zeitlin from Fort Worth), and Ethel Ingalls, to join them on an automobile trip up the coast to Big Sur and Carmel. It was arranged through Fuqua that the group stay at Edward Weston's house in Carmel while he was away. Landacre was impressed by the dramatic, rugged coastline and made sketches all along the way. Later that year, Fuqua took the couple to the Coachella Valley, where Landacre was equally moved by the desert scenery. The resulting wood engravings made from his sketches were published in Landacre's first, and most important, illustrated book, *California Hills and Other Wood-Engravings*, published in 1931. In the foreword, Arthur Millier wrote that "there [is] nothing akin to them in contemporary wood-engraving." The dramatic chiaroscuro, the forceful lines, the weight and power of the images revealed Landacre as one of the nation's best, and distinctive, printmakers at a time when printmaking was undergoing a revival. While other American artists, including Grant Wood and Thomas Hart Benton, chose lithography as their printmaking medium, Landacre opted for the much more difficult task of wood engraving, and he became its undisputed master. *California Hills* was one of the winners of the prestigious Fifty Books of the Year award, and because he came to national attention, he received commissions to illustrate several other books.

Just before *California Hills* was published, Jake Zeitlin gave Landacre his first exhibition, and it was through the bookseller that the artist met many of the people who became his greatest collectors and supporters. With the success of *California Hills*, Landacre's work began to sell. During the Depression, however, Landacre struggled to make ends meet, and it was Margaret's salary that kept the couple going. At times, the artist bartered his prints for household goods, as when in 1933–34 he traded 16 prints to coffee broker James L. Duff for an equal number of packages of coffee. Landacre's prints were selling in galleries for between $6 and $40 apiece, with an average price of $10, of which the artist received two-thirds. Although the Landacres lived modestly, they faced a monthly economic struggle. In late 1933 Landacre joined the WPA, and "for a salary of $26.50 per week, he was obligated to produce one wood-engraving a month." [119] This arrangement lasted for a time, but the Landacres were chronically short of money. Finally in 1936, Zeitlin and Delmer Daves, the movie screenwriter and director, organized The Paul Landacre Association, a group of 12 collectors, each of whom contributed $100 per year in exchange for which each member received a Landacre wood engraving every month. The stated goal of the association was "to help an important artist live by his work and leave him free to develop his art to a greater expression." [120] In 1938 the subscriber list grew to twenty. Among the patrons were Dr. Elmer Belt, Mrs. E.L. Doheny, Kay Francis, Mrs. Samuel Goldwyn, and, of course, Daves and Zeitlin. This financial aid certainly enabled Landacre to continue as an artist. As difficult as his pursuit was, it was equally rewarding, as Landacre expressed in a 1936 letter to Dallas Dupre, an old school friend from Ohio: "This trying to be an artist is a long, long pull, but I'm going to spare both of us all the sordid details. To tell the truth, though, I never expected to be as happy as I have the last ten years, and working like hell all the time, especially the last four or five." [121]

Landacre exhibited locally with many of his friends and fellow artists. In May, 1932 an exhibition of etchings, lithographs and block prints was held at The Community Arts Association at the Public Library and Art Gallery in Palos Verdes, where Landacre's work was on view along with prints by Franz Geritz, Henrietta Shore and Arthur Millier. Landacre was friendly with these artists, and was a vital member of the Zeitlin group. In

Paul Landacre. *Desert Wall*.
Woodengraving, 1930. 8 7/8 x 11 3/8
inches. (Los Angeles County Museum
of Art, Gift of Mr. and Mrs. Joseph M.
Landacre and Mrs. James C. McCreery,
© Estate of Paul Landacre)

addition to being part of The Breakfast Club, Landacre was a member of another group that met every Thursday night at Ward Ritchie's house beginning in 1937. Among the regulars were Zeitlin and Daves; artists Fletcher Martin and Barse Miller; sculptor Gordon Newell as well as friends who were doctors, musicians and lawyers. In 1935 he participated in the exhibition Prints by Living Americans at the Los Angeles Art Association, and in 1940 he had a one-man show at Pomona College where he spent five weeks as a visiting artist in residence. He continued to create prints and to illustrate books, often for the Limited Editions Club, throughout the 1940s, and in 1946 he was elected to membership in the National Academy of Design.

Like the Krasnows, the Landacres lived and worked in the same home for many decades. They were very attached to their house and studio on El Moran and were active in their Echo Park community; as Margaret observed: "You see, 'art' is practiced here along with various other concerns—pruning trees, repairing the roof, watching and feeding wildlife and so on. Of course, other artists live on wooded hillsides, too, and so do other people, and it must be conceded that to some of us this kind of environment is not only valuable but absolutely necessary—a degree of seclusion, the life of growing things, awareness that we are a part of nature." [122]

Landacre concentrated on book illustration in the 1950s, and he began teaching at Otis Art Institute in 1953, continuing to teach there for the next ten years. After Margaret died in early May 1963, Landacre lost his own desire to live and died shortly after, on June 3, of injuries sustained in a suicide attempt.

Paul Landacre's work stands out for its technical virtuosity and modern approach. No one else had conceived of sunny California in such black and white terms. While the California Impressionists were immersed in color, Landacre chose a more discreet, more stringent approach. His prints have a magical quality, inferring in their shadows all the shade and light of the California sunlit landscape. His series on the hills of California show the landscape with its visual, sensual appeal. His rolling hills capture the feel of the land, and after seeing a Landacre print, the landscape seems to be imitating it, rather than vice-versa. Landacre's reputation as one of the greatest of American printmakers is well deserved and his achievement has propelled him beyond the rank of regional artist.

Paul Landacre. *August Seventh.* Woodengraving, 1936. 12 1/8 x 8 inches. (Los Angeles County Museum of Art, Gift of Mr. and Mrs. Joseph M. Landacre and Mrs. James C. McCreery, © Estate of Paul Landacre)

Conclusion

A remote pueblo in 1850, Los Angeles grew into a prosperous city in less than 50 years. After its art museum opened in 1913, Los Angeles had all the accoutrements of a big, modern American city, including a group of resident artists who specialized in rendering the magnificent local scenery. While these landscape artists predominated, a small group of artists with modern ideas about art began to coalesce, and although they faced hostility, they persevered as professionals and became nationally known, adding a distinct Los Angeles facet to American modernism. With few allies, these artists banded together, finding champions in book and art dealer Jake Zeitlin and impresario-turned-designer Merle Armitage, both of whom were instrumental in creating an environment for artists to work and the public to learn. Because art is often more than just the work of an artist, it takes the dedication of a dealer, promoter or writer to create an environment in which the public can approach, investigate and acquire the art. Zeitlin and Armitage provided the means for the modernists in Los Angeles to reach their audience, and while the audience was small, it was influential. Generally, enough collectors, dealers, critics and museums recognized the value of the work of the five artists covered in this study to support their careers as artists. The contributions of these pioneers, recognized by a few who understood their aims during their lifetimes, have been more clearly understood and valued with time.

What distinguishes the Los Angeles modernists from American modernism in general is their concentration on the natural, their exploration of the shape and structure of natural forms. Whereas other aspects of modernism celebrated the machine and other man-made structures, Los Angeles modernism was nature-based. Its ablest practitioners, among them Merrild, Shore, Krasnow, Elise and Landacre, created work that reveals nature both in its simplest and most powerful forms. In a place so lavishly natural as Los Angeles, where plants of all kinds grow profusely, where the sun, nearly always shining, illuminates mountain, desert and valley and sets over a vast ocean, where the ground underfoot can tremble and crack with the might of an earthquake, where wildflowers can appear overnight after a spring rain, where a blazingly hot day can turn into a bone-chilling night, where telescopes on mountaintops can detect the secrets of stars and planets, it is no wonder that artists chose nature as muse and inspiration.

Modernism, not limited to one region, had various manifestations throughout the country. Although New York was the center of the art world, big cities like Chicago, Boston, San Francisco and Los Angeles all developed their own art communities, as did smaller towns like Old Lyme, Provincetown and Taos. Art from such disparate, and often remote places was no longer viewed as provincial; instead, it came to be understood as regional and was valued. Although they sold their work mainly in New York, many important American artists lived elsewhere, including Thomas Hart Benton and Grant Wood, who lived in the Midwest; Georgia O'Keeffe, who abandoned New York for New Mexico; Charles Sheeler, who lived in Pennsylvania; and the adventurous few who lived on the West Coast. Each area created a distinct form of American modernism, and as expected, the art of each region reflected its cultural and geographical attributes. Although they differed in their inspiration, all modernists were committed to paring down forms, to revealing the essentials of an image and to eliminating unnecessary detail. Theirs was a taut, spare ideal, a cleansing and reorganizing of the accumulation of beliefs, theories and attitudes that had built up over time in Western culture. The modernists saw the world anew, and created a new set of values to go along with their fresh vision. The Los Angeles modernists focused their vision on nature, as did the landscape artists who preceded them. In presenting the skeletal elements of natural phenomena, the modernists provided a new foundation upon which to build a radically altered vision of art. In returning art to its primal, basic components, to elemental stones, raw wood and simple, natural forms, the modernists invited art, and Western culture, to renew itself through integrity, simplicity and strength.

Acknowledgements

I could not have completed this book without the help and encouragement of many friends and colleagues, and I wish to express my gratitude to them. Thank you to: Michael Dawson, Terry DeLapp, William Dailey, Andrea Liss, Steve Martin, Tobey Moss, Mary Woronov, Gerald Buck, Whitney Ganz, Royce Foster; the staff at the Archives of American Art; Bruce Whiteman and the staff at the Clark Library; and Sharon Goodman, Ilene Fort, Cheryle Robertson and Shaula Coyl at the Los Angeles County Museum of Art.

Lastly, I thank Steve Turner, my husband, who inspires and informs all that I do, and whose knowledge, insights and guidance have contributed mightily to this work.

[1] Part of the voters' eagerness to obtain more water was a result of the Water Commissioners' report of 1904, in which it was revealed that for "ten days in July the daily consumption of water exceeded the inflow into the [city's] resevoirs by nearly four million gallons." (Allen Kelly, "Introductory Historical Sketch of the Los Angeles Aqueduct" in *Complete Report on Construction of the Los Angeles Aqueduct,* 1916, p. 9.) Voters were unaware, however, of the intrigue and illegal manoeuvers undertaken by city officials to obtain land in the Owens Valley and San Fernando Valley. For a complete summary of these events, see Kevin Starr, *Material Dreams,* 1990, pp.50-61 and Margaret Leslie Davis, *Rivers in the Desert,* 1993, pp.21-32.

[2] The park was also the site of the new State Exposition Building, the State Armory and the Coliseum. For brevity, I will refer to the museum as the Los Angeles Museum of Art.

[3] The proponents of the museum included its original Board of Governors, among whose members were William Bowen, prominent attorney and city council member; George Bovard, President of USC; William Spalding, eminent Los Angeles newspaperman; and Mrs. William Housh, art supporter and wife of the principal of Los Angeles High School. They had their first official board meeting on March 19, 1910.

[4] Los Angeles Graphic, November 1913, clipping from files of the Los Angeles County Museum of Natural History, hereafter referred to as LACMNH files.

[5] The other members of the committee were Everett Maxwell, William Bowen and A.F. Rosenheim.

[6] Unmarked press clipping, November 1913, LACMNH files. Henrietta Housh was president of the Ruskin Art Club, through which she advocated for a museum and for modern American art. (cf. Bessie Beatty, "Los Angeles Club News," in *Club Life,* November, 1905, p.13.)

[7] Los Angeles Times, undated clipping, LACMNH files.

[8] Los Angeles Graphic, undated clipping, LACMNH files.

[9] Guy Rose and Alice Klauber were artists, Robert Harshe had been Assistant Chief of Fine Arts at the PPIE, and Antony Anderson was the Art Editor at the Los Angeles Times.

[10] Von Keith, Joseph H. *Von Keith's Westward or 1000 Items on the Wonders and Curiosities of Southern California,* 1887 as quoted in Nancy Dustin Wall Moure, *Loners, Mavericks & Dreamers* (Laguna Beach: Laguna Art Museum, 1993), p.43.

[11] Theophilus d'Estrella, letter to Granville Redmond, quoted in *Granville Redmond* (Oakland: Oakland Museum, 1988), p.18. The first Kodak cameras were available in 1888, and within six months, thirteen thousand had been sold.

[12] Women's clubs played an important role in the development of the art market in early Los Angeles, and other clubs with art interests included the Friday Morning Club, founded in 1891, the Ebell Club, organized in 1894, as well as the Cosmos Club and the Wednesday Morning Club.

[13] Arthur Millier, "Growth of Art in California" in Frank J. Taylor, *California, Land of Homes,* 1929, p.334.

[14] Merle Armitage. *Accent on Life* (Ames: Iowa State University, 1965), p.238.

[15] F.B. Davison, *Commemorative of the Official Opening. The Los Angeles Aqueduct and Exposition Park,* 1913.

[16] Michael Williams, "Art in California," in *Illustrated Catalogue of the Post-Exposition Exhibition in the Department of Fine Arts, Panama-Pacific International Exposition* (San Francisco: San Francisco Art Association, 1916), p.111 Williams was the art critic for the San Francisco Examiner.

[17] Photography was initially viewed as a scientific medium and photographers were not looked upon as artists; artistic photography did not develop until the beginning of the 20th century, and a long-running debate ensued over the merits of photography as an art form. Conversely, the motion picture developed immediately as an artistic medium (being an offshoot of the theatre), and it was not until later that documentary motion pictures evolved into a legitimate form of cinema.

[17A] The work went through several editions and was the most influential book on color in the 19th century. Chevreul defined 15,000 color tones and was the first to formulate the general principles and effects of the simultaneous contrast of colors. The Impressionists, especially Seurat and Signac, derived their color systems from Chevreul, applying primary colors with intermediate tones as opposing spots, letting the eye of the observer combine them on the canvas.

[18] Saturday Night, (May 17, 1924): 9.

[19] For an overview of the Arensbergs and their life in Los Angeles, see Bonnie Clearwater (editor), *West Coast Duchamp* (Miami: Grassfield Press, 1991).

[20] His collection included work by Kandinsky, Nolde, Pechstein, Grosz, Kokoschka, Modigliani, Archipenko and Schiele, as well as works by Los Angeles artists Boris Deutsch and Lorser Feitelson. The collection was exhibited at the Los Angeles Museum June 16–July 31, 1935. In the foreword to the catalogue, Preston Harrison, Los Angeles first major art collector, remarked, "Los Angeles has been less happy than most other large American cities in having a group of many discriminating art collectors. Mr. von Sternberg is one of the most notable exceptions."

[21] Mabel Urmy Seares, American Magazine of Art 9, no. 2, (December 1917): 58–64. Seares was the sister of Clarence Urmy (1858–1923) first native-born poet of California.

[22] Mary N. Dubois, "The Los Angeles Modern Art Society," The Los Angeles Graphic, 2 December 1916, p.4.

[23] *American Modernists*, exhibition catalogue, (Los Angeles: Los Angeles Museum of History, Science and Art, 1920).

[24] Los Angeles Times, 14 January 1923. Its members included Boris Deutsch, Max Reno and Ben Berlin.

[25] Edward Weston, *The Daybooks of Edward Weston*, ed. Nancy Newhall, (New York: Aperture, 1990), part II, p.4

[26] S. Madconald Wright, *A Treatise on Color*, Los Angeles, 1924, p.27 as reprinted in *The Art of Stanton Macdonald-Wright* (Washington D.C.: Smithsonian Press, 1967).

[27] Jean B. Kentle, "In Educational Circles," Saturday Night (March 31, 1923): 17.

[28] Jackson Pollack, Arts and Architecture (February 1944): 14.

[29] "The WPA Federal Art Project, a Summary of Activities and Accomplishments," as quoted in Marlene Park & Gerald E. Markowitz, *New Deal for Art* (Hamilton, NY: Gallery Association of New York State, 1977), p.28.

[30] Olin Dows to Igor Pantuhoff, Sept. 4, 1936, as quoted in Park and Markowitz, op.cit., p.31.

[31] Los Angeles Times, 12 September 1926.

[32] Armitage and Geritz had collaborated as early as 1924 when Geritz provided a woodcut, composed of portraits of Rosa Ponsell and other opera stars, for Armitage's announcement of his 1924–25 concert season.

[33] Although born in America, Feininger worked in Germany. Kandinsky and Jawlensky were Russian, while Klee was Swiss.

[34] Unsigned review, LAMNH files.

[35] Unsigned review, LAMNH files.

[36] Herman Reuter, Hollywood Citizen-News, Feb. 29, 1936.

[37] Sonia Wolfson, unsourced review, LAMNH files.

[38] *Jake Zeitlin, Books and the Imagination: Fifty Years of Rare Books*, transcript from an oral history, UCLA, p.170

[39] Ibid., pp.175–6

[40] *Daybooks of Edward Weston*, op. cit., p.151

[41] The opening announcement for the shop, "An Unofficial Map of Booklovers' Lane & Environs" has a map of the area which includes Zoitlin's neighbors: Holmes, Lofland, Rogers, Dawson's, and Acadia bookshops, and in a cartouche is a woodcut portrait of Zeitlin by Paul Landacre.

[42] Ward Ritchie, *Jake Zeitlin* (Northridge, CA: Santa Susana Press, 1978), p.5.

[43] Zeitlin, *Books and the Imagination*, p.65.

[44] "The Great Age of Printing, Offered for Sale by Jake Zeitlin," book catalogue, 1929.

[45] Jake Zeitlin: Books… Being The Fifth Catalogue. Book catalogue, 1930.

[46] "Two American Paintings," 4pp. brochure, Jake Zeitlin, c.1930.

[47] Zeitlin, *Books and the Imagination*, p.470.

[48] Ibid., pp. 84–5.

[49] Ward Ritchie, "The Primavera Press," in James D. Hart and Ward Ritchie, *Influences on California Printing* (Los Angeles: William Andrews Clark Memorial Library, 1970), p.53

[50] Ibid., p.64.

[51] Zeitlin, *Books and the Imagination*, pp.534–35.

[52] Ward Ritchie, "A Rush of Memories of Printers Past," in *A Bibilophile's Los Angeles*,

ed. John Bidwell, (Los Angeles: William Andrews Clark Memorial Library, 1985), p.92.

[53] Ibid., p. 96.

[54] Zeitlin, *Books and the Imagination*, pp.111–12.

[55] Zeitlin, op. cit., pp.111-12.

[56] Ibid., p. 449.

[57] Armitage, op. cit., 1965, p.257.

[58] Ward Ritchie, "Merle Armitage, His Many Loves and Varied Lives," in *Of Bookmen and Printers* (Los Angeles: Dawson's Book Shop, 1989), pp. 65 & 74.

[59] Zeitlin, *Books and the Imagination*, p.67

[60] Ibid., p.68.

[61] An article on the murals appeared in California Arts & Architecture, (November 1929)

[62] Zeitlin, *Books and the Imagination*, p.75.

[63] Armitage, op. cit., p.257.

[64] Letter from Merle Armitage to Edward B. Rowan, Oct. 22, 1934, as quoted in Richard D. McKinzie, *The New Deal for Artists* (Princeton: Princeton University Press, 1975), p.31. Rowan was the assistant director of the Public Works of Art Project.

[65] Letter from Merle Armitage to Edward B. Rowan, April 10, 1935, as quoted in McKinzie, loc. cit.

[66] Armitage, *Accent on Life*, p.262.

[67] Touring Topics, (June 1927): 11.

[68] Lustig went on to become a major force in modern typography and was involved with the redesign of California Arts & Architecture in the 1940s.

[69] These include *Libros Californianos Or Five Feet of California Books*, a bibliography and guide to collecting Californiana published in 1931, and *California Through Four Centuries, A Handbook of Memorable Historical Dates*, issued in 1935.

[70] Ritchie, *Of Bookmen and Printers*, p.24.

[71] The founding members were Ainslie Galleries, Bartlett Galleries, Biltmore Salon, Kanst Galleries, Kievits Galleries, Newhouse Galleries, Dalzell Hatfield, Stendahl Galleries and Wilshire Galleries.

[72] Although Elizabeth A.T. Smith, in her article "Arts & Architecture and the Los Angeles Vanguard" in *Blueprints for Modern Living* (Cambridge, MA: MIT Press, 1998), states that "Between 1938 and February, 1939, the date of Entenza's formal listing as editor on the magazine's masthead…", after careful examination, I did not find Entenza listed as editor until the February, 1940 issue.

[73] The Case Study House project was a postwar project aimed at influencing the building of affordable, modern housing. Thirty-six houses were built by leading architects including Richard Neutra, J.R. Davidson, Charles and Ray Eames, Raphael Soriano, Craig Ellwood and others. See *Blueprints for Modern Living*, op. cit, for a detailed account of the project.

[74] Saturday Night, (March 21, 1936): 2

[75] Saturday Night, (June 13, 1936): 2

[76] Los Angeles Times, 25 November 1917.

[77] In 1923 Shore exhibited at the Erich Gallery and O'Keeffe at the Anderson Galleries.

[78] *Daybooks of Edward Weston*, pp.19–20

[79] Ibid., p.20.

[80] Ibid., pp.20–21

[71] Ibid., p.54

[82] Los Angeles Times, 9 October 1927.

[83] Roger Aikin and Richard Lorenz, *Henrietta Shore. A Retrospective Exhibition* (Monterey, CA: Monterey Peninsula of Art, 1986), p.26.

[84] Ibid.

[85] Ibid.,p.27

[86] Ibid.,p.29.

[87] Arthur Millier in *A Private Collection of Paintings Comprising Representative Works of Some of the Living Artists of Southern California* (Rochester, NY: The Memorial Art Gallery, c.1930), p.41.

[88] Merle Armitage, *Henrietta Shore* (New York: E. Weyhe, 1933), pp.9–11.

[89] Roger Aikin, American Art, (Winter 1992): 60.

[90] Aiken and Lorenz, op. cit., p. 38.

[91] Knud Merrild. *A Poet and Two Painters. A Memoir of D.H. Lawrence* (London: Routledge, 1938, p.308.)

[92] Jules Langsner, *Post-Surrealists and Other Moderns*, exhibition brochure from the Stanley Rose Gallery, 1935, p.2

[93] Merrild, op. cit., p.220

[94] Los Angeles Times, 21 July 1935.

[95] Knud Merrild, quoted in Boyer Galleries exhibition brochure, New York, 1939, p.2.

[96] Henry Miller, "Knud Merrild, A Holiday in Paint," in Circle no. 6, Berkeley, 1945, p.39.

[97] Jules Langsner, *Knud Merrild 1894–1954*, exhibition catalogue, (Los Angeles: Los Angeles County Musuem of Art, 1965), p.11

[98] Knud Merrild, *Twenty Five Year Retrospective*. exhibition catalogue, (Bevery Hills: Modern Institute of Art, 1948), p.4

[99] Henry Miller, "Knud Merrild. A Holiday in Paint," in Circle 6, Berkeley, 1945, p.39

[100] Henry Hopkins. "Recollecting the Beginnings," in *Forty Years of California Assemblage* (Los Angeles: Wright Art Gallery/University of California, 1989), p.15

[101] Peter Krasnow. *A Retrospective Exhibition* (Los Angeles: 1975), p.[5].

[102] The other exhibitors were John Coolidge, Jean Mannheim and E. Roscoe Shrader.

[103] Krasnow papers, Archives of American Art.

[104] R.W. Borough, "Slav Painter Starts L.A. Art Row," Los Angeles Express, 28 December 1922.

[105] Saturday Night, (December 23, 1922).

[106] Amy Conger. *Edward Weston: Photographs from the Collection of the Center for Creative Photography* (Tucson: Center for Creative Photography, 1992), Fig.1716/1942.

[107] Clyde Browne (1872–1942), letterpress printer, publisher and organist, built his own stone house and studio, the Abbey San Encino, where he lived a life modeled on that of Elbert Hubbard and the Roycrofters. It was here, beginning in 1930, that the journal of the Cactus and Succulent Society was printed, and Browne rented studio space to various artists and writers throughout the 1930s. Although he was not a modernist, he was friendly with Ward Ritchie and others, and would certainly have known members of the Zeitlin circle.

[108] *Daybooks of Edward Weston II*, p.98

[109] For a complete overview, see Norm Hammond, *The Dunites* (Santa Barbara: South County Historical Society, 1992).

[110] Conger, *Edward Weston*, 797/1934

[111] Pauline Schindler, "Oceano Dunes and Their Mystics," in Westways, (February 1934): pp.12–13 & 36.

[112] *Exhibition by Peter Krasnow*, Stendahl Art Galleries, May 5–17, 1930.

[113] Krasnow, op. cit., p.5

[114] Krasnow papers, Archives of American Art

[115] Krasnow, op. cit., p.[7].

[116] Arthur Millier, *Peter Krasnow, 35 Years of His Art*, 1954, p.4

[117] Letter dated Oct. 26 [1936], Krasnow papers, Archives of American Art

[118] Letter from PL to Carl Zigrosser, July 23, 1936. Paul Landacre Papers, William Andrews Clark Memorial Library, Los Angeles

[119] Anthony Lehman, *Paul Landacre. A Life and a Legacy* (Los Angeles: Dawson's Book Shop, 1983), p.83. This is the authoritative source for information on Landacre.

[120] Ibid, p.86

[121] Letter from PL to Dallas Dupre, Jr. March 22, 1936. Paul Landacre papers.

[122] Lehman, op. cit., p.146

Henrietta Shore. *Cypress Trees, Point Lobos*.
Oil on canvas, c. 1930. 30 1/2 x 26 1/2
inches. (Private collection, courtesy Steve
Turner Gallery)

Henrietta Shore. *Succulents*. Pastel on paper,
c. 1930. 19 5/8 x 23 5/8 inches. (The Buck
Collection, Laguna Hills, Calif.)

Henrietta Shore. *Floripondes*. Oil on
canvas, c. 1925. 24 x 20 1/8 inches.
(The Buck Collection, Laguna Hills, Calif.)

Henrietta Shore. *Two Leaves*. Oil on
canvas, c. 1923. 32 1/2 x 20 2/3 inches.
(Collection of Royce & Jim Foster)

Knud Merrild. *Aesthetic Function In Space*. Painted wood construction with painted cutouts of masonite, painted corrugated cardboard and silvered metal, 1928-33. 31 x 22 3/4 inches.(Courtesy Steve Turner Gallery)

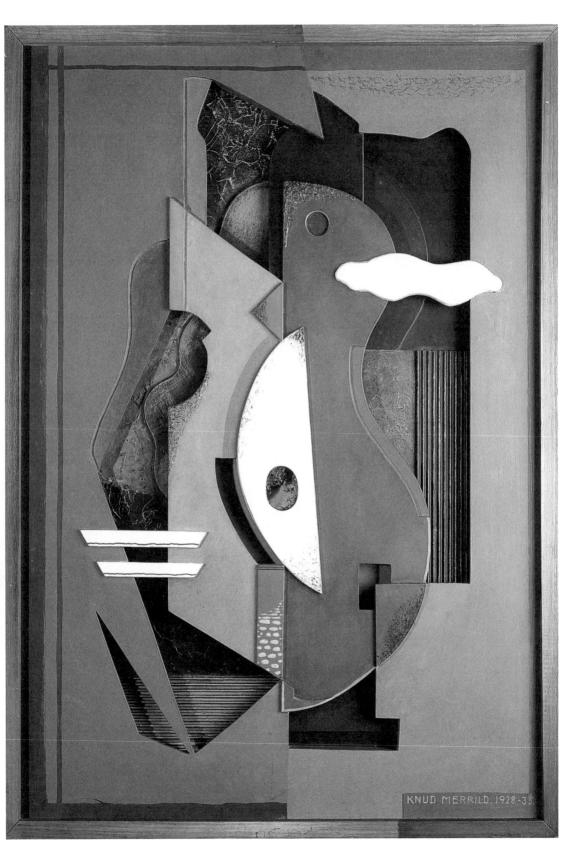

KNUD MERRILD. 1931

Knud Merrild. *Primaries*. Painted wood
construction with corrugated cardboard,
silver foil, painted, unapinted and flocked
paper, 1938. 16 1/4 x 13 1/4 inches.
(Courtesy Steve Turner Gallery)

Knud Merrild. *Untitled Abstraction*.
Construction: oil on wood, 1936.
15 1/2 x 11 3/4 inches. (Ex collection:
May Ray. Courtesy Steve Turner Gallery)

Peter Krasnow. *(Untitled [Demountable]).*
Wood: walnut, 1938. 58 x 13 x 10 inches.
(Courtesy Tobey C. Moss Gallery)

Peter Krasnow. *(Untitled, [Demountable]).*
Wood (walnut, mahogany, oak, paduak and
goncho alves), 1938. Entire piece: 106 x 102 x
24 inches. (Los Angeles County Museum of Art)

Peter Krasnow. *(Untitled figures, Male
Female).* Wood, c. 1935. 20 x 3 x 2 inc
and 17 3/4 x 10 x 2 inches. (The Buck
Collection, Laguna Hills, Calif.)

Elise. *Equilibrium*. Oil on canvas, 1939.
32 x 24 inches. (The Buck Collection,
Laguna Hills, Calif.)

Elise. *Approach*. Oil on canvas, 1939.
27 x 22 inches. (The Buck Collection,
Laguna Hills, Calif.)

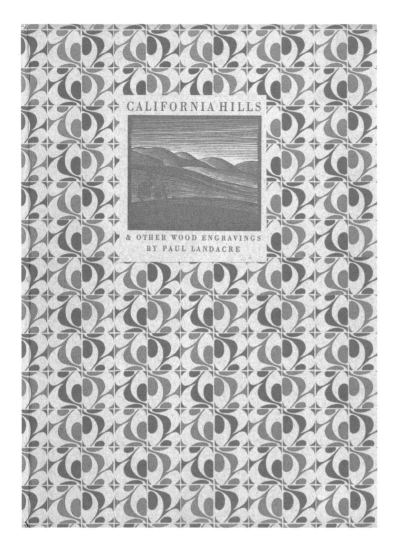

Paul Landacre. *California HIlls & Other
Wood Engravings*, 1931. Front cover.
12 2/4 x 9 7/8 inches. (Private collection)

Paul Landacre. *Nimbus*. Woodengraving, 1934.
8 1/4 x 10 5/8 inches. (Los Angeles County
Museum of Art, gift of Mr. and Mrs. Joseph
M. Landacre and Mrs. James C. McCreery,
© Estate of Paul Landacre)

2

Architecture

A NEW
CREATIVE MEDIUM

by Natalie W. Shivers

Contents:

Foreword

When Swiss emigré architect Albert Frey arrived in Palm Springs in 1934, he exulted in its spectacular landscape: "The sun, the pure air and the simple forms of the desert create perfect conditions for architecture."[1] Frey had come to California to supervise the construction of one of the first modern buildings in Palm Springs. The structure's geometric machine-made forms, a startling contrast to the raw land and rugged mountains, represented the introduction of contemporary European architecture to the desert community.

In the decades before Frey's arrival in Palm Springs, visionary architects had been gathering in Southern California with the self-proclaimed mandate to create a new architecture for the industrial age. As European culture was crumbling between the world wars, the American West seemed to present a "tabula rasa"—a blank slate—where civilization could be re-invented and improved. Designers were inspired by California's sublime landscape and climate to propose new interdependent relationships between living, nature, and shelter.

The region was poised on the edge of its modern future as the world emerged from war in 1918. Architects, convinced of the power of design to revolutionize society, helped lead the charge forward. They saw the Western frontier as the opportunity to build a modern utopia. There progress had equated with physical control of the natural environment—houses built of earth in a place without wood or stone, roads carved through mountains, water piped across the desert. For avant-garde architects the redesign of the man-made environment—its cities, buildings, and landscapes—promised to be the next step in the region's history.

In the era between the world wars, modern design took on the force of an evangelical movement in Southern California: architects saw their mandate as nothing less than to create a total environment for contemporary living. Not content merely to design buildings, architects wanted to re-define ways people would live and work in the industrial era heralded as "The Machine Age." "Real modernity is not a question of a different set of cornices and columns," proclaimed Rudolph Schindler in 1935, "but based on a new aesthetic towards life and its frame, the building." Designers joined a chorus of social and political reformers advocating the improvement of people's lives by improving their dwellings and work places. "We are what our environment makes us," Schindler pronounced, "and if our environment is such as to produce excellent health, beauty, joy, and comfort, it will reflect immediately in our lives."[2]

In the 1920s and 30s, modern architects saw themselves as vital catalysts and collaborators in the creation of the region's future. They aimed to redesign the entire physical setting for contemporary life—from tableware to civic centers, from drive-through banks and drive-up restaurants, to the single-family house and large-scale public housing. They turned their hands to theater and film sets, books and magazines, even cars and airplanes. They wanted to shape all aspects of the region's daily life. "It will be the most interesting phase of architectural development since the Gothic cathedrals," exclaimed industrial designer Kem Weber, "with possibilities never before equalled. We shall be making, not copying, architectural history."[3]

The ambition for a revolutionary new architecture coincided with a pivotal time in the region's history—its physical transformation from a sparsely settled desert area into the largest metropolitan district in the United States. Technologically precocious with the advent of the aircraft, automobile, and movie industries, Southern California was eager to fulfill its promise as a brave new world. At the time, industrialization was unleashing a social and economic

Kocher-Samson Office Building,
Palm Springs, 1934; architects:
Albert Frey with A. Lawrence Kocher.

The Kocher-Samson Office Building
introduced the machine-made forms
of European modern architecture to
the desert community of Palm Springs.
(Architecture and Design Collection,
University Art Museum, University of
California, Santa Barbara)

maelstrom throughout the United States. Nowhere was this felt more keenly than Southern California, where tumultuous historical, social, and technological forces were re-shaping the region's physical form.

These forces converged in a territory with a long-standing tradition of embracing the new. The state's development by settlers who had abandoned the old world to seek fresh opportunities on the Western frontier set the pattern for immigrants in the centuries to come. Throughout the nineteenth and into the twentieth century, Southern California continued to represent a mythic place in the nation's imagination. California was, as one historian suggested, "a moral premise, a prescription for what America could and should be."[4] It promised freedom, a chance for reinvention, and boundless opportunity—for individuals *and* for civilization. This utopian ethos created an ideal environment for generating a unique modern culture for the Machine Age.

Unlike contemporaneous movements in Europe and New York, Southern California's modern architectural movement was in many ways a continuation of, rather than a reaction against, its historical traditions. Since its settlement, the region had been viewed as a paradise where man and nature could co-exist harmoniously. Americans saw California as "a new and better Eden" and attributed therapeutic powers to its natural wonders. Boosters like writer George Wharton James claimed that Southern California was destined to be the home of God's "newer and better 'chosen people.'"[5] And as San Francisco developed a dense metropolitan character similar to Eastern cities, the relatively unsettled and perennially sunny Southern California assumed the imaginative role of the final frontier for the early twentieth century:

"The region was unformed, still capable of being made in the image of its new inhabitants… communities of single family homes for the cold, squeezed-in easterners; economic opportunity for the refugees from the dustbowl; freedom from previous strictures for founders of new religions, and peace from a world at war for Europeans. It was health for the tubercular, wealth for the railroad magnate, and a society whose physical manifestation needed the new forms which reflected its new horizons."[6]

Southern California's Arts and Crafts movement represented a revival of the region's utopian impulses at the beginning of the century. Advocates aimed to counteract the ills of industrialization, which was undermining the beauty and moral character of the frontier civilization. Cultural leaders such as Charles Lummis, editor of the monthly *Land of Sunshine* and founder of the Southwest Museum, proposed a new blend of physical and intellectual culture for Southern California. An offshoot of the British Arts and Crafts movement, the local movement sought inspiration in the region's natural and man-made history as a model for its future. It became widely influential, shaping the area's modern identity and view of its past.

Among the movement's aims was the restoration of moral and aesthetic wholesomeness to design. Improvement of the environment equated with improvement of society, and architecture and art served as tools of social reform. Southern California's natural landscape was the source of inspiration and therapy for revitalizing modern civilization. Houses there fostered a life that was lived mostly outdoors—on terraces and porches and in gardens. Materials were organic and objects were hand-crafted: their authenticity intended to shape a robust life that would counteract industrialization's debilitating effects. Life for all classes would be enhanced and elevated in an environment based on healthfulness, simplicity, informality, love of nature, and the aesthetic treatment of daily life–from household utensils and furnishings to the decoration of rooms and beyond, including the design of buildings and the exterior landscape. These themes of the Arts and Crafts movement served as the founding principles of Southern California's modern design.

While the Arts and Crafts era formed a spiritual and aesthetic base for the region's modern movement, it was one of many styles of the period. As World War I was ending, architects found a landscape of raw land and native building forms, revival styles of all varieties, and rows and rows of bungalows. At the time, the region was far from undeveloped: Los Angeles was the largest metropolis (population 576,673 in 1920)[7], with a substantial business district, an active port, and a large railroad hub. Other cities such as San Diego, Pasadena, San Bernadino, Santa Barbara, and Long Beach were loosely connected by roads and rail lines, forming a spider web of low-scale development across the region. In between were large stretches of desert with occasional oases of irrigated farmland.

Buildings were a mish-mash of historical styles–Romanesque, Gothic Revival, Italianate, Spanish Colonial–suggesting Southern California's ambitions to achieve the stature of older established cultures. The eclecticism of its building styles at the turn of the century also signaled the region's indistinct cultural identity, as well as its ambivalent relationship with its own past. These characteristics, coupled with the area's remoteness from the "old world" and relative lack of development, seemed to offer architects the chance to invent a new architecture–one that belonged to both the industrial age and the magnificent landscape.

The movement to create a new modern architecture for the West started with Irving Gill. In the first decade of the twentieth century, far from avant-garde Europe's trends towards abstraction, Gill developed a revolutionary aesthetic without stylistic references. A contemporary of Frank Lloyd Wright, Gill had one foot in the late nineteenth century's Arts and Crafts movement and the other in the Machine Age. His role in Southern California's history was pivotal. As he translated Arts and Crafts moralism into a new way of building, Gill established the themes of the region's modern architecture: its emphasis on healthful design; the merging of indoor and outdoor living; the ingenious use of industrial technologies; a passionate belief in the morality of architecture and its ability to do social good. He found inspiration in the West's natural landscape and its adobe missions, as well as the materials of modernism. Experimenting with new building systems, Gill created an architecture that belonged both to indigenous traditions and to the twentieth century. His flat-roofed geometric forms signaled the dawning of Southern California's modern architectural movement.

Gill's urging of architects to "break through convention and get down to fundamental truths"[8] resonated with a new generation: Rudolph Schindler and Richard Neutra, and then with his own and their protegés: Lloyd Wright, Harwell Hamilton Harris, Gregory Ain, and Raphael Soriano. In the eras before and after World War II, these avant-garde designers, as well as colleagues such as Albert Frey in Palm Springs, built on Gill's efforts in their experiments with low-cost housing, new technologies, and an architecture that mediated between the man-made and natural landscape. Other architects–J.R. Davidson, Kem Weber, Jock Peters–called themselves industrial designers and aimed to develop a commercial vernacular as representative of Southern California's modern age as its domestic architecture.

All found in Southern California a society and climate that nurtured their ideas and provided opportunities for realizing them. As Dione Neutra wrote

Los Angeles, view from Olive Hill, c. 1926.

Modern architects viewed Los Angeles'
spectacular natural setting and unimpres-
sive assortment of historical styles and
bungalows as an opportunity for an entirely
new architecture for the Machine Age.
(Security Pacific Collection/Los Angeles
Public Library)

to her mother in Switzerland soon after her arrival in 1925, "the future of Los Angeles seems immense."[9] While the directions their experiments took varied widely, these visionary architects shared a common conviction in the importance of a new architecture for the modern West.

By most measurable standards, however, the revolution was a failure—at least in terms of its impact at the time. With the exception of a few hundred enlightened patrons, modern architects failed to persuade Southern California's fundamentally conservative population of their vision. Instead of conceiving entirely new cities for the new world, their work was mostly limited to singular projects, isolated symbols of a modern utopia. Their medium for experimentation was primarily the single-family house, though they also developed multi-family housing, stores, restaurants, nightclubs, drive-in markets, and an occasional small office building. Their designs for gas stations, drive-in restaurants, motels, airports, and cities, however, would mostly remain on paper.

Even so, the efforts of this small avant-garde group represented a moment of brilliance in the region's development—a formative era that has proven inspirational to later generations of architects who continued to promote their cause to post-World War II Southern California. Although it took several more decades and a world war, the seeds of modernism scattered in the 1920s and 30s eventually did root and become a vigorous movement. Observers who know where to look can trace the region's contemporary identity to this formative era between the world wars.

Keyes House, Altadena, 1911.

Arts and Crafts bungalows in Southern California promoted outdoor living and communion with nature as an antidote to the stresses of modern civilization. (Courtesy of Kennon G. Miedema)

Lewis Courts, Sierra Madre, 1910; architect: Irving Gill.

Irving Gill's flat-roofed, geometric forms signaled the start of Southern California's modern architectural movement. Lewis Courts combined Arts and Crafts themes of healthful design and outdoor living with a modern aesthetic based on indigenous adobe forms and industrial technologies. (Esther McCoy Files on Architects 1945-1989, Archives of American Art, Smithsonian Institution)

1

The Historical Backdrop
for Modern Architecture

The labors of these revolutionary architects took place against the backdrop of a rapidly modernizing region. The period between the world wars witnessed an unprecedented wave of immigration: more than 1.5 million people moved to Southern California between 1920 and 1930.[10] This enormous new population required urban and community infrastructures on a scale previously unimagined there.

The region's growth was fueled by the 1913 construction of the aqueduct from the Owens River. This monumental public works project brought water to Southern California and allowed huge swaths of barren land to be developed for the first time. Besides enabling widespread colonization, irrigation created, as one visitor observed, "a certain air of unreality and impermanence," noting that the unexpected presence of palms and gigantic geranium bushes, hummingbirds and swallow-tailed butterflies conveyed the sense of "having strayed into one of Mr. Wells' Utopias."[11]

Just as the region was being transformed by the arrival of water, the discovery of oil caused a frenzied "oil rush" akin to Northern California's gold rush the century before. An enormous influx of people from around the country swarmed into Southern California, turning it into a twentieth century El Dorado. At the same time, the aviation and motion picture industries were becoming established. These brand-new businesses attracted design and engineering talent from all over the world, catapulting Southern California from a cultural backwater into international consciousness. Oil-refining, automobile, and tire manufacturers drew legions of new workers as Southern California became an industrial center on the order of Chicago.

The era after World War I was a critical period in the development of urban Los Angeles. City leaders were anxious to fashion a metropolis to rival the great cities of the East and Midwest. They envisioned a grand Beaux Arts-style civic center with an opera house, museum, and public library that would put Los Angeles on the cultural map. At the same time, oil millionairess Aline Barnsdall arrived in the West to establish an avant-garde community that would include an experimental theater and cinema. These efforts to create important cultural and counter-cultural institutions signaled Los Angeles' coming of age.

The forces influencing the growth of Southern California's urban areas were different from those affecting older cities in the East and Midwest. Not only was there pressure to expand exponentially

Hollywood Bowl, Hollywood, 1927;
architect: Lloyd Wright.

The establishment of the Hollywood Bowl
in 1919 signaled Los Angeles residents'
conviction in the civic value of an outdoor
amphitheater for the performing arts. The
open-air venue was considered especially
conducive to building community spirit
while entertaining and educating patrons.
Lloyd Wright's first shell for the Bowl
recalled ancient Mayan architecture in its
stepped pyramidal shape. (Eric Wright,
courtesy of Getty Center for the History
of Art and the Humanities)

and immediately, but also the region's embrace of the automobile became the major factor in the development of a new kind of metropolis. This auto-dependent, decentralized city would have been impossible in an area with the constraints of dense pre-existing urban fabric. But Southern California, only recently opened to development by the arrival of water and with two of its major cities leveled by earthquakes—Santa Barbara in 1925 and Long Beach in 1933—presented a relatively clean slate to planners and builders.

Continuing the existing pattern of decentralized communities established by Pacific Electric's railroad lines, Los Angeles spread out in a series of far-flung communities, filling in gaps between neighboring towns and cities with developments of single-family houses and commercial strips. Its 1915 annexation of the San Fernando Valley was equivalent to the city's "Louisiana Purchase," exponentially expanding the city's physical and imaginative possibilities. As the city leap-frogged over existing communities, the incorporated metropolitan area grew from 337 square miles in 1916 to 450 square miles in 1930—the largest in the United States.[12]

Just as Southern California developed the need for it, the automobile was becoming widely available. The car provided the means for the region to achieve its modern form and character. As one journalist observed in 1937, the car was to Los Angeles what the sailing ship had been to Boston: it facilitated the colonization of the western landscape with low-density communities.[13] By 1927 there was one car for every 3.2 people in Los Angeles County.[14] New auto-oriented buildings—drive-in service stations, markets and restaurants—sprang up to serve passengers rather than pedestrians. And new kinds of streets—freeways and "linear downtowns" like Wilshire Boulevard—extended the sprawling decentralized city into the future.

Other buildings evolved to serve the car by the late 1920s. Department stores like Bullocks Wilshire and the May Company turned to face parking lots as well as streets; theaters offered grand porte cocheres for automobile drop-offs; shopping centers changed the streetscape as they retreated from urban sidewalks to create their own precincts with off-street parking. At the same time, the forms and decoration of buildings were beginning to reflect the car's influence. Architectural elements such as towers, cantilevered canopies, and billboard-scale signs increased dramatically in

Hattem's Shopping Center, Los Angeles, 1930-31; architect: Walter Hagedohm.

By 1930 buildings had begun to reflect the car's influence, as architectural elements such as towers and signs grew in size to attract the attention of people driving by. The Art Deco style used geometric forms and ornament to imitate the car's aesthetic in a decorative moderne style scorned by modern architects. (Security Pacific Collection/ Los Angeles Public Library)

Project, *Union Oil Company Service
Station Prototype,* 1932-34; architect:
Rudolph Schindler.

Schindler developed prototypes for
Standard Oil Company and Union Oil
Company service stations, although
none were constructed. (Architecture
and Design Collection, University Art
Museum, University of California,
Santa Barbara)

size to attract the attention of people driving by. Materials and ornament simulated the car's machine-made aesthetic: sleek, fast-paced, geometric forms unencumbered by useless decoration and traditional detail. A genre of commercial architecture—buildings in the shapes of the items they sold such as doughnuts, tires, oranges, and hot dogs—also appeared at this time. Those structures turned emporia into giant three-dimensional billboards in order to lure passengers to stop and shop.

Modernists waged heroic, but losing, battles to create a new architecture for Southern California. Most buildings, including ones that served brand new functions such as service stations and supermarkets, continued to be clad in familiar period revival styles. Other buildings celebrated the Machine Age by adopting the gimmicks of Art Deco fashion—zigzag ornament and zooty materials that evoked the glamour of rapid transit—without altering conventional planning and construction methods.

Disdainful of the "moderne" Art Deco mode, the avant-garde wanted not only to change the way buildings looked, but also to revolutionize the ways buildings were conceived, designed, built, and inhabited. For them, the appearance of truly modern buildings would be generated by their structure and program, not a superficial application of machine-made imagery. In its 1935 issue devoted to modern architecture, *California Arts and Architecture* magazine scorned "modernistic" design, a term that included Art Deco, Streamline Moderne, and other decorative styles of the Machine Age, as "a superficial stylism, a fashion of empty geometrizing." Modern design, on the other hand, was based on profound principles of structure and spirit. "Between 'modernistic' and 'modern,'" editorialized the magazine in 1935, "there is the difference which separates the distorted echo from the authentic voice." [15]

Buildings designed by Southern California's pioneering architects looked like none that had existed in the region before them. They did, however, bear some relationship to modern buildings in other American and European cities. In the early decades of the twentieth century, the avant-garde was upending the Old World's cultural traditions in a series of overlapping movements—Russian Constructivism, Italian Futurism, the Viennese Secession, the German Bauhaus, the Dutch De Stijl. All shared the goal of expressing in built form the new possibilities of industrialization, rejecting age-old architectural conventions in favor of mod-

Apartment house, Stuttgart, Germany, 1927; architect: Ludwig Mies van der Rohe.

Mies van der Rohe's design for multi-family housing in Germany was typical of European avant-garde architects' interest in the design possibilities of industrialization. They rejected traditional styles in favor of modern materials and abstract forms. (Architecture and Design Department, The Museum of Modern Art, New York)

ern materials and abstract forms. Aiming to re-shape the existing social order through progressive design, early twentieth century avant-garde movements had a strong reformist agenda. They proposed a new integration of arts, industry, and society that would address low-cost housing for the masses, the design of functional objects, and well-planned healthier cities.

European modernism came to Southern California with the influx of avant-garde designers from Austria and Germany. They had been schooled in the new European movements and had trained in the classrooms and offices of such well-known modernists as Otto Wagner, Adolf Loos, Erich Mendelsohn, Le Corbusier, and Peter Behrens. Some came seeking new opportunities, others were forced into exile by the aftermath of World War I and premonitions of World War II. A letter written by Richard Neutra to Rudolph Schindler, by then working in America, suggested the widespread despair shared by European architects in 1919. Neutra complained that the European crisis was "beyond description":

"The building trade is stagnant… in contrast to America—every state here is autocratic, has no raw materials or consumer articles, the turnover is strangled through horrible inflation, the prohibitions of export and import, the closing of frontiers, and an unimaginable rail-road misery which you cannot fathom in your wildest imaginations."

Anxious to join the exodus to America, Neutra declared that all of Europe's revered cultural values and traditions had disappeared. They had been "discredited, refuted." His self-prescribed cure for his depression was to repeat the mantra, "CALIFORNIA CALLS YOU," over and over again.[16]

Los Angeles became known as "the new Weimar" as it attracted dozens of Austria's and Germany's leading designers, dramatists, musicians, filmmakers and writers after World War I. They brought with them strong leadership and a powerful constituency for the region's modern movement. Swelling the ranks of Southern California's avant-garde, they provided vital stimulus to the fledgling movement. Their settlement far from their homeland solidified their break with age-old social and cultural traditions. Shortly after arriving in Los Angeles in 1923, Jock Peters wrote his family back in Germany:

"I have decided for sure to stay here. I shall try to forget, for the present, that there is more of culture over there… Here it will be possible to live simply and contentedly, and to give form to inward things. One does not vegetate here. People who are spiritually rich do not need the whole ballast of art and ideas in order to feel themselves human and happy. With much less it goes better."[17]

2

The Dawn of the Revolution

Scant information about European or American movements had reached California, however, when Irving Gill was proposing a revolutionary architecture at the beginning of the century. Although his buildings are often viewed as imitations of his more famous European contemporaries, he probably did not know of their work.[18] The son of a contractor in Syracuse, New York, Gill had studied building design in practitioners' offices rather than schools. It was in the Chicago office of Adler and Sullivan, where he worked before moving to San Diego in 1893, that he had learned about an emerging American architecture based on new structural systems like the steel frame. He absorbed Louis Sullivan's interest in both the "luminous idea of simplicity" and the development of an architecture appropriate for a new time and place. Gill's "place," however, was twentieth century Southern California, not the nineteenth century Midwest of Louis Sullivan. So his abstract concrete buildings extending long arcades into the western landscape bore more resemblance to ancient southwestern missions and pueblos than to Sullivan's steel-framed skyscrapers looming over the Chicago prairie.

Gill's ideas developed in direct response to the new requirements of the Western frontier. His references were the adobe structures and the wood frame bungalows around him. From those traditions, Gill forged a new vernacular using modern concrete technology. His buildings reduced historic missions to their essential forms—the masonry block, the arch, and the arcade—and enriched them with a strong sense of craft and material. They were integrated into the Southern California landscape by pergolas and "green rooms," as well as actual leaf imprints in stucco walls and concrete floors.

Gill's earliest buildings in San Diego, designed with his partner W.S. Hobbard, were large houses in a variety of styles for San Diego's business and civic leaders. Over the course of his career, his work evolved from popular historical genres to a machined aesthetic of geometric purity. In its development—from an architecture of styles to one based on moral precepts, from conventional wood frame construction to innovative concrete technology, from status-conscious houses for the upper class to a social architecture for the working class—Gill's work mirrored the development of Southern California's modern architectural identity.

The fundamental premise of Gill's buildings was that architecture could act as a vehicle of social

La Jolla Women's Club under construction, La Jolla, 1912-14; architect: Irving Gill.

Gill experimented with "tilt-up" concrete walls for the La Jolla Women's Club. The walls were poured on platforms that were tilted by jacks. Metal frames for windows and doors were placed in the forms before the concrete was poured. (Esther McCoy Files on Architects 1945-1989, Archives of American Art, Smithsonian Institution)

La Jolla Women's Club completed,
La Jolla, 1912-14; architect: Irving Gill.

Gill's one-step tilt-up construction
system combined structure, form,
and aesthetic. Its design was based on
the missions of California, abstracted
into pure forms of straight lines, arches,
and cubes. (Private collection)

change. This new architecture would be based on honest expression of structure and progressive standards of efficiency, economy, hygiene, and beauty. Just as the Arts and Crafts movement had campaigned for design reform, suggesting that social reform would go hand-in-hand, Gill crusaded for morally pure design as a means to improve people's lives. His goal—to create low-cost buildings that would also be beautiful and functional—drove his technological innovations. These in turn produced a new aesthetic for all classes. He developed a democratic architecture that bridged socio-economic strata, providing working class tenants and wealthy homeowners alike with well-detailed, simplified construction.

Gill began his experiments with concrete early in the twentieth century. He was intrigued with the new material's possibilities for low-cost, fireproof construction. Other concrete structures mimicked the styles of stone and wood frame buildings. Gill's designs derived from the nature of the material itself. Gill's interests were far from the issues of style that preoccupied most American architects at the time. Instead, he urged architects to discard conventional structural beliefs and standards of beauty and to return to "the source of all architectural strength—the straight line, the arch, the cube and the circle." [19] He developed a radical new vocabulary of geometric shapes, flat roofs, simple details, and plain surfaces devoid of surface ornamentation.

Gill experimented with "tilt-up" poured concrete walls, a system developed by Robert H. Aiken in 1907 and used for the construction of a number of structures in the Midwest and Southern California. [20] In 1912 Gill formed the Concrete Building and Investment Company and purchased the patent rights to the Aiken system, setting up business as his own contractor. He tested the technology on several smaller structures before he built the Banning House in Los Angeles, his first major commission constructed of tilt-up slabs in 1913. That was followed by the La Jolla Women's Club in 1914 and the La Jolla Community Center in 1916. Although Gill was almost bankrupted by the process, later generations of architects continued his exploration of one-step construction systems that combined modern structure, form, and aesthetic.

Gill focused his reformist zeal on planning the low-cost house. Convinced that well-designed dwellings would help low-income groups to lead better lives, Gill was the first West Coast architect to turn his attention to workers' housing and com-pany towns. In 1900 he began developing his new ideas about design, construction, and ways of living in a series of experimental cottages in San Diego. He tested their premises by living in them himself. There he challenged conservative building codes to develop techniques for economical wall construction, which he called "thin-wall construction." He also simplified details to make housekeeping easier and planned private garden spaces that functioned as outdoor rooms, which he considered essential to a fulfilling and creative life, translating Arts and Crafts' precepts into modern design.

Gill's goal to develop "a perfectly sanitary, labor-saving house… where the maximum of comfort may be had with the minimum of drudgery" [21] was realized in such projects as Lewis Courts in Sierra Madre, constructed in 1910. In his homes for working-class families, Gill placed kitchens at the front facing the garden courtyard, installed skylights in bathrooms and hallways, and created both private and shared outdoor spaces in arcades and patios. (He was distressed to learn that the rents charged for the Lewis Courts units were beyond the means of working class tenants.) Treating each project as an opportunity to refine his theories, Gill gradually eliminated traditional moldings like baseboards, cornices, and door and window trim to rid houses of their dust-catching ledges. He developed built-in vacuum systems, kitchen garbage disposals that emptied into basement incinerators, and automatic car-washing devices in garages. He even replaced the traditional claw-foot bathtub with one boxed in magnesite that made bathrooms easier to clean.

Mary Banning, Gill's client for an early tilt-up house, boasted to the *Los Angeles Times* of her liberation from housework: "You see I'm tired of the everlasting pursuit of the grain of dust," she told her interviewer in 1914. "I'm tired of the gingerbread work that characterizes our American houses. I wanted something quite simple, easy to care for, but I wanted the best of materials and the best of craftsmanship." The *Times* heralded the modernity of the Banning house:

"…it stands today in its naked truth, a protest against jigsaw ornament, and shoddy workmanship, and all the flimsy pretense under which American architecture too often tries to hide its insincerity… In its outward form the house is merely an expression of the spirit within—that of absolute simplicity, absolute sincerity, absolute independence." [22]

Interior, *Dodge House,* West Hollywood, 1914-16; architect: Irving Gill.

Gill eliminated traditional moldings like baseboards, cornices, and door and window trim that required constant dusting, making housekeeping easier while also simplifying the aesthetic. (Photograph by Julius Shulman)

While some of Gill's patrons like Mary Banning shared his reformist passion, not all of his working-class clients agreed with his means of improving their world. One of Gill's few opportunities to realize his ideas on a city-wide scale, the model industrial town of Torrance planned in 1912, was halted by the protests of laborers building and living there. Although managers of the companies that sponsored the town—Pacific Electric, Union Tool, and Llewelyn Iron Works—supported Gill's innovative architectural ideas, most workers did not. They felt threatened by the elimination of traditional details from construction trades, and they objected to the simplicity and economy of Gill's flat-roofed cubes. Work on Gill's houses stopped after only ten were constructed. The rest of the town was built with traditional wood-framed cottages with pitched roofs.

Gill's efforts to develop low-cost housing persevered, however. In 1911 he asked the Riverside Cement Company to allow him to design barracks for Mexican laborers and their families. One quadrangle, enclosed by continuous walls and opening onto a central garden, was built. In the late 1920s he tried to interest officials in Baja in group dwellings for Mexican families, to no avail. And in 1932 he was hired by the Office of Indian Affairs to design cottages for the Rancho Barona Indian Resettlement in Lakeside. Gill moved to the site and designed the project to be built by unskilled Indian workers under his supervision.

Gill's experience in Torrance was indicative of his reception during his lifetime. He owed his occasional successes to enlightened patrons like journalist and newspaper heiress Ellen Browning Scripps, who embraced Gill's architecture as a tool for her crusade to leave the world a better place. As one of La Jolla's most committed philanthropists, Scripps used Gill's architecture to help realize her social goals. Together they established a strong modern tradition for this young city. Gill developed for Scripps a fireproof house, a naturally lit and ventilated laboratory (Scripps Institution of Oceanography's first building), several preparatory schools, a community center and playground, and the progressive La Jolla Women's Club. Each building defined a prescriptive model for how people should live and work in the modern age. As the Woman's Club president, Dr. Mary B. Ritter, announced at the opening ceremony, their building would stand for what Ellen Browning Scripps intended it for: "progress toward higher citizenship, spreading the gospel and the fact of

fraternity, of mutual helpfulness." To that end, Scripps often paid membership dues for women who couldn't afford them, hoping that "every citizen of the town should in some way be benefited by this building."[23]

Although he lived until 1936, by 1916 Gill's career was on the wane. The decorative Spanish Baroque style of San Diego's 1915 Panama California Exposition proved to be far more popular than Gill's abstractly moral architecture, no matter how righteous it was. And the architectural press, when it did pay attention to his work, labeled it simplistically as "cubist" or "secessionist." Gill died in poverty and obscurity, identified as a "laborer" on his death certificate.[24] However, in his determination to create a new way of building for the twentieth century West and in his fusion of industrial technologies with the region's natural and man-made traditions, Gill's work established an enduring foundation for Southern California's modern architecture.

3

Leaders of the New Movement

Gill's experiments took place in relative isolation in the first decades of the twentieth century. It wasn't until after World War I when two Austrian architects, Rudolph Schindler and Richard Neutra, emigrated to Los Angeles that themes introduced by Gill were adopted by a wider movement. Thoroughly modern in outlook and ambition, Schindler and Neutra became charismatic leaders of the region's avant-garde. Among its most vocal evangelists, they used their designs for cities, buildings, landscapes and furniture, along with lectures, exhibitions, and informal salons in their own living rooms, to promote modernism in all aspects of life. Schindler and Neutra shared Gill's fundamental goal: to create a new architecture for this new place and time—one that merged living and building with nature.

Schindler arrived in Southern California in 1920, Neutra in 1925. Both were fascinated by the industrialized America that had been mythologized in the European press. Trained in Vienna, the two studied modern forms of expression being developed by leading European architects, Otto Wagner and Adolf Loos. Frank Lloyd Wright, known to Europe through his 1910 Wasmuth portfolio, was held up as the hero of this new movement. "His freedom is perfection," wrote Schindler in a letter to Neutra in 1919. "It had no tradition to overcome or prejudice to fight. His work grows quietly out of itself. He is the master of each material, and the modern machine is at the base of his form-giving." [25]

Drawn by Wright's work and America's potential for generating an architecture for the Machine Age, Neutra and Schindler both headed for Chicago after finishing school. Schindler's great hope was to apprentice with Frank Lloyd Wright, who he felt was the one architect making the "space architecture" required for the twentieth century. Wright's revolutionary designs "exploded the box" of conventional rooms. To Schindler they seemed the realization of his own manifesto written in 1912: "These old problems have been solved and the styles are dead… The architect has finally discovered the medium of his art: SPACE. A new architectural problem has been born." [26]

Schindler worked with Wright in Chicago and at Taliesin from 1917 until 1920, absorbing his mentor's philosophy of developing a new architecture from modern technologies, without reference to styles of the past. It was through Wright that Schindler came to Southern California in 1920. He appointed Schindler construction supervisor

Richard Neutra, Rudolph Schindler, Dione
Neutra, Dion Neutra (clockwise, from top
left), at the Schindler House, 1928.

The Neutras moved into the Schindlers'
house in 1925. Neutra and Schindler set
up practice there under the name of
AGIC—Architectural Group for Industry
and Commerce. (Esther McCoy Files on
Architects 1945-1989, Archives of
American Art, Smithsonian Institution)

Aline Barnsdall in front of *Hollyhock
House,* Olive Hill, Hollywood, 1920-21;
architect: Frank Lloyd Wright.

———————

Barnsdall urged Frank Lloyd Wright to
create a new architecture for the region,
just as she was trying to create a new
theater for America. Wright looked to
the area's pre industrial traditions,
evoking Mayan monuments of Pre-
Columbian Mexico in the sloped
stuccoed walls and stylized ornament
of Barnsdall's Hollyhock House.
(Security Pacific Collection/Los Angeles
Public Library)

for Aline Barnsdall's new cultural acropolis in Los Angeles when he went to Japan to work on the Imperial Hotel.

Barnsdall's theater project was to be located on a 36-acre knoll in Hollywood known as Olive Hill. Her goal "to play a part in the coming American drama" [27] spurred her move from Europe to Chicago (where she met Frank Lloyd Wright) and then to Los Angeles to establish an experimental theater community. For Barnsdall, the theater could only become a great force in the world where there would be freedom of thought and action, a situation promised by California—not New York City, which Barnsdall considered "the worst possible place for creative people." [28]

Collaborating with Wright, Barnsdall conceived a scheme of theaters, performance spaces, and artists' studios and residences to be sited within the existing olive grove. In her "art park," theater patrons would stroll during long intermissions, and teas and theater suppers would be held in a roof garden. Barnsdall's own "Hollyhock House" would be located at its apex. Barnsdall proposed in 1919 "to keep my gardens always open to the public that this sightly spot may be available to those lovers of the beautiful who come here to view sunsets, dawn on the mountains, and other spectacles of nature, visible in few other places in the heart of the city." [29]

Barnsdall abandoned her experimental enterprise in the mid-1920s, frustrated by Frank Lloyd Wright's neglect while he was in Japan and his obstinate refusal to design the kind of progressive theater she wanted. But her attempt to give the region's modern movement an institutional base had sparked a potent mix of activities. She introduced the region's avant-garde to each other and to artists of international renown. The theater complex, for instance, was planned by Wright with his architect son, Lloyd, manager/director Richard Ordynski from Max Reinhardt's theater in Berlin, and set designer Norman Bel Geddes, who became one of America's foremost industrial designers. Although the theaters were never built, Barnsdall's dramatic troupe performed in local venues for audiences that included Hollywood's D.W. Griffith, Cecil B. DeMille, and Erich Von Stroheim. [30]

Olive Hill also housed a progressive kindergarten for Aline Barnsdall's daughter and children of other forward-thinking parents. Here new methods of "free association" and "learning by doing" were taught by Leah Press Lovell, her sister Harriet

Press Freeman, and Rudolph Schindler's wife, Pauline. The kindergarten formed a nucleus of the region's modern architectural movement, introducing Leah Lovell and Harriet Freeman to Frank Lloyd Wright and Rudolph Schindler. The Freemans then hired Wright to design a house in the Hollywood Hills; the Lovells hired Schindler (whom Leah considered to have the genius of Wright but to be more affordable) to design three vacation houses.

Wright described the socially unconventional and politically radical Barnsdall as "neither neo, quasi nor pseudo… as near American as any Indian… as domestic as a shooting star." [31] She was committed to social change through art theater, progressive literature, feminism, and birth control. She opposed war and contributed funds to radical groups in Los Angeles, including Tom Mooney's defense fund after his imprisonment for the Preparedness Day bombings in 1916 and Upton Sinclair's campaign for governor in 1934. Barnsdall hired Clarence Darrow to defend Emma Goldman, as she lectured the country on the merits of anarchy, and Margaret Sanger in her efforts to establish birth control clinics. Barnsdall also underwrote Margaret Anderson's *The Little Review*, which aimed to improve the human race through poetry. [32]

Until her death in 1946, Barnsdall continued her attempts to establish facilities to help the oppressed at Olive Hill: a recreation center for young women working as nursemaids and housekeepers, a home for soldiers, a senior citizens' center, an art museum, and a "radical center." When she gave Barnsdall Park to the city in 1927, Barnsdall declared, "No country can be great until the least of its citizens has been touched by beauty, truth and freedom; unless all three radiate from this little hill it is as nothing." [33]

Aline Barnsdall's most enduring legacy may have been her commission of Frank Lloyd Wright, for he gave a vital push to the development of Southern California's modern architecture. Her conviction that a new country like the United States should create its own drama served as Wright's mandate to develop the region's own architecture. She commanded that he put his "freest dreams" into her project, "for I believe so firmly in your genius that I want to make it the keynote of my work." [34] She also hoped that Wright's association would provide a feeling of permanency and inspire local and national confidence in her enterprise. Wright called Barnsdall's project his "California Romanza" and, like Gill, turned to the region's pre-industrial traditions for architectural inspiration. Gill had looked to adobe missions; Wright to Mayan monuments of Pre-Columbian Mexico, evoked in the sloped stuccoed walls and stylized ornament of Hollyhock House.[35]

Wright's theories of a new native architecture were refined in his series of "textile block" houses built in the early 1920s: three in the Hollywood Hills, including one for Harriet and Samuel Freeman, and "La Miniatura" in Pasadena for anti-quarian book dealer Alice Millard. The ageless yet modern forms of Wright's houses were important landmarks in the region's architectural develop-ment. For these houses Wright invented a system of textured concrete block walls that acted as supporting structure as well as exterior and interior finished surfaces. (The combination of structure, enclosure, and aesthetic in one system was similar to the challenge Gill took on with his tilt-up slab technology.)

Like Hollyhock House, the blocks' terraced masses and textile-like patterns recalled buildings of the ancient Mayans. Wright also planned a 411-acre development of concrete block houses on a hillside site. Although never built, the Doheny Ranch project culminated his fascination with this construction technology that integrated form and structure with the natural landscape. Indeed, Wright's concrete block buildings seemed to be fragments of the earth itself.[36]

The Freemans' residence, built in 1924–5, was Wright's third textile block structure in Southern California. After Harriet Freeman met Wright at Olive Hill, she and her husband hired him to design their extraordinary house. (They knew enough to stipulate in his contract that he would be responsible for any overages in the construc-tion cost beyond the $10,000 budget in return for a proportionate share in the ownership of the house. The house ultimately cost $22,000, though it is unknown whether Wright ever made up the difference.) Sam Freeman owned a jewelry store in downtown Los Angeles, while Harriet taught adult-education dance-exercise classes at various schools and studios. She also held classes in her Wright-designed living room, which she consid-ered "the most beautiful room in the country!"[37]

Located in a community of artists, actors, musicians, and arts clubs, the house became the center of a group of creative free-thinkers. The Freemans' circle of friends, neighbors, and tenants embraced a miscellany of modern artists and

Freeman House, Hollywood, 1924-5; architect: Frank Lloyd Wright.

The Freeman House, one of a series of "textile block" houses designed by Frank Lloyd Wright, recalled buildings of ancient Mayans in the blocks' terraced forms and geometric patterns. (Security Pacific Collection/Los Angeles Public Library)

performers: Serbo-Croatian artist Gjura Stojano; Jean Negulesco, director of "How to Marry a Millionaire," "Daddy Longlegs," and "Titanic"; photographer Edward Weston and his former mistress and muse, Margrethe Mather, an important artist in her own right; dancer/choreographer Lester Horton, whose troupe became a pet project of Harriet Freeman's; art dealer Galka Scheyer, agent for "The Blue Four" artists, Klee, Kandinsky, Feininger, and Jawlensky; and architect Rudolph Schindler, who succeeded Wright as the Freemans' family architect. (Schindler equated his contribution in architecture—"the modern California frame for living"—with Harriet Freeman's in dance—"the motion with which to fill it.")[38] Added to this mix were a series of bohemian tenants: dancer Wyn Evans, who slept on the Freemans' living room couch; Xavier Cugat, a Cuban bandleader at the Cocoanut Grove known as "the Rhumba King"; and actor Albert Van Dekker and his wife Esther, who later hired Schindler to design a house for themselves.[39]

Although Wright's buildings had few local imitators, his fundamental philosophy of a new native architecture gained many followers. His influence was spread by disciples like Rudolph Schindler, Richard Neutra, and his son, Lloyd Wright, all of whom had worked for him. (Gill too had worked with Wright in the office of Adler and Sullivan; both were inspired by Sullivan's ideas of architectural simplification.) These men committed their lives to developing Southern California's new architecture, distilling Wright's principles into their own sensibilities and, ultimately, a local building tradition. Wright must also be credited with introducing Schindler to Los Angeles, who in turn persuaded Richard Neutra to join him. "This climate and character, together with a further true development of Space Architecture," Schindler pronounced, "will make Southern California the cradle of a new architectural expression."[40]

After Schindler's work on the Barnsdall project ended, he stayed in the West to open his own practice. Returning to a Europe still reeling from World War I seemed impractical, and he was intrigued by California's opportunities for architectural invention. Schindler's first experiment after he left Wright's office was a house for himself and his wife Pauline. As Gill had done twenty years earlier and Richard Neutra would do ten years later, Schindler used his own home to test new theories of design, construction, living, working, and socializing. The contemporary house, for Schindler,

would be "not a new variation in style but a radically new conception."[41] (The design was so unorthodox, in fact, that the Building Department would only grant him a provisional building permit that could be revoked at any time during its construction.)

The house was conceived in 1921 as a cooperative dwelling for two couples, the Schindlers and their friends, Marion and Clyde Chace. As Schindler described its planning:

"The ordinary residential arrangement providing rooms for specialized purposes has been abandoned. Instead each person receives a large private studio; each couple, a common entrance hall and bath. Open porches on the roof are used for sleeping. An enclosed patio for each couple, with an out-of-door fireplace, serves the purposes of an ordinary living room."[42]

Schindler intended the house to fulfill the basic requirements of the camper's shelter: a protected back, an open front, a fireplace, and a roof. Half cave-half tent, the house was a spiritual descendent of a Yosemite camp structure that Schindler had seen on a trip to Northern California. Bare concrete walls faced the street and neighboring lots, providing a protective barrier against the outside world. Other exterior walls served as interior walls for outdoor living spaces. Around these private courtyards, light canvas sliding screens barely separated interior from exterior rooms. Living quarters also extended outside to the roof, where sleeping "baskets" (porches) allowed residents to camp out year round—even in the rain, which required carrying umbrellas to their beds.

Rejecting the "onion-like" method of covering structural members with layers of finish materials, Schindler's house was made of a few elements that retained their natural color and texture. Load-bearing walls were constructed of tilt-up concrete slabs, the same technology used by Irving Gill.[43] The slabs were battered, or sloped, to reduce their weight, and the three-inch slits between them were glazed or filled with concrete. The result, Schindler noted, had "all the repose of the old type masonry wall, without its heavy, confining qualities. It permits light and air to filter through the joints…"

In its cave and tent-like aspects, the house represented the ideal that was fundamental to the region's modern movement: that mankind could be restored by communion with nature. And in its evocation of the region's adobe buildings, Schindler's

residence was as firmly rooted in Southern California as Gill's houses had been:

"I came to live and work in California. I camped under the open sky, in the redwoods, on the beach, the foothills and the desert. I tested its adobe, its granite and its sky. And out of a carefully built up conception of how the human being could grow roots in this soil—unique and delightful—I built my house. And unless I failed it should be as Californian as the Parthenon is Greek and the Forum Roman."[44]

This startling modern house in western Hollywood's outer reaches became the nexus of a group of bohemian artists—poets, playwrights, dancers, photographers, musicians, socialists, reformers, intellectuals of all sorts—in the 1920s and 30s. They congregated around Pauline and Rudolph Schindler, who were the very embodiments of modern lifestyles. (Legend has it that the couple had met leaving a concert of Sergei Prokovief's "Scythian Suite" in Chicago, both overcome with excitement at its new sounds.) Together they were catalysts for new ideas. The Schindlers' Sunday evening open houses attracted "adventurers reaching out for the new," as one friend described them. "These people weren't rebelling against the old, they were disregarding it."[45]

Regular guests included Edward Weston, John Cage, Theodore Dreiser, and Lloyd Wright. John Bovington, who established his "dance laboratory" in one of the Kings Road studios, often performed his "psycho-hygenic" dances in the "Schindler Shrine-Garden." One audience member described Bovington's "Dance of the Evolution": "Beginning with his naked-breasted female partner as a mass of quivering protoplasm on the grass in the patio, the dance developed through various stages of lower animal forms to the ultimate human."[46] Bovington frequently invited audience participation after the formal program. Sunday afternoon musical events also included chamber music performed by Lloyd Wright, pianist Doris Levings accompanied by Dione Neutra who sang and played cello, and pianist Richard Buhlig with his protegé John Cage.

Members of the Schindlers' social set became tenants of the living/sleeping/working studios after Clyde and Marion Chace left in 1923. New residents included artist Hilaire Hiler, lawyer John Packard, and art collector/dealer Galka Scheyer, who lined her concrete studio with enormous paintings by her "Blue Four" artist-clients.

Schindler House, West Hollywood, 1921-22; architect: Rudolph Schindler.

Rudolph Schindler's house was conceived as a cooperative dwelling for two couples. Like a camper's shelter, the house had solid walls facing the street and neighbors and an open front of light screens facing private courtyards. (Landscaping to create courtyards was installed after this photograph was taken.) The walls were constructed of "tilt-up" concrete slabs, the same technology used by Irving Gill. (Esther McCoy Files on Architects 1945-1989, Archives of American Art, Smithsonian Institution)

Outdoor Patio, *Schindler House,* West Hollywood, 1921-22; architect: Rudolph Schindler.

Private courtyards served as outdoor living rooms to be shared by each couple. They were planned as extensions of the interior studios, separated only by thin canvas and glass screens and with exterior fireplaces. Schindler's notion of "indoor-outdoor" living became a hallmark of Southern California's modern architecture. (Photograph by Julius Shulman)

Schindler considered Scheyer his soul mate, likening her efforts to introduce modern painting and sculpture to Los Angeles to his own in architecture. She, in turn, thought he was brilliant and introduced him to like-minded clients. She did not, however, enjoy living in his unorthodox house, complaining that her $60 per month rent presupposed "livable conditions," namely "circulation which does not necessitate climbing on the roof to open or close a window."[47] She declared she was "not a Bohemian" and ultimately hired Neutra to design her house in the Hollywood Hills.

Among Schindler's most significant patrons were Philip and Leah Lovell, who were members of the Schindlers' avant-garde circle. Vowing to introduce "a modern type of architecture and establish it firmly in California, where new and individualistic architecture is necessary,"[48] the Lovells commissioned two residences that brought Southern California's new architectural movement to the world's attention: their beach house designed by Rudolph Schindler and "The Demonstration Health House" designed by Richard Neutra.

The Lovells' elevation of health and fitness to the status of "physical culture," a preoccupation shared with many of the region's modernists, was the basis for the designs of their dwellings. As a professional naturopath, Philip Lovell was—and wanted to be seen as—progressive in all aspects of life. His radical attitudes towards health and diet provided his entrée into the circles of other radicals, including artists and architects. Lovell preached the virtues of body-building, nude sunbathing, and outdoor living from many pulpits: the Lovell Physical Culture Center in Hollywood, a weekly health column in the Los Angeles Times entitled "Care of the Body," and his family's modern residences. These would be "a social school" for his children, "in which they will learn their life habits. Their customs will be molded and shaped therein."[49] Both Schindler and Neutra shared Lovell's passionate belief in the relationship between a well-designed physical environment and a healthy life. Their experimental dwellings provided the "frames" for the Lovells' experiments in modern living.

Schindler's design for the Lovells' house in Newport Beach, completed in 1926, was unlike anything the region—or the world—had seen before. Set on a beachside lot, the house was raised above the sands on massive concrete piers, leaving the ground free for outdoor recreational activities. Elevation of the main living quarters allowed residents to take advantage of the views and natural breezes and provided privacy for their glass-walled interiors. There was no ornament, no decoration—the appearance of the house was determined by its structure and the spaces within. The interior living areas were as unorthodox as the exterior suggested. There were few conventional rooms, corridors, walls, or doors. In contrast to the enclosed box-like spaces of traditional houses, the Lovells' home had an open plan with a two-story living/dining area that extended outside onto exterior decks. Instead of individual bedrooms, it had a communal outdoor sleeping porch, from which the Lovells could hear pedestrians below discussing their "upside-down" house.

While the beach house was under construction, Schindler issued its design principles as a manifesto to Lovell's Los Angeles Times readers:

"Our rooms will descend close to the ground and the garden will become an integral part of the house. The distinction between the indoors and the out-of-doors will disappear. The walls will be few, thin, and removable. All rooms will become part of an organic unit, instead of being small separate boxes with peepholes… Our house will lose its front-and-back-door aspect… Each individual will want a private room to gain a background for his life. He will sleep in the open. A work-and-playroom, together with the garden, will satisfy the group needs. The bathroom will develop into a gymnasium and will become a social center."[50]

These characteristics would become hallmarks of the modern California house: the integration of house and landscape, the celebration of physical culture, the informal plan that eliminated rooms with specific functions in favor of free-flowing multi-use spaces.

For their residence in Los Angeles, the Lovells commissioned Richard Neutra, who went on to become Southern California's most influential modern architect. Neutra had arrived in Los Angeles in 1925 via New York and Chicago after fleeing Europe's worsening economic and political conditions. Like Schindler, Neutra had come to America to explore the design possibilities of industrialization, intending to stay only two years. Neutra too was fascinated by the revolutionary architecture proposed by Frank Lloyd Wright. He worked for Wright before heeding Schindler's urging to come West. (Neutra's reverence for

Lovell Beach House, Newport Beach,
1925-26; architect: Rudolph Schindler.

The Lovells' Beach House was raised
on massive concrete piers, leaving the
ground free for recreational activities.
The house had an open plan with a
two-story living/dining area and an
outdoor sleeping porch rather than
individual bedrooms. (Photograph by
J.R. Davidson, courtesy of Esther McCoy
Files on Architects 1945–1989, Archives
of American Art, Smithsonian
Institution)

Richard Neutra in front of the Lovells'
"Demonstration Health House,"
Los Angeles, 1927–29; architect:
Richard Neutra.

The Lovells' town house, designed
by Richard Neutra, was the first all-
steel-frame residence in America.
Its radical program for indoor-
outdoor living included exterior
exercise spaces, open sleeping
porches, and private sunbathing
decks. (Security Pacific Collection/
Los Angeles Public Library)

Wright was so great that he named his first son after him.) In Southern California Neutra found "what I had hoped for, a people who were more 'mentally footloose' than those elsewhere, who did not mind deviating opinions... where one can do most anything that comes to mind... All this seemed to me a good climate for trying something independent of hidebound habitation."[51]

In 1925 Richard Neutra and his wife Dione moved into the studios vacated by the Chaces in the Schindlers' house, and Neutra and Schindler set up a partnership they called the Architectural Group for Industry and Commerce (AGIC). Although AGIC designed a number of innovative projects—a highway bungalow hotel, an airplane flyers' club, a drive-in market, a skyscraper, an explosives complex, a competition entry for the new League of Nations—few were actually built. One of them was the Jardinette Apartments (1927) in Los Angeles, which was heralded in the Museum of Modern Art's 1932 "Modern Architecture" exhibition as "the first practical application in America of a consistent scheme of design based on modern methods of construction."[52] The building's industrial image and its reinforced concrete structure, ribbon windows, cantilevered balconies, and rooftop terrace represented the introduction of European modern architecture to Southern California.

Also featured in MOMA's exhibition was Neutra's design for the Lovells' town house in Los Angeles, completed in 1929. Described in the catalogue as "stylistically the most advanced house built in America since [World War I]," the Lovells' "Demonstration Health House" was the epitome of Machine Age architecture. Everything about their Los Angeles dwelling was modern: its program for indoor-outdoor living that included exterior exercise spaces, open sleeping porches, and private sunbathing decks; its pre-fabricated steel structure—the first all-steel-frame residence in America (supervised by Bethlehem Steel during its erection); its industrial aesthetic that even Neutra described as a "strange unheard-of apparition" next to its Spanish Colonial neighbors.[53] (Proving that modern building technology did not necessary equate with low costs, however, the house went almost 100% over budget.)[54]

Lovell saw his residence as a model for healthful living. He invited readers of his Los Angeles Times column to see it for themselves and to adapt its features for their own homes. The house was opened to the public on four Sundays with personal tours by Lovell and Neutra to explain the building's "multiple meanings." Lovell posted a notice announcing proudly: "The architecture [Neutra] espouses is Modernistic in more senses of the word than one. That is, it is unquestionably the very best combination of the utmost in utilitarianism and beauty."[55] The house caused a sensation. Thousands of people came to marvel at its novel features, requiring auto club officials to conduct traffic up and down the narrow hilly street. And the press spread the news world-wide of the brand new architecture in Los Angeles.

Although Schindler's and Neutra's philosophies diverged after the dissolution of AGIC in 1931, their belief in the absolute value—the moral correctness—of modern design did not. They shared a passionate conviction in Southern California's need for a fresh architecture. Their determination "to make true the promise of the grand revolution" spurred messiah-like efforts to preach their gospel.[56] Both lectured to reformist groups and social clubs tirelessly, organized exhibitions of modern work in every available venue, and tried to enlist local architecture schools in their campaign. In their matching air-cooled Franklin cars, Neutra and Schindler appeared as "twin freaks," as one of their colleagues described them, with "their peculiar dress, hair, nature-dancer friends, food-faddism, etc."—charismatic figures to an avant-garde elite perhaps, but undoubtedly strange to the general public.[57]

Schindler included appraisers' and bankers' groups on his lecture circuit, stating that, "every building had to be supported by an educational campaign reaching everyone concerned, and in many cases the owners."[58] In the late 1920s most bankers, contractors, and local architectural committees considered modern architecture unmortgageable, unbuildable, and unattractive. Even architectural colleagues were skeptical and/or ignorant of their efforts. A 1927 survey of local architects by the film industry's Hi-Hat Magazine determined that 82% hadn't heard of a "modern trend," 11% had neither heard of the trend nor were they interested in it, and 7% were attempting "in every way to create along modern lines."[59]

That 7% met enormous resistance from finance companies, who refused to provide mortgages for homes that would have little resale value, according to their conservative standards. They insisted on conventionalizing unconventional features before they would commit to a loan. Philip Lovell claimed that no bank would lend money for any of his modern houses. When he needed additional funds for his Health House, he had to borrow money from *Los Angeles Times* publisher Harry Chandler. (The conservative Chandler replied that he would give Lovell money for friendship, but he would not give him a dime for the house.)[60]

Similarly, tract and homeowners' associations often prescribed traditional massing, setbacks, rooflines, and styling. Local building departments objected to construction materials and details that didn't follow codes. And contractors rebelled against new techniques, which they considered "custom," often driving up the costs of the very measures modern architects invented to improve the economy and efficiency of construction.

The public was also stubbornly resistant to modernists' campaigns. Even after national and international accolades were showered on the Lovells' Health House, Neutra found himself without commissions. On his post-Lovell House lecture tour in Europe and Asia in 1930, Neutra was greeted enthusiastically at each stop by throngs of supporters who had heard about his revolutionary architecture in Los Angeles. Yet, when he returned to America, Neutra despaired of his prospects: "What is in the offing? Lectures, playing a role with nothing to back it up. The famous modern architect has no office, no organization, no jobs. Where can he rest his weary head?"[61]

Not sure that Los Angeles could offer him anything, Neutra returned nevertheless. He was concerned by the rumblings of National Socialism in Germany, especially after he had experienced the freedom of America. Also, tired of months of rain, he and Dione were anxious to get back to the blue skies and clear mountain air of California. But, as Neutra had pessimistically predicated, in 1931 only eight students signed up for the modern architecture seminar he was co-teaching with Schindler, although the school had advertised all over the country. "The prospects here are miserable," Dione Neutra despaired. "He is not a fashionable architect. He is an experimenter, way ahead of his time and, for this reason, not fashionable."[62]

Prototypes for Production

In spite of the general public's conservatism, however, by the 1930s modern architects' efforts to reform the environment were being cheered on by professional and shelter magazines, building products manufacturers, and housing organizations. They sponsored competitions and exhibitions of model houses to encourage good design for the average homeowner. Although many of the houses presented were historical in style, by the mid-1930s modern models were frequently featured as well. At the same time, Depression-era government agencies began funding programs to develop low-cost workers' housing and commissioned innovative designs for economical and efficient dwellings.

Architects like Schindler and Neutra jumped at these opportunities to develop new prototypes for large-scale production. Their goal was to create an architecture that was high-quality, low-cost, mass-producible, and available to all classes. Just as building products were made cheaper by standardization, industrialization, and wide distribution, they suggested that architecture itself should be standardized, industrialized, and widely distributed. (Their buildings simulated these qualities even when they weren't actually constructed with machine-made parts. Neutra, for instance, often specified wooden windows and posts painted with metallic silver paint.)

Pre-fabrication seemed the most promising way to achieve modern design for the masses. Neutra's first project for pre-fabrication in 1926 was an expandable dwelling called "One Plus Two," designed as two units with a shared movable wall. The house was to be constructed of lightweight "diatomaceous earth" panels made from steam-hardened earth and seashell deposits. The panels would be suspended from cables attached to central masts. Pre-fabricated metal foundations could be adjusted to the contours of any site, a design Neutra later patented.

Schindler's experiments produced the "Schindler Shelter" in 1933. Constructed of reinforced hollow concrete units similar to Frank Lloyd Wright's textile block system, the house was essentially a single large space subdivided by movable closets. Costs would be limited by pre-fabrication of the closets and doors and by grouping the kitchen, bathroom, and utility room together to keep the plumbing in one wall. Although Schindler proposed his design for the government's Depression-era housing programs, its $1800 construction cost was higher than conventional construction. Later he developed a modular wood "panel-post" system as a substitute for the labor-intensive masonry walls. Still, none were built.

Neutra was more successful than Schindler in realizing entire communities of his low-cost prototypes. In his campaign to build large-scale

SCHINDLER-SHELTER B-TYPE 4 R'MS © R.M SCHINDLER · ARCHITECT   5° UNITS

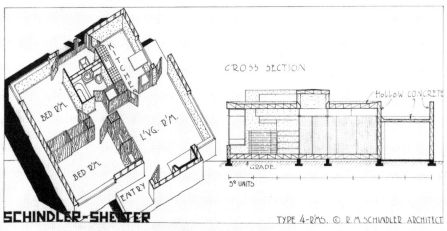

CROSS SECTION

HOLLOW CONCRETE

GRADE

5° UNITS

SCHINDLER-SHELTER   TYPE 4-R'MS. © R.M SCHINDLER ARCHITECT

Project, *Schindler Shelter Residential Prototypes for B-type, 4 rooms,* 1933-39; architect: Rudolph Schindler.

Top: Perspective Elevation and Plan. Bottom: Cutaway Axonometric and Section. (Architecture and Design Collection, University Art Museum, University of California, Santa Barbara)

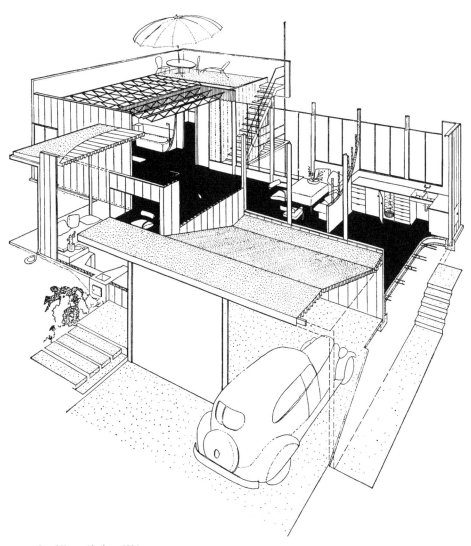

Beard House, Altadena, 1934;
architect: Richard Neutra.

Neutra's design for the Beards'
all-metal house included "self-
cooling" walls made of metal
flooring and built-in furniture—
beds, couches, desks, bureaus,
shelving—which shaped the ways
the Beards would live and work in
the house. (James and Katherine
Morrow Ford. *The Modern House
in America.* NY: Architectural Book
Pub., c. 1940, reprinted by Dover
Publications)

housing, he solicited ideas from socialist writer Upton Sinclair (author of *The Jungle*) and supported Sinclair's 1934 failed run for governor on the End Poverty in California (EPIC) platform. The Department of Labor's Consumers Division asked him in 1936 to produce a "Consumer's Manifesto on Housing" that would include designs, photographs, plans, specifications, literature, and an argument for modern, low-cost, high-efficiency housing. A spokesperson for the Labor Department considered Neutra's ideas and achievements on the subject the "most carefully thought out, balanced, original, and practicable" of any in America.[63] In his practice Neutra designed cooperative subsistence homesteads for unemployed and migrant farm workers, collaborated on two of Los Angeles' earliest public housing projects—Hacienda Village and Pueblo del Rio, and developed several of the first defense workers' communities. For Avion Village, a defense community in Grand Prairie, Texas, Neutra helped to invent a pre-fabricated house that could be constructed in 57 minutes.

Neutra had first experimented with his urban theories in a "test tube" model metropolis, "Rush City Reformed," for a population of 1,000,000. (Its name was meant to evoke the fast pace of American life.) Designed over the course of the 1920s, the plan was organized around modes of transportation similar to Le Corbusier's 1922 "Ville Contemporaine" and his 1930 "Ville Radieuse." Speedways, elevated trains, railroads, airports, docks, helicopter landing strips, and pedestrian walkways linked the city together and with other urban centers in a web of modern transportation systems. Rush City's residents would live in apartment towers, pre-fabricated houses, and patio houses clustered together. Shared parks would serve as front lawns, and property lines would be erased to eliminate "the self-centered confinement" of the individual home.

Neutra's appetite for the new—building types, structural systems, industrial materials—was insatiable. He treated each commission as a prototype for industrial production, testing innovative ways to achieve maximum design for minimum cost. Between 1934 and 1937 he experimented with pre-fabricated steel walls for the California Military Academy, aluminum-coated steel for the skin of the Von Sternberg house, plywood for a demonstration house at the California House and Garden Exposition, and diatomaceous earth panels for the Beckstrand House. Neutra's "all-metal" house constructed in 1934 for California Institute of Technology engineering professor and his aviator wife, William and Melba Beard, was the first modern residence to win the "Better Homes in America" Gold Medal Award in the "small house" category. Its "self-cooling" walls were built of metal flooring with channels that served as vertical flues for exterior air. The Beards considered it "as easy to operate as a car."[64]

As Neutra was testing the architectural possibilities of new industrial products, Schindler was turning away from progressive construction technologies in the mid-1930s. In the decade before, he had followed Gill's lead and experimented with concrete on a variety of projects: tilt-slab construction for his own house, concrete frames for the Lovell beach house, slip-form construction (concrete poured in movable forms) in the Pueblo Ribera Courts, slab-gun construction (gunite blown against vertical panel forms to create self-supporting walls) for the Packard House. Schindler's interest in "space architecture" (and perhaps his experiments' numerous technical glitches) spurred his conversion in the '30s to conventional wood frame and stucco construction.

Hoping to gain a larger clientele for his theories by using the more economical methods of speculative builders, Schindler focused on spatial rather than technological innovations. He obtained his general contractor's license and trained non-union, unskilled laborers to build the way he wanted them to, finding that easier and cheaper than retraining skilled labor. This allowed clients to afford an architect-designed house for the price of a contractor-built one. It also required Schindler to be on site throughout construction, limiting his output to several buildings at a time, a very different way of making modern architecture than Neutra's philosophy of mass-production.

Schindler expanded his architectural theories into other media, including a line of "unit furniture." His furnishings, which he described as "floor terraces," were designed to merge with the architecture and to leave the room "free to express its form." Like Schindler's buildings, they were modular, informal, and flexible, and could be assembled in a variety of configurations. Also like his buildings, Schindler's furniture had a strong element of social reform, designed to promote informal and more genuine human interactions. "It has ceased to be a sign of politeness to assume the most uncomfortable position in front of our friends," he wrote in 1926 for Philip Lovell's

"Care of the Body" column. "Instead of impressing each other with a series of conventional postures and manners, certifying good ancestors and upholding our social prestige, we are trying to relax together, as the only way of getting real human contact." [65] Schindler's unit furniture also represented his view of the machine's role in modern design: individual components, rather than entire objects, would be made by machine; the components themselves would then be assembled by hand. This, for Schindler, was the only way to subdue the "mechanical ferocity" of the machine to individual expression.

Modern Architecture Gains a Public
By the mid-1930s, modernism had gained increased legitimacy and a broadened constituency in Southern California. The sea change in public opinion coincided with the arrival in Los Angeles of the Museum of Modern Art's traveling "Modern Architecture" exhibition in 1932. Neutra spearheaded the effort to find a site and funding for the exhibition, since he was the only invited participant west of Chicago. Rejected by established cultural institutions, Neutra persuaded Los Angeles' new modern department store, Bullocks Wilshire, to sponsor the show. He used the occasion to enlist the city's cultural elite in the modern cause, beginning by inviting the president of the conservative University of Southern California (USC) to chair the honor committee. Invitations were also sent to the mayor, governor, bank presidents, newspapers, and members of "the upper 10,000"—several hundred of whom actually attended the opening. As Dione Neutra reported to her mother, "No rotten eggs were thrown, no disparaging remarks were made, at least not publicly, and the ten exhibition models and photographic enlargements were stared at as one gazes at exotic animals." [66]

The exhibition made Neutra famous in his adopted home city and spurred a growing interest in modern architecture. Although Neutra had not had any work for a year, his wife reported that he had become a figure of importance and was invited to dinners and openings, requiring him "to wear his tuxedo quite often." That year USC asked Neutra to conduct their graduate course, which, according to Neutra, was the first time an American university would offer a degree based on modern design. Dione noted in a letter to her mother that "the interest in modern architecture has grown tremendously in this last year, and the exhibition has helped materially." [67] Nevertheless, it wasn't until

1936 when Neutra received the commission from the prominent John Nicholas Brown family for their house on Fishers Island, New York, that he purchased his first new suit since his move to California eleven years before.

As Neutra's fame was growing, so was the recognition and acceptance of modern architecture. Significantly, *California Arts and Architecture* magazine, a bellwether of local taste, devoted an issue in 1935 to modernism. At the same time, art schools were flourishing as designers, artists, and intellectuals from all over the world gathered in Southern California to explore the expression of new technologies and lifestyles. Otis Art Institute, Chouinard, UCLA, Occidental, USC, California Institute of Technology, and the Claremont Colleges also developed intellectual communities of ideas and experimentation that contributed to the movement's growth.

This new architecture was beginning to enjoy a certain vogue among Southern California's "progressives," as they were known. While avant-garde residents like the Lovells had gravitated to experimental architecture a decade earlier, commercial clients who wanted "modern to the minute" styling were also beginning to recognize its advertising value in the 1930s. Schindler designed a number of smart restaurants and retail shops in this period: Sardi's Restaurant, auto-mobile showrooms for Maddux, Inc. and Brown, Smith & Moore, a cafe dansant and restaurant for impresario Sid Grauman (of Grauman's Chinese Theater fame), as well as the interior of a Lockheed Model 27 airplane and prototypes for Standard Oil Company's and Union Oil Company's gas stations.

But it was Neutra who invented Southern California's commercial modernism that gained international fame. By the mid-1930s, Neutra had become the avant-garde architect of choice. Over the course of the decade, Neutra received almost 100 commissions, more than 50 of which were built—a record for any modern architect of that period. He designed stores, factories, schools, theaters, museums, airports, houses, and cities, as well as an aluminum bus for the White Motors Company in 1931. His industrialized aesthetic—generic, machine-made, and infinitely replicable—was more like the fashionable "International Style" than Schindler's idiosyncratic designs.

Neutra became the modern West's ambassador to the rest of the world, just as he served as the ambassador of European modernism to the West. He wrote articles for Austrian and German maga-

Interior, *Westby House,* Los Angeles,
1938; architect: Rudolph Schindler.

Schindler's design for the Westby
House interior combined built-in
"floor terraces" for seating with
plywood dining room furniture
that complemented the architectural
design. (Photograph by Julius Shulman)

zines and circled the globe on world-wide lecture tours, teaching a studio at the Bauhaus in Germany, attending CIAM (Congrés International d'Architecture Moderne) conferences about city planning and housing in Brussels, and proposing his small office as CIAM's first American chapter. In 1927 Neutra also published a book documenting America's technological prowess, *Wie Baut Amerika? (How America Builds),* and made plans to establish a school for large-scale planning. Signaling the country's embrace of his ideas, Neutra's buildings received at least one award a year beginning in 1934 and culminating in his appearance on the cover of *Time* magazine in 1949.

Neutra's and Schindler's growing roster of clients shared an interest in experimentation, a commitment to modernism, and, in many cases, near-infatuation with their architectural muse. Schindler's patrons included "millionaire hobo" James Eads How, grandson of inventor James Eads and founder of colleges for hoboes around the United States. Another of Schindler's clients, Peter Yates, was music columnist for Southern California's progressive *Arts and Architecture* magazine (formerly *California Arts and Architecture*). Yates' "Evenings on the Roof" experimental concert series, held in his Schindler-designed rooftop studio, aimed to introduce new music to Los Angeles. The modern studio, with its plywood-lined walls, great windows overlooking the city, and ceiling pitched to the angle of the piano's lid, suited Yates' weekly informal recitals which were given "to all comers, free or at local movie prices… without bows, entrances, or exits." [68]

Neutra's brand of International Style modernism appealed to residents who, like his commercial clients, wanted to show off their own "modern to the minute" self-image. Among them was art collector Galka Scheyer, who sought the "most modern" architect for her new house/exhibition gallery in Santa Monica Canyon, located on Blue Heights Drive (named for her "Blue Four" clients). Grace Lewis Miller also chose Neutra for the progressive image he could bring to her Palm Springs home/studio, where she taught the Mensendieck System of Functional Exercise. Like his client Bertha Mosk, they believed that Neutra's architecture gave them "freedom to breathe and grow." He was their pied piper leading them into the modern era: "It was a great privilege to have been closely associated with a person who is so far ahead of his time," Mosk stated, "who has given us an instrument so that we can keep up with his

vision." [69] Mona Hofmann described the process of designing her house with Neutra as "second only to my psychoanalysis as a major experience." The Barshas declared that after they moved into their Neutra-designed house, modern architecture had become "practically a religion" for them; they had grown "intolerant of everything in life that isn't thoroughly modern." [70]

Neutra also became the favorite architect for members of the film community who wanted to identify themselves as avant-garde: screenwriter Anita Loos, director Josef von Sternberg, writer/producer/director Albert Lewin, and actress Anna Sten and her husband, director Eugene Frenke. Neutra's house for Eugene Frenke and Anna Sten, Russian rival to Greta Garbo, was the first modern house to win the *House Beautiful* competition in 1934. [71] Her studio publicists sent out a press release announcing that her house had received a special award and that its progressive design and construction "is as interesting a departure from the usual film stars' homes as Miss Sten herself is different from other screen actresses." [72]

Neutra's design for Josef von Sternberg's residence, clad in aluminum and enclosed by a shallow moat and curved wall cooled by artificial rain, later became the home of Ayn Rand, author of modern architecture's own story in *The Fountainhead.* His Santa Monica house (1937) for Albert Lewin, head of MGM's story department and producer of Irving Thalberg's pictures, was featured in Charles Reznikoff's modern Hollywood novel, *The Manner Music.* His Strathmore Apartments in Westwood, constructed in 1938, at various times housed Orson Welles, Dolores Del Rio, Luise Rainer and playwright Clifford Odets, and designers Charles and Ray Eames, who molded their first plywood chairs in a "kazam machine" there.

Fellow emigrés also gravitated to Neutra, who seemed to represent a familiar European modernism. After composer Arnold Schoenberg moved to Los Angeles in 1934, he talked with Neutra about building a house in the style of the renowned avant-garde Austrian architect Adolf Loos: "He also appears to be of Loos' circle and does very nice houses, even if a bit more doctrinaire than Loos, more studied, and not uninfluenced by Bauhaus principles. Still, anyway, he has Viennese taste and knows what a scribe needs." (The deal was never executed and Schoenberg purchased a Spanish Colonial house in Brentwood Park.) [73]

Galka Scheyer in her house,
Los Angeles, 1934-5; architects:
Richard Neutra, Gregory Ain.

Galka Scheyer, a modern collector
and dealer for the German "Blue Four"
artists, hired Richard Neutra and
Gregory Ain to design her house/
exhibition gallery in the Hollywood
Hills. (Courtesy of Tino Hammid)

Corona Avenue School, Bell, 1935;
architect: Richard Neutra.

Neutra's design for the Corona Avenue
School aimed to encourage different
ways of learning in classrooms that functioned as "living" rooms. Each classroom
had a garden patio that could be used
as an outdoor schoolroom. Sliding glass
walls and portable furniture allowed
students to move back and forth easily
between inside and outside classrooms.
(Security Pacific Collection/Los Angeles
Public Library)

In the 1930s modern architecture was also find-ing support among social reformers. Nora Sterry, a school principal in Bell, California, and an advo-cate of progressive educational theories, enlisted the League of Women Voters in her campaign to build one of Neutra's open-air schools. He had developed the model "Ring Plan School" with individual classrooms encircling an open lawn for Rush City Reformed. Sterry and Neutra shared the same goals: to establish a more informal rela-tionship between teacher and student and to encourage different ways of learning by creating classrooms that functioned as "living" rooms.

Thanks to Sterry's efforts, a real version of a Ring Plan School, the Corona Avenue School, was built in Bell. The school board and other principals had been skeptical—one-story schools on multi-acre lots were unheard-of. They asked Neutra to prove his theories with comparative research on one-story bilateral-light schools on large lots. He made speeches to school administrators at educational conventions and published his "scientific theories" of school planning in journals. He invited doubting principals to his Silver Lake house, demonstrating the "hominess" of his proposed school by throwing open the sliding door onto his patio with its sweeping semi-circular bench: "Why could a classroom not be and look as does this kind of a living room?" asked Sterry of her colleagues.[74]

When it opened in 1934, the Corona Avenue School was featured on Hearst's "Metronome News" and "The March of Time" newsreel. The Los Angeles Times declared that it differed "from the customary school building like a 1936 model automobile from the original horseless carriage."[75] Unlike the typical multi-story school with long interior hallways and a small playground, Neutra's design offered individual detached classrooms, connected by open-air walkways and garden patios used as outdoor schoolrooms. Sliding glass walls and portable furniture allowed students to move back and forth easily between roofed and unroofed classrooms. The Corona Avenue School, typical of Southern California's modern buildings, offered a model for social reform. Decades after it was built, a nursery school teacher stated, "I have yet to find in Los Angeles or anywhere else a building which can measure up to the primary grade building at Corona… May many more such school rooms be built in the years that lie ahead."[76]

Although it wasn't until after World War II that modern architecture was widely accepted in Southern California, the generation that matured in the 1930s and 40s built on the work of the movement's founders and spurred development of a regional modern building tradition. A handful of architects—the "second generation," as architectural historian Esther McCoy christened them—took up the early revolutionaries' crusade, distilling their doctrinaire aesthetic into an architecture that was less dogmatic and more accommodating. They defined architecture broadly and sought its wide distribution: movie and theater sets; mass-produced furniture; prototypes for drive-in restaurants, markets and gas stations; and large-scale city plans and public housing projects.

Architects like Lloyd Wright, Hamilton Harwell Harris, Gregory Ain, and Raphael Soriano trained in the offices of the region's pioneering modernists. Schindler's and Neutra's studios in the 1930s and 40s especially were magnets for young architects searching for something new, while Frank Lloyd Wright continued as spiritual mentor. Wright, Neutra, and Schindler treated their practices and building projects as forms of pedagogy as well as platforms for evangelism. Their students formed a loose-knit, but clearly identifiable, band of apostles. Each developed a distinctive philosophy of form and materials—their buildings could not be mistaken for each other's—yet their work shares common themes with the work of their predecessors.

Lloyd Wright worked for Irving Gill as well as his father, Frank Lloyd Wright; Ain, Harris, and Soriano apprenticed with both Schindler and Neutra (though their terms with Neutra were longer). Together they formed the nucleus of the group that expanded the legacy of Gill, Wright, Schindler, and Neutra and extended its influence to shape post-World War II Southern California. Other architects—J.R. Davidson, Albert Frey, Kem Weber, Jock Peters—were pioneering at the same time. They too helped further Southern California's avant-garde architectural development between the world wars.

Like their mentors, most of the second generation's built projects were one-of-a-kind residential and commercial buildings. Although they developed models for mass-produced building types and technologies, many more of their plans were conceived than realized in the era between the wars. However, in their hands modern design—through a variety of media from housewares to urban planning—began to achieve a familiarity and

Neutra with students at *Lovell Health House* construction site, photograph c. 1928; architect: Richard Neutra.

Richard Neutra (with roll of plans) used the Lovell "Demonstration Health House" as a laboratory for his students from the Academy of Modern Art, including Hamilton Harwell Harris (second from right) and Gregory Ain (right). (Esther McCoy Files on Architects 1945-1989, Archives of American Art, Smithsonian Institution)

degree of comfort as architects balanced dogma with clients' needs in their efforts to popularize the new aesthetic.

While the second generation's clientele included arch modernists like *California Arts & Architecture* publisher John Entenza, they also included middle-class families who were less concerned with the styling of their houses than with the flexibility of open plans and indoor-outdoor living; office building developers who found auto-oriented planning and industrialized building technologies resulted in cost savings and increased rentability; and store owners who realized that progressive design sold their products, whatever else they might think of it. As modern architecture both suited—and was perceived to suit—the functional needs of everyday life, it gained acceptance. And architects recipro-cated by making designs that clients would find acceptable.

At the same time, the gap between progressive and traditional architecture was narrowing. Floor plans were becoming freer and more informal, hous-es were opening up to the landscape, and ornament was becoming more abstract. Also modern details such as corner windows, glass walls, and exterior patios treated as outdoor rooms were being seen more and more on otherwise conventional houses. Even the design of public buildings, under the influence of the PWA, was becoming more abstract and geometric, shedding stylistic appliqués in favor of a stripped-down modern esthetic.

The cultivated landscape was also casting off historical styles. Its magnificent natural geography and climate and its tradition of outdoor living were turning Southern California into a center for land-scape design in the 1930s. This landscape-based movement was the region's unique variation on modernism. The European avant-garde paid scant attention to the natural setting—most buildings were depicted as hermetically sealed boxes on generic sites. However, in Southern California, where people actually lived in "outdoor rooms," the relationship between building and site pre-occupied most designers—not just the avant-garde. Over the course of the 1930s, modernists' rejection of his-torical forms in favor of abstraction and their combination of formal elements with informal lifestyles gained favor. An interest in native plants and materials that had begun with the Arts and Crafts movement seemed to make more and more sense in a Depression-era economy which demanded practical approaches to gardens that emphasized function and low maintenance.[77]

A Nature-Based Modernism

Lloyd Wright, who trained as a landscape archi-tect, advocated a holistic design approach that merged buildings, site, plantings, and pools into an overall composition. (He made a landscape plan for each building project, whether the clients asked for it or not.)[78] Houses like Wright's 1936 ranch house for actor-producer Raymond Griffith demonstrated his interest in integrating man-made structures with nature. With its low-slung rambling form extending into the landscape via long garden walls, vine-covered trellises, wide eaves, and horizontal planes, Wright's architectural treatment of Griffith's residence anticipated the post-War California ranch house.

Wright's aim to develop a near-seamless inte-gration of building and landscape also produced one of the first modern landmarks in the Southern Californian desert. The Oasis Hotel, constructed in 1923, heralded the rise of Palm Springs as a pop-ular resort and established a toehold for modern architecture there. Using an innovative slip-form method of building concrete walls, Wright devel-oped a kind of modern adobe structure. Soil from the site was mixed with concrete and poured into movable forms that were raised and lowered on reinforcing rods.[79] These thick earthen walls helped to insulate interiors against 120-degree summer temperatures and proposed a kind of modernism that grew out of indigenous forms. Similarly, the composition of ramadas and court-yards arranged around an expressionistic tower was based on native planning traditions. The result was a contemporary interpretation of an Indian pueblo: "a dramatic and striking expression of a new land," as writer Anaïs Nin described Lloyd Wright's work.[80]

The eldest son of Frank Lloyd Wright, Lloyd Wright was educated in music, engineering, and agronomy before working in his father's office. After helping their father complete drawings for the Wasmuth portfolio, Lloyd and his brother John moved to San Diego in 1911 to work with Olmsted and Olmsted on the landscaping of the Panama California Exposition. Wright then worked as a draftsman and landscape designer in Irving Gill's office from 1912 until 1915. While there he lived in one of Gill's experimental cottages. Of his attraction to Gill's work, Wright later noted, "I had been seeing Gill's work around the town and I had admired it; it seemed to me to contain the same ideas as the buildings of my father."[81] It wasn't until much later that Wright discovered that Gill

Raymond Griffith Ranch House, Canoga Park, 1936; architect: Lloyd Wright.

The Griffith Ranch House anticipated the post-War California ranch house with its low rambling form that extended into the landscape. Wright's intention to merge building and site into an overall composition was achieved with long garden walls, stone foundations, vine-covered trellises, and wide horizontal eaves. (Department of Special Collections, Charles E. Young Research Library, University of California, Los Angeles) and Frank Lloyd Wright had both worked in the office of Louis Sullivan and that Sullivan was the source of those ideas.

As Gill's fortunes dwindled, Wright left to open practice with another landscape architect, Paul Thiene, and then to run Paramount Studios' Design and Drafting Department in 1916. There he designed sets ranging from medieval to classical in style and advocated more realistic 3-dimensional representations. After moving to Los Angeles, Wright joined Aline Barnsdall's avant-garde circle where he met Rudolph Schindler and married a member of Barnsdall's theatrical troupe, actress Kira Markham.

Lloyd Wright also was a member of bookseller Jake Zeitlin's circle, which included some of the region's most innovative artists and intellectuals: photographer Will Connell, graphic designer Grace Marion Brown and her beau, Louis Samuel (actor Ramon Novarro's business manager and a client of Wright's for his own house), impresario Merle Armitage, *Los Angeles Times* art editor Arthur Millier, opera singer Lawrence Tibbett, and industrial designer Kem Weber. Congregating in Zeitlin's bookshop/gallery, the group would rope in anyone interesting who came into town, take them to Will Connell's studio where he would shoot their photograph, then they would all go to dinner at a cheap French restaurant nearby, where dinner cost 75 cents and a bottle of wine 50 cents. "We would then gather at my shop," Zeitlin recalled, "and talk and make a lot of noise and argue and generally have a hell of a good time." [82]

Lloyd Wright designed three of Zeitlin's shops, in spite of what Zeitlin considered a certain impracticality that included inattention to maximizing shelf space. Describing his shop on Sixth Street, Zeitlin remarked:

"It was a very beautiful place, but it was no more practical than the previous one. He [Lloyd Wright] always had a great love for putting in lighting arrangements which created a very soft, diffused light. But when the light bulbs went out, you couldn't get at them to replace them, and so gradually, as one after the other of the light bulbs expired, the place got darker and darker. And finally we couldn't use the ceiling fixtures at all, and we had to set lamps around the place in order to keep the shop lit well enough for people to see the books they thought they might buy." [83]

Zeitlin considered Lloyd Wright the creative working member of the father-son partnership: Frank Lloyd Wright did the selling and Lloyd did the design. He applauded Lloyd as ingenious, creative, and able to produce the most effect for the least money. Ultimately, how-ever, Wright's inventive designs distracted Zeitlin's customers from his purpose:

"After a while, the interest was focused so much on the architecture and the interior design of my shops, the customers couldn't look at the books. A great many people would come and look at the architecture and "oh" and "ah" and walk away, and that wasn't really what I was there for." [84]

While working on his own projects like Zeitlin's stores, Lloyd Wright continued to supervise construction of his father's textile block projects—inspired perhaps by his own block system for the 1922 Henry Bollman house. From Gill, Lloyd Wright had learned the function and aesthetic of concrete. However, after watching Gill struggle with his tilt-up system, Wright turned instead to reinforced concrete blocks which were easier and cheaper for workers to handle. The Bollman block system, used to ornament a conventional stucco and frame house, comprised two separate walls of 4-inch-deep blocks tied together by steel. Frank Lloyd Wright then went on to develop a monolithic system of textile blocks—first for the Millard House in 1923, without steel reinforcement, and then for the Storer House that same year. Using a system similar to the Bollman House, the Storer, Freeman, and Ennis Houses all had exterior and interior walls of 4-inch-deep patterned concrete blocks, tied together vertically and horizontally with steel. Unlike Lloyd Wright's decorative textile block system, however, Frank Lloyd Wright's block system served as structural bearing walls.

Lloyd continued to propose the use of blocks for houses as well as a Catholic cathedral sky-scraper project. In most cases the blocks were ornamental rather than structural: none used a homogeneous system like his fathers' knit-block houses. These had proven considerably more costly than standard wood frame construction and had fatal technical flaws. Such buildings as the Carr house (1925), the Sowden house (1926), the Farrell house (1926), and his own studio-residence (1927) showed Gill's influence, as well as Frank Lloyd Wright's. In form, they resembled

Gill's cubic concrete buildings with simple punched openings. However, unlike Gill's structures, large blank wall surfaces were juxtaposed with sculptural ornament of textile blocks, evoking Pre-Columbian associations. These early buildings of Lloyd Wright's suggested his ambitions to forge his own version of a new modern architecture for the West.

Writer Anais Nin praised Lloyd Wright's appeal "to the spirit of grandeur in the American character."[85] Indeed, Wright's commissions could be theatrical in ways that his modernist colleagues' were not. Clients such as actress Jobyna Howland and impresario John Sowden came to Wright for spectacular houses that provided stage sets for their own theatrical lives. The Sowden house (1926), for instance, was centered around a stage-like courtyard that served as an exotic backdrop for dramatic productions, musical performances, and films. The Sowdens' furnishings, also designed by Wright (in collaboration with Sowden), included Roman-style barrel chairs and gold-faceted bedroom furniture.

The scenographic aspect of Wright's architecture in the 1920s was an extension of his work in the movies and theater. Not only did he design sets for Paramount Pictures, but he also created sets and two band shells for the Hollywood Bowl—the first in 1927, the second in 1928. (His introduction to the Bowl may have been through Aline Barnsdall, who donated money for acquisition of the property as well as improvements to the structure.)[86] Lloyd Wright's commission to develop the Hollywood Bowl's first music shell followed his design of the Bowl's productions of "Julius Caesar" in 1926 and "Robin Hood" in 1927. Using plaster board and wood leftover from sets, Wright aimed to invent a shell "characteristic of the southwest."[87] The shell's pyramidal shape and treatment evoked Mayan architecture, merging regional and age-old Greek theater traditions.

When patrons of the Bowl asked for a second, more permanent (and conventional) circular shell in the "pseudo Spanish" style of the time, Wright used their request as a springboard for a modern form and a new structural concept. The design comprised concentric segmental arches shaped according to a "reflected ray" model of sound transmission and constructed of light-weight, prefabricated standard parts that could be rapidly assembled and disassembled and tuned, panel by panel, using rods and turnbuckles like a drum. Ingeniously countering the circle's tendency to

Jake Zeitlin's Bookstore, Los Angeles, 1936-38; architect: Lloyd Wright.

Lloyd Wright designed three bookstores for Jake Zeitlin (Zeitlin appears in the background of the photograph), which also functioned as a gallery and gathering place for the region's avant-garde. The photograph was taken by a member of Zeitlin's and Wright's coterie, Will Connell. (Department of Special Collections, Charles E. Young Research Library, University of California, Los Angeles)

Aliso Village Public Housing Project,
Los Angeles, 1941-43; architects: George
Adams, Walter Davis, Ralph Flewelling,
Eugene Weston, Jr., Lewis Eugene
Wilson, and Lloyd Wright.

Wright developed an innovative site
plan and landscape design for the Aliso
Village Public Housing Project to maxi-
mize open space for light, air, and
recreation areas. Large apartment blocks
were located at the perimeter, lower
blocks were grouped at the interior of
the site, leaving generous areas for
parks, playgrounds and parking. Wright
used trellises, pergolas and ramadas
to connect the simple buildings to the
climate and landscape. (Security Pacific
Collection/Los Angeles Public Library)

focus sound in its apex, Wright's elliptical design successfully transmitted music to the back seats without electronic amplification. He claimed that his shell represented "the very essence of the democratic spirit that begot the Bowl… to distribute the great works of man to the many." [88]

Wright's interests in public-scale projects spurred him to design a conceptual modern civic center for Los Angeles in 1925. He had developed his urban planning skills while working in the Olmsteds' office, which had established the field of regional planning and was responsible for most of the large city plans in the United States. Wright's early interest was furthered by his work on Gill's schemes for Torrance. As an alternative to the Allied Architects' traditional plans for Los Angeles, Wright prepared a design for an industrial and transportation hub laid out in an axial City Beautiful format. Its setback composition of modern high-rises and terraced gardens was interlaced with multi-level transportation systems linking the city to the harbor, transcontinental railroad, and truck lines. Elevators connected underground subways and high-speed motorways to rooftop helipads and airplane landing fields.

Wright's theoretical "City of the Future," also published in 1925, offered a radical alternative to his father's suburban Broadacres City. In contrast to the elder Wright's Jeffersonian community of single-family houses on individual lots, Lloyd Wright's metropolis comprised one 1000-foot-high, cruciform-shaped, earthquake- and tornado-proof concrete, bronze, and glass tower, ringed by multi-level streets and freeways and crowned by a seven-level airplane landing field. The tower would be surrounded by vast open spaces of farms, forests, and parks. Its 40 acres of floor space would house 150,000 people under one roof, with transportation, industries, and stores on lower levels and residential units, cultural and recreational spaces above.

Like his modernist colleagues, Wright too was concerned with the design of low-cost housing. He collaborated on the design of several of Los Angeles' earliest public housing projects: Ramona Gardens (1939-40) and Aliso Village (1941-3). Budget constraints and long-term maintenance requirements dictated simple unornamented row-house and apartment units. The main innovations were the site plan and landscape design, which were Wright's responsibility. His plan for Aliso Village maximized open space for light, air, and recreation areas. Large apartment blocks were located at the perimeter, and lower blocks were grouped in the interior of the site, concentrating buildings in specified areas to leave large portions of the land free for parks, playgrounds, and parking. Besides the main access and service roads, a tree-lined "paseo" provided continuous pedestrian and recreational space with wading/spray points at regular junctures. Wright's main contributions were elements connecting the simple economical buildings to the climate and landscape: trellises, pergolas, and ramadas. As Gill had before him, Wright considered his chief achievement the landscaping—"that most essential requirement for tolerable human living conditions… for upon it depends in large measure the future livability of the project." [89]

Like Lloyd Wright, Hamilton Harwell Harris developed a new architecture for the West based on a reciprocal and integral relationship with the natural landscape. Harris was grandson of a '49er and early homesteader and son of an architect-rancher in Redlands. He credited his family's roots in San Bernardino, a town laid out by the Mormons with a grid of numbered and alphabetized streets precisely 1/8 of a mile apart, for his affinity for the modular unit system of design. And he cited the natural landscape for his way of building: "The variety in nature is something that is very much a part of me and something I like to take into account as far as possible in any building that I do… it wasn't a nature that had to be dominated… it was simply something to accommodate oneself to and to develop in what [I] built as a means of making more complete and general living possible." [90]

Like Lloyd Wright, and his early mentors, Rudolph Schindler and Richard Neutra, Hamilton Harwell Harris was introduced to modern architecture through Frank Lloyd Wright. Harris had no particular interest in architecture until he visited Wright's Hollyhock House with Ruth Sowden, a client of Lloyd Wright's and a classmate at Otis Art Institute where Harris was studying sculpture. Harris wrote of that fateful encounter with Wright's Southern California "Romanza":

"It was in the late afternoon, and the sun was getting low, and the walls—which were sort of a golden tan—were very gold in the light of the setting sun. And the building was very horizontal and had wings that came toward you and away from you, this way and that way, and the movement of these wings was paralleled with the movements of bands of repeated ornament…

and I simply couldn't stand still. I just had to move. As the building moved, I moved. That was all. I had to follow its development… This building was something I had never been able to imagine before." [91]

Harris credits his 1925 visit to Aline Barnsdall's house with his architectural epiphany. He went to the Los Angeles Public Library, looked up Wright's work in the 1910 Wasmuth portfolio (the same publication that had introduced Wright's work to Schindler and Neutra when they were students in Austria), and decided to become an architect. Sixty years later he wrote that he "never escaped from the influence of the Wasmuth Folio plans." [92]

After his encounter with Wright's work, Harris made a practice of going to look at new buildings in Los Angeles. His visit to the Jardinette Apartments under construction led him to AGIC, Schindler's and Neutra's Kings Road studio. Schindler's house made an indelible impression: "If any building can fire one with the passion for simple living and high thinking, this is it." He wrote of the house's air of unreality and enchantment enhanced by Dione Neutra's appearance in a toga, suggesting that he had arrived on Mount Olympus. [93]

Harris had registered for the architectural program at Berkeley, but was persuaded to apprentice with Schindler and Neutra instead. Neutra convinced him that he could learn more working on a drawing board on a trunk in their drafting room while taking engineering courses at night. After Neutra opened his own office, Harris continued drawing his visionary plans such as the Lehigh Portland Cement Airport Competition, Rush City Reformed, the Ring Plan School Project, and CIAM projects. Harris wrote of the education he and Gregory Ain received at that time: "The marvelous thing was that Neutra was doing his thinking, his musing, his proposing, his adopting, his rejecting with me and Ain as ringside watchers." [94] Harris claimed that he and Ain learned more in several weeks with Neutra than they could in years on their own. (Harris and Ain set up practice together in 1936, but none of their collaborative projects was built.) Harris also admired the spontaneous, provisional nature of Schindler's designs, his inventiveness with materials that had never been used before in buildings, as well as his adaptation of standardized parts for unique solutions.

While he learned fundamental lessons of modernism from Neutra, Wright, and Schindler, of his generation Harris was unique in also looking to local architectural traditions, such as the Greene Brothers' bungalows, Japanese art and architecture, and Bernard Maybeck's work, as well as Synchromist painter Stanton Macdonald-Wright with whom he studied at the Art Students League. Ultimately Harris proposed an architecture that was evocative of all of them, yet was like none of them. "By avoiding the clichés of the moment—whether 'modern' or 'traditional,'" noted The Architectural Forum in 1940, Harris "has succeeded in establishing an idiom of his own that is as fresh today as it was five years ago." [95]

After a few experiments in steel framing, Harris worked primarily in wood, a material that many clients favored over Neutra's machine-made imagery. When financing agencies rejected his modern designs, Harris turned easily to hipped roofs and conventional stucco and wood siding instead of the flat roofs and experimental materials preferred by his avant-garde colleagues. Harris' ability to accommodate the exigencies of site, clients, and banks, and to achieve an architecture that was modern without seeming doctrinaire made him one of the most popular of Southern California's progressive architects. As he joked about his 1934 house for Pauline Lowe, the redwood siding was chosen by the client, the roof by the loan company, the circulation owed something to Frank Lloyd Wright and the fenestration to the Japanese, but the L-shaped floor plan was his own. [96]

Like Schindler's and Neutra's houses for themselves, Harris' own house—a simple wood-framed pavilion high up in the trees of Fellowship Park—represented his deeply-held philosophy of architecture. Barely enclosed by a structure of redwood posts and sliding screens, the house comprised one large room, with a small kitchen, bath and dressing room to one side. Its structural supports were external to the walls: wood and iron compression-tension buttresses that were connected to ceiling girders and cantilevered floor joists allowed the walls to open wide to embrace the woods outside. Levitating above the hillside, the structure seemed to float in the foliage.

On the interior natural redwood panels with black rails, grass floor matting, a gold leaf screen, and dark blue and vermilion upholstery—as well as high-gloss blue, vermilion, and yellow-green enameled walls and ceilings in the bathroom and kitchen—provided, as one article noted, "the background for the existence of two modern people." [97] Serving as filters for light and air rather than enclo-

Fellowship Park House, Los Angeles, 1935;
architect: Hamilton Harwell Harris.

Harris's own house was a simple wood-
framed pavilion in Fellowship Park, with
permeable exterior walls of glass, cloth and
insect netting that could be interchanged
with solid panels in harsh weather. It
represented the modern version of the
traditional vine-covered cottage. (Esther
McCoy Files on Architects 1945–1989,
Archives of American Art, Smithsonian
Institution)

Greta Granstedt House, Los Angeles,
1938; architect: Hamilton Harwell Harris.

Harris, one of the most popular of the
region's modern architects, developed
an architecture that accommodated
informal lifestyles and indoor-outdoor
living. His houses were modern in an
unprepossessing way and proposed
innovations such as turning the garage
sideways so its doors faced the
driveway rather than the street.
(Harwell Hamilton Harris Papers,
The Alexander Architectural Archive,
The General Libraries, The University
of Texas at Austin)

sure, exterior walls comprised light screens of glass, cloth and insect netting. These were interchangeable with each other and with solid celotex and masonite panels for harsh weather. Beyond the screens hung bamboo shades from the edge of the wide eaves, extending the interior space into the outdoors. Almost Japanese in its simplicity, order, and expression, the pavilion captured America's imagination when it was constructed in 1935. It was widely praised for its poetic beauty and economy ($430 construction cost, plus plumbing and electrical work)[98] and was awarded a number of design honors.

With few exceptions Harris' clients, unlike Neutra's or Schindler's, shared an apparent disinterest in affiliating with the avant-garde. Clients did not find him by driving by architectural masterpieces. Rather they saw his homes in popular magazines like House Beautiful and admired his facility for working with small budgets. The Architectural Forum also showcased his houses: typically built for young middle class families with children, they were cited for their accommodation of "informal effortless living" and their lack of overt style.

The Bauers, for whom Harris designed a house in Glendale in 1939, were typical of his clients. They asked Harris to create a house for a family that liked to play together, with a close connection between indoors and outdoors, and providing seclusion from the street and neighbors. Accordingly, Harris planned a house that turned away from the street and opened up with glass walls to the rear garden. Its flexible plan allowed living, dining, play, and garden areas to function separately or together, as glass walls could slide open or be curtained to provide varying degrees of privacy. As the Bauers described their new home,

> "We wanted a house that was simple, open, and which did not require a lot of furniture to make it livable. We did not discuss the question of modern versus traditional. We like the openness of the house, its airiness, and informality. It is homey and lacks pretense. It fits into its surroundings. We think our house a good investment because it suits the site, is comfortable to live in, and is not dated."[99]

Harris' work bridged the worlds of high and popular culture. His projects were featured in a number of exhibitions, from a traveling show sponsored by House Beautiful and installed in department stores around the country, to the Paris International Exposition in 1937, exhibitions at New York's Museum of Modern Art, even the 1939 New York World's Fair. His work was heralded by both the popular and the architectural press—it suited the time and the place: progressive, not radical; up-to-date without being uncomfortable; modern but not startling. His innovations made sense to homeowners: for instance, turning the garage in front of the house sideways, so its doors faced the driveway rather than the street, and providing a covered walk from the garage to the front entry instead of the side door. This change to the conventional suburban site plan was quietly revolutionary—and widely accepted.

Harris' impact can be measured by how familiar his houses seem now, with their box-like masses, low overhanging pitched roofs, high wood fences enclosing private gardens, and garages integrated into the composition of the site plan. His fundamental principles have resonated throughout the history of Southern California's residential design, linking the work of the early modernists and the post-War California ranch house.

An Aesthetic of Economy

Like Harris, Gregory Ain practiced a deliberately straightforward modernism. His objective to create well-designed, low-cost housing superceded any desire for architectural effect. Focusing his efforts on developing economical construction technologies, Ain's aesthetic evolved into a "builder's modern" that bridged the contractor's vocabulary of economics and the high art of his colleagues. Ain's architectural apprenticeship began in 1928 as a student in Neutra's class at the Academy of Modern Art. The Lovell Health House, under construction at the time, served as the class laboratory.

Attracted by Neutra's aesthetic of scientific rationalism, his commitment to industrial technology, and his view of architecture as a social tool, Ain joined Neutra to work on his theoretical projects: the Ring Plan School project, the Lehigh Cement Airport Competition, and Rush City Reformed. Ain continued to work on and off for Neutra between 1928 and 1935, and he and his wife lived with the Neutras in their VDL Research House. Ain was cited as "associate" or "collaborator" on a number of projects, including Neutra's own VDL Research House, the all-metal Beard house, and art dealer Galka Scheyer's house. He also worked occasionally for Schindler in the early 1930s, helping him to develop low-cost houses and a prototype service station for Standard Oil.

Ain first encountered modern architecture in 1925 when he was still in high school and visited Schindler's studio. Schindler's left-wing politics and his philosophy of architecture's social promise struck a spark in him. After that fateful encounter, Ain went on to study design at the University of Southern California. Named for Menshevik hero, Gregory Gershuny, Ain had grown up in a socialist community in East Los Angeles. His father was a founding member of the utopian Llano del Rio cooperative farming community in Antelope Valley, and as a child Ain had lived in a tent there. That experience informed his practice of architecture as a form of socialism throughout his career. Forty years after he first encountered Rudolph Schindler, Ain still described architecture as a "social art," declaring that "its aesthetic power must be derived from a social ethos." [100]

Ain was far more interested in developing a practical modern architecture than an artistic one. For Ain, his designs were "…always intended to be a precise solution to prior stated problems, rather than Architecture." [101] He deliberately designed houses that could be built by any carpenter using conventional construction technologies: most were wood frame with stucco finish. His view of design as a problem-solving process prompted his rejection of machine-related imagery in favor of an imagery of pragmatism after he left Neutra's office. Ain's designs were almost artless, even mundane—disinterested in effect for the sake of effect. His work in the mid-1930s anticipated merchant builders by simplifying framing and reducing the number of structural components. His Dunsmuir Flats of 1937, for instance, used two-story four-inch by four-inch posts, which also served as door and window jambs, eliminating many elements and their costs. By the late 1930s Ain's houses shared both the spirit and the vocabulary of the contractor/builder house: highly efficient plans of economical construction without superficial details.

Like his $4800 house for a postman's family constructed in 1936, many of Ain's houses were designed for middle-class clients without servants (unlike Neutra's clients). They provided access to the kitchen directly from the entry rather than a service porch and playrooms next to kitchens so mothers could oversee their children while cooking. Ain shared planning and aesthetic interests with his modernist colleagues: open, flexible layouts that had few corridors; subdividing living

Dunsmuir Flats, Los Angeles, 1937; architect: Gregory Ain.

Ain's interest in developing a practical modern architecture, realized in the Dunsmuir Flats, used a builder's vocabulary of wood framing and stucco. His plan provided each unit with separate entries and private patios. (Photograph by Julius Shulman)

spaces with built-in furniture and fireplaces rather than fixed walls; expansion of the interior to the exterior through glass walls and balconies; controlling and manipulating natural light through the use of clerestory windows, trellises, and skylights; and providing privacy from neighbors and the street.

These design principles were achieved for relatively low costs. Ain would re-design, often for free, until he came up with a plan the owner could afford. Many of his clients shared his socialist goals. (One of Ain's colleagues observed that most kept copies of The People's World newspaper, a local Communist paper, on their coffee tables.)[102] Dunsmuir Flats resident Dorothy Kahan was the niece of a member of the Llano del Rio community. She and her husband, Bob Kahan, became committed supporters of Ain's and went on to develop and move into Ain's Park Planned Homes in 1946–7. Ain's other clients included a number of women with servantless households, bookstore/gallery owner Jake Zeitlin, and Rita and Max Lawrence, founders of Architectural Pottery which manufactured local artists' pots that were often featured in modern interiors.

Ain's primary concern, however, was the development of low-cost housing. His first social housing project, designed in 1935 for agricultural workers, served as the genesis for much of his experimentation. Using elements from Buckminster Fuller's Dymaxion House as well as the "Schindler Shelter," the prototype house comprised a one-room, 20-foot by 20-foot concrete structure with four corner concrete pylons, factory-made partitions with built-in closets and storage, a pre-packaged plumbing/heating core for a back-to-back kitchen and bathroom, and pre-fabricated doors and windows. Ain's 1940 design for a "One Family Defense House," sponsored by a Guggenheim grant and developed in collaboration with Joseph Stein, was a refinement of the first design. Constructed of precast concrete corner slabs and 4-inch by 4-inch posts, with plywood wall and roof panels, the house was primarily an assembly of shop-built standardized parts. Only the concrete pylons required semi-skilled labor. The house could be completed in six days for $1000.

Ain's interest in experimental technologies focused on prefabrication, which he saw as the means to achieve good, cheap, and rapidly constructed dwellings. He aimed to standardize the general layout in order to achieve economical and efficient construction, providing exterior variety with different roof treatments, site plans, and land-scaping. He advocated using products that were widely available, easily transported, inexpensive, and would allow small-scale production—all factors that had previously hampered mass-production of small houses. Not only would pre-fabrication save in time and labor, Ain felt, but it would also assure greater precision and, thus, superior strength and durability and better quality of finishes and details.

Other systems—pre-assembled bathrooms, prefabricated wall systems, pre-cut studs, pre-drilled holes in studs for wiring—were tested in his later cooperative housing projects. Ain hadn't counted on contractors' resistance to labor-reducing systems or pre-fabricated components, however. Because builders priced any deviation from conventional construction methods as "custom," Ain finally had to concede, as Schindler had, that the contractor-built house would remain cheaper than his proposed housing with pre-assembled components. Although Ain's efforts to disseminate modern design led to a number of multi-family housing projects after World War II, he never realized the large-scale commissions for pre-fabricated housing that he had committed his career to researching and developing. And, although his homes of the mid-to-late 1930s received a number of design awards, his "builder's modern" single-family houses didn't achieve the popularity of the more commodious modernism of contemporaries like Harwell Hamilton Harris.

The machine-based aesthetic of another of Neutra's apprentices, Raphael Soriano, also proved to have a limited audience. Of the second generation, Soriano may have been the most devout subscriber to the early modernists' belief in new technology: McCoy called him "a romantic technologist, the true missionary of Southern California."[103] Soriano, more than any of his peers, took up the crusade for structural experimentation, spending twenty years perfecting economical steel framing for housing and office buildings to bring its costs below wood framing. He then turned his efforts to developing a framing system of aluminum, which he considered easier to fabricate, cheaper to ship, and less work to install and maintain since it could be permanently finished by anodizing. (Nevertheless, according to at least one client, efficient and economical construction did not necessarily translate into low costs on Soriano's buildings.)[104]

Soriano practiced in the tradition of Gill and Schindler. His office remained small and each commission was treated as a means to further his research into structural innovation and economical modern design. He did not design large buildings nor buildings with large budgets. However, he developed construction systems using mass-produced, pre-fabricated parts that would suit wide-scale production.

Soriano freely acknowledged Neutra's influence in his fascination with progressive technologies and orderly planning. Along with Gregory Ain and Hamilton Harwell Harris, Soriano worked on Neutra's Rush City and other visionary projects in the early 1930s after studying architecture at the University of Southern California. (Soriano almost flunked out for refusing to design in styles.) He also spent a brief period in Schindler's office, but had little empathy for his work which he considered too personal and sculptural. Schindler, in turn, thought Soriano's work was "too functional." [105]

Soriano's buildings realized theories advocated, but rarely practiced, by Neutra. More concerned with economy and functionality than architectural effect, Soriano did not set out to create self-consciously avant-garde architecture. Instead, unlike the work of early modernists, Soriano's buildings intended to provide unobtrusive back-drops for living, working, and socializing—often on minimal budgets. Soriano had little interest in innovative planning or spatial dramatics. Many of his buildings had traditional box-like rooms with full-height walls and eight-foot ceilings. The vocabulary was generic modern: smooth stucco surfaces, ribbon windows, flat roofs, built-in furniture, indirect lighting, and large areas of glazing and continuous soffits to merge indoors and out. For Soriano, architecture was "more than just surfaces, more than styles… It's the thinking; it's the structuring of all the totality of the elements in the unified concept." [106] Soriano compared his precise modular planning that encompassed interiors as well as landscapes to Bach's fugal compositions.

Soriano dates his last use of wood to 1936, the year he met Fritz Ruppell, developer of the Lattisteel framing system. Soriano's work with the Lattisteel system of welded steel angles and steel plumbers' straps was the beginning of a long career of experimentation with steel framing.

"What do you do with wood? Well, the same old stuff, and all you do is just put those little sticks all over the place. And I said this is not the way to build. This is uneconomical, clumsy, costly, the labor, and then the result is wrong. You have four walls to hold a little room with these two by

Project, Exterior and Interior Models, *One-Family Defense House,* 1939-40; architect: Gregory Ain in collaboration with Joseph Stein.

———————

Ain's commitment to the design of low-cost housing produced the "One-Family Defense House." Constructed of pre-cast concrete corner slabs and wood posts, with plywood wall and roof panels, the house could be built in six days for $1000. The interior plan comprised a pre-packaged plumbing/heating core for a back-to-back kitchen and bathroom, factory-made partitions with built-in closets and storage, and prefabricated doors and windows. (Exterior photograph by Julius Shulman; interior photograph courtesy of Esther McCoy Files on Architects 1945–1989, Archives of American Art, Smithsonian Institution)

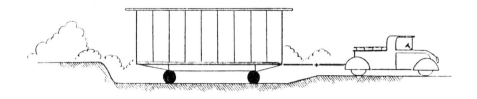

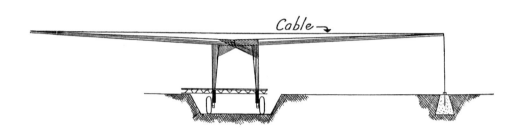

Cable →

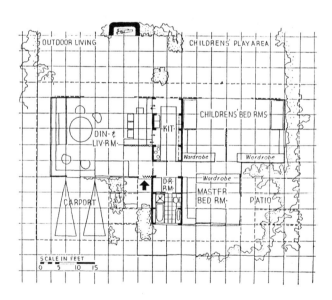

OUTDOOR LIVING   CHILDRENS' PLAY AREA

CHILDRENS' BED RMS

KIT·

DIN· ¢
LIV·RM·

Wardrobe   Wardrobe

Wardrobe

D·R·
RM·

CARPORT

MASTER
BED RM·   PATIO

SCALE IN FEET
0   5   10   15

Project, Mobile Unit, designed c. 1939,
published 1942; architect: Raphael Soriano.

Raphael Soriano's commitment to new
technologies and low-cost housing
produced a project for a mobile house
that could be delivered by a small
truck and erected without foundations.
(Esther McCoy Files on Architects
1945–1989, Archives of American Art,
Smithsonian Institution)

fours. In mine, I don't need that. I liberated right away. I went into complete freedom having… no obstacles." [107]

Soriano built without bearing walls, but instead with steel columns and beams allowing 20-foot by 40-foot modules and long cantilevers. In 1939 he developed prefinished, pre-fabricated walls and ceiling assemblies that could be stacked together like chairs for shipping and bolted in place on site. Constructed this way, Soriano's buildings could be put together by unskilled workers at the rate of four housing units a day. [108]

Soriano's interest in pre-fabrication generated a project for a mobile house that could be delivered by a small truck and erected without foundations. Constructed of plastic or wood-faced panels that could be snapped into place on walls, ceilings, and floors, the building would be supported on wheels or struts anchored to concrete bases. Utilities would be located in a trench underneath. No painting would be required, since surfaces would be covered with a membrane of plastic, light metal or canvas. A heater would not be needed; instead warm air generated by the hot water unit would circulate between beams and radiate heat from the ceiling. Rather than installing expensive electrical wiring and light fixtures, specially treated areas of the ceiling would be activated by "black light" from the underground electrical system. The plan would be flexible: all rooms would open to outdoor patios and to each other. Furniture would be sectional and modular, so it could be moved and re-combined. Rooms would be separated by wardrobes with snap-in connections for doors. Infinitely flexible and modular, houses could be expanded with additional panels.

In spite of—or because of—Soriano's determination to create the most efficient and economical designs for each client, he experienced the same denials by financing agencies and homeowners' boards that Schindler and Neutra suffered. Sometimes the FHA would approve less than the requested loan amount, and Soriano would contribute half the difference in order to realize the project. The Gogol House was actually stopped mid-construction by homeowners' petitions, which caused the lending agency to threaten to withdraw the loan since the flat-roofed house did not "conform to the neighborhood." After his door-to-door lobbying failed to sway neighbors, Soriano directed the builder to add a flimsy hipped roof to the penthouse studio, barely tacking down the shingles so they would blow off in the first wind after the loan was re-secured. In another instance when he was told his design didn't conform to the neighborhood, Soriano showed the lender photos of the half dozen different types of nearby housing, asking him which type his house should conform to. The lender finally approved Soriano's design. But, as Soriano observed many years later, "it used to take pains and aggravations." [109]

Another advocate of a machine-based modernism for the new age was Albert Frey, who moved to Palm Springs from Switzerland in 1934. Frey's earliest desert buildings were the epitome of pure functionalism, derived from the European modernism of Le Corbusier. He felt that machine technology would provide the precise means to develop buildings that would meet "exactly, definite requirements"—in his opinion a tremendous improvement over the haphazard results of individual handicraft.

After graduating from the Institute of Technology in Switzerland, Frey had worked from 1928 until 1930 in the office of Le Corbusier, then came to New York in 1930. He achieved almost instant international renown with his design, in partnership with A. Lawrence Kocher, of the Aluminaire house for the 1931 Allied Arts and Building Products Exhibition. The first American house designed by a Corbusier-trained architect, as well as the first all-light-steel and aluminum house, the Aluminaire established Frey's reputation as a standard-bearer of European modernism. It also demonstrated his keen interest in conceiving a new architecture to suit new lifestyles and developing affordable housing through modern technology.

After moving to Palm Springs to oversee construction of a building for Kocher's brother, the city's first physician, Frey wrote to Le Corbusier:

"The California desert continues to charm me, continues to nourish me, to give me an opportunity for modern architecture, from time to time. It is a most interesting experience to live in a wild, savage, natural setting, far from the big city, but without losing contact with civilization, thanks to the car… to the radio, to the plane, and to the intellectual milieu in Palm Springs due to the presence of visitors and inhabitants from all parts of the world… We are confident that the future holds more and more opportunities to do modern work." [110]

Frey's architecture transposed Le Corbusier's rhetoric to the Western landscape, spreading the forms out across the desert, rather than raising them up on stilts. As other California modernists like Gill and Neutra had depended on the natural landscape to soften and humanize their buildings, Frey suggested that "plants and mountains with their curved and irregular contours create a welcome contrast to the rectilinear practical house form."[111]

Frey's first efforts were pure examples of the International Style. His pristine machine-made structures, in contrast to the rugged irregularity of the natural landscape, found their ideal setting in Palm Springs, which was just beginning to develop its urban character when Frey arrived. His rectilinear buildings were inspired by the simple cubic volumes of the native Indian pueblos, which he considered to be living areas that were merely "walled in and roofed-over." Just as the needs of inhabitants dictated the width, length, and height of the rooms, Frey's volumes were precisely sized and arranged according to their use and importance.

The Eastern architectural press viewed Frey as a leading exponent, along with Richard Neutra, of European modernism in the West. *Architectural Record's* 1936 article on the apartment interior featured a kitchen designed by Kocher and Frey, along with the stair hall in Le Corbusier's Villa Savoye, Gropius' dining room for Moholy-Nagy in Dessau, and Neutra's VDL Research house.[112]

As Neutra had done, Frey was inspired by his experience in America to write an architectural manifesto, *In Search of a Living Architecture*, published in 1939. In it he theorized about the fundamentals of design for the industrial age, affirming the lessons of America's and other nations' most rudimentary structures to fulfill modern needs. As Gill and Neutra had done in their treatises, Frey couched his rhetoric in the words of a technician, equating architectural progress with scientific progress. He felt that this made new forms more palatable to Americans, declaring that in the U.S. "only mechanical, scientific, and technical progress"—not architecture—"is accepted without hesitation."[113]

As his counterparts in Los Angeles were doing, Frey experimented with industrial materials and standardized components—aluminum, steel, corrugated metal, asbestos cement board—to develop affordable modern design. Like his colleagues, Frey used his own house as a laboratory for experimenting with new products and ideas. His first house, constructed in 1941, was sheathed in corrugated metal, which wouldn't shrink and expand with drastic desert temperature changes as wood and stucco would. Walls of glass extended out towards the pool, enlarging the tiny 320 s.f. volume. Windows were precisely situated, based on calculations of the amount of sunlight each opening would receive throughout the year. In one of Frey's houses, the bathroom had a light fixture on one side of the medicine cabinet, not both, since natural light would illuminate the other. Frey was neither concerned with symmetry nor with people needing even light to shave or apply make-up, if it meant adding a feature he felt was extraneous.[114]

Frey worked with his partner John Porter Clark to develop new building types for the modern West. These included a drive-in dairy adjacent to the highway with a cinema, restaurant and milk processing area, surrounded by a counter where visitors could sit and watch the process while eating. After Clark was licensed in 1940 and the firm could solicit public projects, Clark and Frey also developed prototypes for modern schools such as Cathedral City Elementary School (1940) and Cahuilla Elementary School (1941): one-story, flat-roofed pavilions with outdoor work areas, connected by covered walkways. With their glass walls facing north and clerestory windows facing south, indoor-outdoor classrooms, and informal plans, Clark and Frey's schools seemed particularly suited for the desert climate. Not only could this scheme be expanded exponentially as schools grew, but it could also be replicated from site to site.

After World War II, Frey became one of Palm Springs' leading architects, designing hospitals, schools, churches, and the city hall, as well as projects in other desert communities. He came to Palm Springs at a formative time in its development and made his imprint on the city, shaping its distinctive modern tradition.

Frey House 1, Palm Springs, 1941;
architect: Albert Frey.

Clad in corrugated metal with glass
walls that extended out towards the
pool, Frey's first house was a 320-
square-foot laboratory for testing
new ideas and products. (Photograph
by Julius Shulman)

5

Modern Commercial Design and the Industrial Arts

As Southern California's modern residential architecture was achieving international renown, at least with the avant-garde, the region's commercial design and applied arts were also undergoing a metamorphosis. In this arena J.R. Davidson, Kem Weber, and Jock Peters were among the chief protagonists. Born and educated in Germany, all three designers called themselves "industrial designers" first and architects second. They transposed their aesthetic and interest in modern materials to a wide range of scales: from the design of furniture and fixtures to interiors, graphics, buildings, landscapes, and large-scale site plans, working in commercial as well as residential genres. Moving to Southern California in the early decades of the twentieth century, they brought with them a Bauhaus-like determination to merge modern architecture with the industrial arts to create contemporary environments.

Davidson's, Peters', and Weber's work represented new approaches to the conventions of retail development. They led commercial design into the future by inventing a new retail aesthetic that was both modern and popular based on the imperatives for large signs and glass display windows:

> "Advertisement—lettering—signs—electrical light—effects—reflections—movements and other attractions hitherto superimposed upon the classical architectural efforts of our store fronts have now become the basis for store front design—copies of classical columns, pilasters, cornices and antique stone structures are replaced by designs evolved from modern steel and concrete construction, and advertising necessities are the means of enrichment, variation, and character." [115]

Jock Peters, who moved to Los Angeles from Germany in 1922, had an aptitude for the stage-craft of commercial design as well as a sensuous appreciation of industrial materials, forms, and colors. Having apprenticed with a stonemason, studied at a building trades school, and directed a school for the applied arts in Germany, Peters had a strong background in applied arts that continued to inform his architectural projects. In 1913-14 he worked in the office of Peter Behrens, whose fusion of classic design and industrial materials was considered the ultimate expression of modern theories and construction methods at that time. (Before World War I, Behrens' office was almost a required rite of passage for young European architects interested in developing a new architecture for the twentieth century: Walter Gropius, Mies van der Rohe, and Le Corbusier all worked in his studio before striking out on their own.)

Peters' frail health and Germany's post-World War I economic and political collapse propelled him to Los Angeles, where his brother had moved ten years earlier. He was 33 years old, knew no English, and left behind his wife and five children to seek new opportunities in the American West. Like many other emigrés, Peters soon turned to movie studios for employment. Famous Players/Lasky (later Paramount Pictures), with its powerful, tight-knit German community, offered him employment as an art director for a number of years (1924-1927 and then off and on into the early 1930s). While there he designed sets for "City of the Future" (never made), "Road to Reno," "This is the Night," and "What Price Glory?" (for William Fox), as well as stage sets for productions of "Mars" and "The Mystery of Life." [116]

In 1927 Peters and his brother George opened Peters Brothers Modern American Design, a studio for the design of modern furniture, residential interiors, and stores. They solicited work from Schindler's and Neutra's AGIC, among others. His early commissions were for conventional period interiors, but Peters was able to demonstrate his progressive sensibilities with a series of model interiors and furnishings for *Hi Hat Magazine*, a magazine published by and for the film industry. The editors heralded his designs: "they typify precisely the kind of furniture which is being built for the present-day home," noting that "Peters follows the fundamental practice of any applied art in his designs—which is to make furniture adapted to the habits and needs of our time with little or no reference to past forms." [117]

At the same time, Peters entered competitions for rug and furniture designs, including one sponsored by S. Karpen & Brothers in 1927 whose brief requested submissions strong enough to withstand use by the modern American household, combining comfort with beauty, durability with structural economy, and encouraging designs "unhampered by traditional motifs." Peters' design was praised as "a type of modern furniture where the frank use of wood in its natural straightness and a dependence on arrangement of line are stressed rather than development of detail." [118] During this period Peters designed carpets for Mohawk Mills and furniture for Universal Assembling Furniture, while working off and on

with store planners, Feil and Paradise, to produce designs for Desmond's storefront (1928) and Maddux Air Lines building (1928). When Feil and Paradise were commissioned in 1929 for the interiors of a new department store, Bullocks Wilshire, they enlisted Jock Peters to create its brand new look.

In its luxuriant materials and opulent effect, Bullocks Wilshire offered a sensuous modernism distinct from the ascetic esthetic practiced by Neutra, Schindler, and other avant-garde architects. Yet, beyond its elegant finishes, the store represented a revolution in modern retail development. Designed by architects John and Donald Parkinson, Bullocks introduced a site plan that for the first time was oriented to both car and pedestrian, accommodating automobiles with a main entry and porte-cochere facing the parking lot in the rear. Bullocks also provided a series of distinctive specialty shops rather than departments, merchandising each boutique with its own accessories so that customers could be completely outfitted in each area. Each shop had its own identity, courtesy of Peters, from the Sportswear Department, which heralded the freedom of speed and movement, to the cubist volumes and rich textures of the Saddle Shop.

The inspiration for the interiors came from the 1925 Paris Exposition Internationale des Arts Décoratifs et Industriels Moderne, which Bullocks executive P.G. Winnett had visited. Jock Peters' interpretation drew on sources that ranged from the Bauhaus to cubism to industrial machinery to Frank Lloyd Wright's textile block houses. His elegant materials and refined detailing belied their simple modern forms and industrial references, proposing a new vocabulary for commercial interiors. Incorporating artwork by well-known artists such as Gjura Stojano and Herman Sachs, Bullocks' interiors were a testimonial to the integration of modern design and commerce.

After working on Bullocks Wilshire, Peters collaborated with Schindler on the planning and designs of model houses for William Lingenbrink's 140-acre development in Calabasas. Lingenbrink wanted to establish an artists' colony to be called "Park Moderne," where all buildings would be developed "along modern lines" and traditional styles and applied decoration were forbidden. Schindler designed several houses in 1929, followed by Peters' Community Building and model house in 1931. In an effort to encourage artists to move there, Lingenbrink offered to trade

Interior of *Sportswear Department,*
Bullocks Wilshire, Los Angeles, 1929;
architects: John and Donald B. Parkinson,
Jock Peters.

Jock Peters' design for Bullocks Wilshire's
Sportwear Department created an identity
of freedom and movement and featured
a mural, "The Spirit of Sports," by artist
Gjura Stojano. (California State Library's
Mott-Merge Photograph Collection)

lots for artwork that he sold in a gallery on Sunset
Boulevard designed by Schindler. He also offered
to donate building materials to prospective residents. Sculptors Archipenko and Jan de Swart
took Lingenbrink up on his offer, although
ultimately the experimental development failed
to attract enough artistic buyers interested in a
community of modern design. (The timing of the
development during the Depression may have
contributed to its failure.)

Although Peters died in 1934, he is viewed as
an important contributor to the development of
modern design in Los Angeles. In her 1932 article
on "Modern California Architects" for *Creative Art*
magazine, Pauline Schindler noted that while
Neutra, Schindler, and Lloyd Wright were "at their
best in the organization of the whole and its inner
relationships of form and function," Peters and J.R.
Davidson contributed "items of detail"—a flower
shop lighting fixture or a drinking fountain—each
"a distillation of the modern temper... the totality
reduced to a single clear and distinct syllable of
utterance."[119]

Before moving to Southern California in 1925,
J. R. Davidson had worked in London, Paris,
Berlin, and New York. His first several years in Los
Angeles were spent in the office of a local period
revival architect, Robert D. Farquhar, and designing sets for movies, including "It" for art director
Cedric Gibbons and "The Golden Bed" directed
by Cecil B. DeMille. Davidson's aesthetic sensibilities had been shaped by his work on sophisticated
Paris interiors. His use of color and materials as a
means of architectural development represented
the merging of interior decoration and architecture
that traditionally had been two separate domains.
Davidson cited the influence of his Paris training
in his use of colors and his experiments with
montage and cubism. From his work for a London
architectural firm specializing in ocean liner interiors, he learned to develop the simplest solutions
that maximized function and effect in the minimum
of space. There too he invented elegantly flush
details and indirect lighting fixtures to enlarge and
dramatize small spaces. Davidson brought this
sensibility to his 1930s and 40s commercial and
residential projects in Southern California.

Davidson's avant-garde designs and sophisticated aesthetic earned him more commercial
commissions than any other modernist during the
1930s.[120] Projects like Sardi's Restaurant in 1936
and the Feingold and Harris Medical Building in
1941 were landmarks of modern commercial

design, just as his hotel nightclubs such as the Nickabob Cafe and the Cocoanut Grove at the Ambassador Hotel shaped the modern cocktail lounge.

In his commercial designs Davidson used new materials in innovative ways for striking effects. He also developed indirect lighting fixtures that manufacturers then mass-produced. His facade for C.R. Hite, developed in 1929, used light green chemically stained cement with aluminum reveals, sand-finished and lacquered bronze, and indirectly lit glazing. He tried cadmium-plated steel and copper for the Hite-Bilike shops, copper and redwood for the Satyr Bookshop. His facade for Jay Bari on Hollywood Boulevard comprised a cubistic collage of solid and transparent rectangles and stripes. His exterior for Lora Lee had a recessed entry with a forecourt lined by a ziggurat of neon-lit showcases. After a fire destroyed Schindler's design, Davidson's 1936 remodel of Sardi's Restaurant featured a facade of water-blue and wine-red Carrara glass with extruded aluminum trim and a base and sidewalk of purple terrazzo.

Davidson also designed prototypes for drive-in markets: a curb market with large glass display windows directly on the street and a "DRIV-IN-CURB-Market" (1931) that provided drive-in parking. Both treated the building as a giant display window. Other architects, such as Richard Neutra and Lloyd Wright, also developed designs for this new type of market that was becoming popular in the 1920s. Wright, for instance, designed the Yucca-Vine Market in 1928, one of the region's earliest shopping facilities that treated a group of stores as a unit, oriented to the car.

Kem Weber, a close friend of Davidson's from Berlin, was also instrumental in developing Southern California's modern commercial aesthetic. He designed not only store interiors and facades but also their furniture, fixtures, and even their products. His commercial projects ranged from the interiors and a mural for the Vultee Aircraft Corporation to a photography studio for avant-garde photographer Will Connell (1936), a roadside restaurant and gas station (developed with Art Center students in 1935), and a number of stores—Hartfield Hosiery, Kerr Sport Shop, Colburn's Fur Store, Zacho's Store, Hudson's Credit Jewelers, Roos Brothers shoe store, Sommer and Kaufmann Store—in Los Angeles and San Francisco. He also joined Jock Peters at Paramount Pictures where they designed modern sets under German art director Hans Dreier in the 1930s.

Kem Weber's training in Germany was in the applied arts: he apprenticed with the Royal Cabinetmaker in Potsdam and studied at the Academy of Applied Arts with Bruno Paul. He moved to the United States in 1914 to work on the German section of the Panama-Pacific International Exposition in San Francisco. Prevented by World War I from returning to Germany, Weber stayed in California and opened a design studio in Santa Barbara to produce interior fixtures, furniture, and artwork. Especially interested in developing consumer products for the household that were popular and affordable, in 1921 he joined the design department of Barker Brothers store in Los Angeles, working first as a draftsman and then as art director, a post he kept until 1927.

Weber launched Barker Brothers' efforts to develop modern design for home furnishings and accessories, which they heralded in 1926 as "the beginning of an American period of design and expression."[121] While at Barker Brothers, Weber created the new "Modes and Manners" shop, the first large modern interiors and furniture retail outlet in Southern California. He invited other manufacturers to use his Barker Brothers atelier, offering to develop new designs for their furnishings that would consider the larger environment of room, house and grounds. After opening his own studio, he continued to work with Barker Brothers, creating the "Tempo" shop in 1934. With 12 new display rooms and 22 settings, Weber intended to create "styles so beautiful and settings so adapted to 1934 living, that the furnishings in countless homes become obsolete."[122] Both a curiosity and a success, the new Tempo displays attracted 25,000 visitors on opening day.

Weber was also an organizer and participant in the first exhibition of the American Union of Decorative Artists and Craftsmen (AUDAC) at the Brooklyn Museum in 1931. The exhibition comprised modern domestic and office furniture, fabrics, decorative paintings, photographs, typography and graphic arts, developed by "practical modernists," i.e. artists, designers and architects designing for business and industry and applying art to commercial practice. Established in 1927, AUDAC's founding principle was that "contemporary life demands appropriate setting and that it is the work of the artists of all ages to mould the external world to suit the life of their time."[123] As late as 1925, Secretary of Commerce Herbert Hoover had declined to participate in the International Exposition of Industrial and Decorative Arts

Sardi's, Los Angeles, 1936;
architect: J.R. Davidson.

J.R. Davidson's many commercial
commissions included a design for
Sardi's Restaurant, after the Schindler-
designed version was destroyed in a
fire. Davidson's sophisticated modern
restaurant and bar interior used a
range of elegant, contemporary
materials for striking effects.
(Photograph by Julius Shulman)

The Bachelors' Haberdashery,
Los Angeles, 1935; architect:
J.R. Davidson.

Davidson's Bachelors' shop featured
Makassar ebony panels set in aluminum channels, combined with
red lacquered screens, brown and
tan carpeting laid in stripes of
varying widths, and pigskin-covered
stools with chrome bases. (Photograph
by Will Connell, courtesy of Esther
McCoy Files on Architects 1945–
1989, Archives of American Art,
Smithsonian Institution)

held in Paris, declaring that the United States had no modern design to submit. Through the efforts of such participants as Donald Deskey, Paul T. Frankl, Gilbert Rohde, Kem Weber, Edward Steichen, and Rockwell Kent, AUDAC aimed to establish a modern tradition in American industrial arts.

Weber's first venture into mass-produced, machine-made furniture was his Bentlock furniture line. Manufactured by the methods of "Fordized furniture construction," a nine-piece dining room suite cost less than $250, a six-piece breakfast suite less than $100—a "change of economic significance," according to one commentator, that could not be "disrelated from the esthetics of the machine age."[124] The Bentlock line replaced traditional mortise and tenon and doweled joints with a bent machine-made member, reinforced with an oval lock of solid wood. Based on this elementary principle, Weber created 125 different pieces of furniture from a few basic units that could be combined into tables, chests of drawers, and boudoir cabinets.

Over the course of his career, Weber designed a wide range of furnishings and household products that were mass-produced: lamps for Brilliant Glass, silverware for Friedman Silver, pewter and silver for Porter Blanchard Silver, clocks for Lawson Clocks, tubular steel furniture for Lloyd Manufacturing, the "Fleetwood Line" for Mueller Furniture, and the famous "Airline Chair" for Haskelite Manufacturing, as well as products for Berkey and Gay Furniture, Karpen Furniture, Baker Furniture, Widdicomb Furniture, and Grand Rapids Furniture Manufacturing.

His efforts to elevate the industrial arts earned him chairmanship of the first Department of Industrial Design at the Art Center School in 1931, where he aimed to train students to meet the new needs of industry with contemporary techniques and materials. Problems given to beginning students at Art Center School included gas stations, markets, radio cabinets, electric clocks—all types unrelated to historical or traditional building forms, so students could gain an understanding of materials and purpose by designing freely. They were also taught the rules of commercial success: sales, sales, and more sales. If objects didn't sell, they were failures according to Weber, no matter how beautiful:

"Commodities are manufactured and distributed for profit… Therefore, an industrial design can only be considered good, if it finds public acceptance sufficient to satisfy the producer and the dealer. If from the standpoint of a trained designer a commodity is perfect in form, color and function and is discontinued by the producer due to lack of public acceptance, then such design is not a solution for industry and the designer did not function as an industrial designer."[125]

Beyond the design of stores, furniture, and household products, Weber was determined to develop an all-encompassing modern aesthetic appropriate for the place and the age. His designs for Walt Disney's 51-acre animation studio in Burbank realized his efforts to merge planning, architecture, interior design, graphic design, and the industrial arts into a modern environment. Weber was involved with the designs of buildings, interiors, signs, and furnishings for the studio in 1939–40.[126] With stages, office buildings, a restaurant, a service station, a penthouse gym and lounge for artists, and custom-designed furniture, Disney Studios was one of the largest and most cohesive modern architectural projects built in Southern California before World War II.

Conclusion

By the late 1930s, the experiments of Southern California's modern architects were increasingly drawing the world's attention. Both the architectural and popular press heralded the ways they were re-shaping the region's homes and work places, and their projects received design award after design award. More importantly, they were viewed as a cohesive group creating a distinctive body of modern architecture.

Hamilton Harwell Harris explained why modernism "took" in Southern California and became integrated into the regional tradition: "In California in the late 1920s and 30s modern European ideas met a still developing region-alism. What was relevant was accepted and became part of a continuing regionalism." [127] Harris theorized that the Northeast accepted European mod-ernism wholesale, since its own regionalism was so rigid and restrictive that it "first resisted and then surrendered." Modernism quickly became just another style in the Northeast's architectural development. In Southern California it evolved into local designers' and builders' vernacular because modernism helped shape the region's identity at a formative stage of its development.

Post-World War II Southern California proved an ideal arena to realize modernists' ideas. The imperative to build enormous factories and housing complexes for the defense industry kick-started new building technologies into mass-production. Architects' early experiments with pre-fabrication, standardi-zation, and the development of prototypes for large-scale production were put to the test. World War II forever changed how communities were planned and buildings were made—not just in Southern California, but across the country. Once the region's industries had geared up for war, they continued post-War building production at the same scale. But it was in Southern California, more than in any other region, that post-War building and design were a continuation of, rather than a break from, the region's pre-War modern tradition.

Southern California's experimental architects had used the freshly develop-ing land as a laboratory for testing radical new theories about design and living—ones that combined nature, living, and building. The early modernists' philosophical similarities attest to the identity and integrity of the region's avant-garde tradition; their stylistic differences demonstrate the movement's richness and variety. Their legacy distilled into a few key lessons: "that a good house could be made of cheap materials, that outdoor living was as valued as indoor spaces, that a dining room was less necessary than two baths and glass walls…" [128]

Acknowledgements

In the years between "The Architecture of Modernism's" conception and publication, I have accumulated a number of debts of gratitude to people and organizations. Foremost among them is the James Marston Fitch Charitable Trust, which provided a generous research grant. Others who were instrumental in this effort: Carolyn Cole of the Los Angeles Public Library Photo Collection and volunteers with Photo/Friends Architecture Committee: Judy Artunian, Silvia Orvietani, Busch, Colleen Davis, Kathy Hummer, Terra Ishee, Katy Lane, and Steve Moga; David Gebhard and Kurt Helfrich of the Architecture and Design Collection at the University of California, Santa Barbara; Victoria Steele and Simon Elliott at the Department of Special Collections, University of California, Los Angeles; Judy Throm and Wendy Hurlock at the Smithsonian Institution's Archives of American Art; Barbara Hoff and Linda Dishman with the Los Angeles Conservancy; Greg Hise and Howard Smith at the University of Southern California; Rick Starzak of Myra Frank, Associates; Vicky Komie with the City of Los Angeles Bureau of Engineering; Eric Lutz; Pete Moruzzi; and Richard Rowe. Among the people who read the essay along the way and provided important editorial guidance were: Donald Albrecht, John Chase, Fred Jacobs, Christian Kiillkkaa, and Frank R. Shivers Jr. And many thanks to Julius Shulman who contributed insights as well as images, my colleagues Victoria Dailey and Michael Dawson, and to Ann Gray for her enthusiasm for the subject and her commitment to the project.

While the footnotes provide specific bibliographic citations for sources used in the research and writing of "The Architecture of Modernism," many other resources, published and unpublished, provided ideas and information for the chapter. Following is a summary and acknowledgement of a selection of those resources.

Unpublished and Miscellaneous Sources

Unpublished sources in the archives of several institutions were valuable lodes of information. These included the Archives of American Art, Smithsonian Institution, Washington, D.C.; the Architecture and the Design Collection, University Art Museum, University of California, Santa Barbara (UCSB); the Department of Special Collections, Charles E. Young Research Library, University of California, Los Angeles (UCLA); and the Security Pacific Collection, Los Angeles Public Library.

Esther McCoy's archives in the Archives of American Art include letters; unpublished manuscripts; photographs; notes on conversations with architects and their friends, clients, and critics; and taped interviews with Gregory Ain, Hamilton Harwell Harris, Leah Lovell and Philip Lovell, Richard Neutra, and Lloyd Wright. In UCSB's Architecture and Design Collection are the papers of Gregory Ain, J.R. Davidson, Jock Detlef Peters, R.M. Schindler, and Kem Weber. UCLA holds the papers of Lloyd Wright and Richard Neutra. The Security Pacific Collection of the Los Angeles Public Library offers architectural photographs, as well as documentation of the region's history. Other archives that proved useful were R.M. Schindler's Papers at the Avery Library, Columbia University, New York City, and the Historic American Buildings Survey, Library of Congress, Washington, D.C., which has documented significant landmarks of the region's modern architectural tradition, including a number of buildings by Irving Gill.

Oral histories completed under the auspices of the Oral History Program at UCLA provided first-hand glimpses of the modernists' time and place. These include interviews with Dione Neutra, "To Tell the Truth," by Lawrence Weschler (c. 1983); Raphael Soriano, "Substance and Function in

Architecture," by Marlene L. Laskey (c. 1988), and Jake Zeitlin, "Books and the Imagination: Fifty Years of Rare Books" by Joel Gardner (c. 1980). Also, interviews were conducted by the author with photographer Julius Shulman in Los Angeles on July 7, 2001 and July 14, 2001.

Other unpublished manuscripts that provided insight into architects, clients, and their cultural milieu include: Jeffrey Mark Chusid, "Samuel and Harriet Freeman House," Historic Structure Report (School of Architecture, University of Southern California, July 1989); Barbara Giella's dissertation, "R.M. Schindler's Thirties Style: Its Character (1931-1937) and International Sources (1906-1937)" (Vol. 1, Dissertation submitted to the Graduate School of Arts and Sciences, New York University, 1985).

Periodicals

Professional and shelter magazines provided important information about trends of the period, the context for Southern California's modern architects' work, and how they were viewed by their colleagues and critics. Magazines that were especially useful included *Arts and Architecture* (formerly *California Arts and Architecture*), *The Architect and Engineer, The Architectural Forum, The Architectural Review, Arts and Decoration, California Arts and Architecture, California Southland, Camera Craft, The Craftsman, Creative Art, Hi-Hat Homes, House and Garden, House Beautiful, The Journal of San Diego History, L'Architecture d'Aujourd'hui, Pencil Points, Popular Mechanics, Southwest Builder, Southwest Builder and Contractor, Studio, Sunset Magazine,* and *The Western Architect.*

Published Books

A number of cultural and social histories of the region and the time provided background information for the chapter. These included: Donald Albrecht's *Designing Dreams: Modern Architecture in the Movies* (New York: Harper & Row in collaboration with The Museum of Modern Art, 1986); Timothy J. Andersen, Timothy J., Eudorah M. Moore, Robert W. Winter, editors, *California Design 1910* (Pasadena: California Design Publications, 1974); Michael Buckland and John Henken, eds., *The Hollywood Bowl: Tales of Summer Nights* (Los Angeles: Balcony Press, 1996); Dorothy Lamb Crawford, *Evenings On and Off the Roof: Pioneering Concerts in Los Angeles, 1939-71* (Berkeley: University of California press, 1995); Tom Dardis, *Some Time in the Sun* (New York: Charles Scribner's Sons, 1976); Anthony Heilbut, *Exiled in Paradise: German Refugee Artists and Intellectuals in America from the 1930s to the Present* (New York: Viking, 1983); Richard Longstreth, *City Center to Regional Mall, Architecture, the Automobile, and Retailing in Los Angeles, 1920-1950* and *The Drive-In, The Supermarket and the Transformation of Commercial Space in Los Angeles, 1914-41* (Cambridge: The MIT Press, 1997,1999); Carey McWilliams, *Southern California: An Island on the Land* (Salt Lake City: Gibbs M. Smith, Inc., Peregrine Smith Books, 1983); Kevin Starr's California history series: *Americans and the California Dream 1850-1915; Inventing the Dream: California Through the Progressive Era; Material Dreams: Southern California Through the 1920s; Endangered Dreams: The Great Depression in California* (New York: Oxford University Press, 1973, 1985, 1990, 1996); David C. Streatfield, *California Gardens: Creating a New Eden* (New York: Abbeville Press, 1994); John Russell Taylor, *Strangers in Paradise: The Hollywood Emigres 1933-50* (London: Faber and Faber, 1985); Kenneth R. Trapp, *The Arts and Crafts Movement in California: Living the Good Life* (Oakland, California: The Oakland Museum; New York:

Abbeville Press, 1993); Robert Winter, *The California Bungalow* (Los Angeles: Hennessy & Ingalls, 1980); and Sally B. Woodbridge, *California Architecture: Historic American Buildings Survey* (San Francisco: Chronicle Books, 1988).

Books that helped to elucidate the work of Southern California's modern architects and patrons include: Vivan Endicott Barnett and Josef Helfenstein, *The Blue Four: Feininger, Jawlensky, Kandinsky, and Klee in the New World* (Dusseldorf: Kunstmuseum Bern and Kunstsammlung Nordrhein-Westfalen; Cologne: Dumont Buchverlag,1997); Norman Bel Geddes, *Miracle in the Evening* (edited by William Kelley; Garden City, New York: Doubleday & Co., 1960); Marla C. Berns, ed., *The Furniture of R.M. Schindler* (Santa Barbara: University Art Museum, University of California, Santa Barbara, 1997); *Blueprints for Modern Living: History and Legacy of the Case Study Houses* (Los Angeles: The Museum of Contemporary Art; Cambridge: The MIT Press, 1989); *Concrete in California* (published by the Carpenters/Contractors Cooperation Committee of Southern California in conjunction with the School of Architecture at the University of Southern California, 1990); Margaret Leslie Davis, *Bullocks Wilshire* (Los Angeles: Balcony Press, 1996); Albert Frey, *In Search of a Living Architecture* (Facsimile of 1939 ed. Reprint, Santa Monica: Hennessy + Ingalls, Art and Architecture Books, 1999); Alice T. Friedman, *Women and the Making of the Modern House: A Social and Architectural History* (New York: Harry N. Abrams, 1998); Lisa Germany, *Harwell Hamilton Harris* (Austin: University of Texas Press, 1991); Jennifer Golub, *Albert Frey/Houses 1 and 2* (New York: Princeton Architectural Press, 1999); Thomas S. Hines, *Richard Neutra and the Search for Modern Architecture* (New York: Oxford University Press, 1982); Donald Hoffman; *Frank Lloyd Wright's Hollyhock House* (New York: Dover Publications, 1992); Bruce Kamerling, *Irving J. Gill, Architect* (San Diego: San Diego Historical Society, 1993); *Modern Architecture International Exhibition* (New York: The Museum of Modern Art, 1932); Dione Neutra's compilation and translation of Richard and Dione Neutra's letters in *Richard Neutra, Promise and Fulfillment, 1919-1932: Selections from the Letters and Diaries of Richard and Dione Neutra* (Carbondale and Edwardsville: Southern Illinois University Press, 1986); Peter Noever, ed. *MAK Center for Art and Architecture: R.M. Schindler* (Munich: Prestel Verlag, 1995); Joseph Rosa, *Albert Frey, Architect* and *A Constructed View: The Architectural Photography of Julius Shulman* (New York: Rizzoli, 1990, 1994); August Sarnitz, *R.M. Schindler Architect* (New York: Rizzoli, 1988); Julius Shulman, *Architecture and its Photography* (Koln: Taschen, 1998); Kathryn Smith, *Frank Lloyd Wright, Hollyhock House and Olive Hill, Buildings and Projects for Aline Barnsdall* (New York: Rizzoli, 1992); Robert L. Sweeney, *Wright in Hollywood: Visions of a New Architecture* (New York: The Architectural History Foundation; Cambridge: the MIT Press, 1994); and Alan Weintraub, *Lloyd Wright* (New York: Harry N. Abrams, 1998).

Esther McCoy and David Gebhard's seminal research into the region's modern architects and their projects merits special thanks. Without their pioneering work to identify, document, and champion the work of many of these designers, their buildings may have been consigned to obscurity. Of Esther McCoy's many books, key were *Richard Neutra* (New York: George Braziller, Inc., 1960); *Five California Architects* (1960. Reprint, New York: Praeger Publishers, Holt, Rinehart and Winston, 1975); *Case Study Houses 1945-1962* (Second ed. Los Angeles: Hennessy + Ingalls, 1977); *Vienna to Los Angeles: Two Journeys* (Santa Monica, California: Arts + Architecture Press, 1979); and *The Second Generation* (Salt Lake City: Gibbs M. Smith, Inc.,

Peregrine Smith Books, 1984). David Gebhard's invaluable books include *Schindler* (New York: The Viking Press, A Studio Book, 1971) and, in collaboration with Harriette Von Breton, *Los Angeles in the Thirties 1931-1941* (Second ed. Los Angeles: Hennessy + Ingalls, 1989). Gebhard also co-curated and co-wrote catalogues for exhibitions at the University of California Santa Barbara Art Museum on the work of Gregory Ain, Kem Weber, Lloyd Wright. With Harriette Von Breton, Gebhard produced *Kem Weber, The Moderne in Southern California 1920 Through 1941* and *Lloyd Wright Architect, 20th Century Architecture in an Organic Exhibition* (Weber catalog - Reprint 1976; Wright catalog - Reprint, Santa Monica: Hennessey + Ingalls, 1998). With Harriette Von Breton and Lauren Weiss, David Gebhard produced *The Art of Gregory Ain: The Play Between the Rational and High Art* (Reprint, Santa Monica: Hennessy + Ingalls, 1997). Collaborating with Robert Winter, Gebhard wrote *A Guide to Architecture in Southern California* (Los Angeles: Los Angeles County Museum of Art, 1965) and subsequent editions that focused on Los Angeles. These guides offer a road map for people who want to learn first-hand about Southern California's modern architectural tradition.

Footnotes

[1] Albert Frey. Letter to Le Corbusier, 10 November 1935, quoted in Joseph Rosa, *Albert Frey, Architect* (NY: Rizzoli International Publications, Inc., 1990), 78.

[2] Rudolph Schindler, "About Furniture" essay for "Care of the Body" column, *Los Angeles Times*, 18 April 1926, quoted in August Sarnitz, *R.M. Schindler, Architect 1887-1953* (NY: Rizzoli International Publications, Inc., 1988), 46.

[3] Kem Weber, *California Arts and Architecture* 49 (January 1935): 1.

[4] Kevin Starr, *Americans and the California Dream 1850-1915* (NY: Oxford University Press, 1973), 47.

[5] George Wharton James, quoted in *The Arts and Crafts Movement in California: Living the Good Life* (NY: Abbeville Press Publishers with the Oakland Museum, 1993), 107.

[6] Jeffrey Mark Chusid, "Samuel and Harriet Freeman House," Historic Structure Report (School of Architecture, University of Southern California, July 1989), 15.

[7] Kevin Starr, *Material Dreams, Southern California Through the 1920s* (NY: Oxford University Press, 1990), 69.

[8] Irving Gill, *The Craftsman*, May 1916, quoted in Bruce Kamerling, *Irving J. Gill, Architect* (San Diego: San Diego Historical Society, 1993), 46.

[9] Dione Neutra. Letter to Muetterli, August 1925, quoted in *Richard Neutra, Promise and Fulfillment, 1919-1932, Selections from the Letters and Diaries of Richard and Dione Neutra*, compiled and translated by Dione Neutra (Carbondale and Edwardsville, Illinois: Southern Illinois University Press, 1986), 142.

[10] Kevin Starr, *Material Dreams*, 69.

[11] Maxwell Armfeld, quoted in Carey McWilliams, *Southern California: An Island on the Land*, Peregrine Smith Edition (Salt Lake City: Gibbs M. Smith, Inc., Peregrine Smith Books, 1983), 367.

[12] Kevin Starr, *Material Dreams*, 60, 83.

[13] Douglas Haskell, "Architecture on Routes U.S. 40 and 66," *The Architectural Review*, vol. LXXXI, no. 484 (March 1937): 101–131.

[14] Kevin Starr, *Material Dreams*, 79.

[15] Editorial, *California Arts and Architecture* (January 1935): 11.

[16] Richard Neutra. Letter to Rudolph Schindler, September 1919; Richard Neutra. Letter to Dione Neutra, December 1923, quoted in *Richard Neutra, Promise and Fulfillment*, 5–7.

[17] Jock Peters. Letter to family, 24 December 1922, Jock Peters Papers, Architecture and Design Collection, University Art Museum, University of California, Santa Barbara.

[18] Gill's buildings are often compared with the work of Austrian architect, Adolf Loos, author of the famous modernist treatise, "Ornament and Crime." Gill began developing his abstract geometric buildings around 1907, a year before Loos' essay was published in Vienna. Loos' first building to represent his theories about elimination of ornament from architecture, the Hugo Steiner house in Vienna, was constructed in 1910. Given San Diego's remote location and Gill's apparent lack of interest in what his contemporaries were doing elsewhere, there is no evidence that Gill's architecture referred to Loos' buildings or his essay. However, in an interview with Esther McCoy, Lloyd Wright suggested that Gill was aware of the modern movement in Germany and Austria, including the work of Adolf Loos and Josef Hoffman.

[19] Irving Gill, *The Craftsman*, May 1916, quoted in Kamerling, *Irving J. Gill*, 125.

[20] Roger Hatheway and John Chase, *Concrete in California* (Carpenters/Contractors Cooperation Committee of Southern California with the School of Architecture, University of Southern California, 1990), 22–24.

[21] Irving Gill, *The Craftsman*, May 1916, quoted in Kamerling, *Irving J. Gill*, 126.

[22] Article by Mrs. Bertha A. Smith, *Los Angeles Times*, 1 November 1914, sec. VI, p. 1, quoted in Chase and Hatheway, *Concrete in California*, 25.

[23] Dr. Mary B. Ritter, quoted in La Jolla Woman's Club, Historic American Building Survey, CA–1957, prepared by Albert E. Outcalt (Library of Congress, Washington, D.C., June 1971), 2.

[24] Kamerling, *Irving J. Gill*, 112.

[25] Rudolph Schindler. Letter to Richard Neutra, 1919, quoted in Esther McCoy, *Five California Architects*, 1975 ed. (Holt, Rinehart and Winston, Praeger Publishers, Inc., 1975), 155.

[26] Rudolph Schindler, "Modern Architecture: A Program," 1912, quoted in Sarnitz, *R.M. Schindler*, 42.

27 Aline Barnsdall, *New York Times*, 2 January 1915, p.9, quoted in Donald Hoffman, *Frank Lloyd Wright's Hollyhock House* (NY: Dover Publications, 1992), 8.

28 Aline Barnsdall, quoted in Norman Bel Geddes, *Miracle in the Evening*, ed. William Kelley (Garden City, New York: Doubleday and Co., 1960), 152, 156.

29 Aline Barnsdall, *Los Angeles Examiner*, 1919, quoted in Alice T. Friedman, *Women and the Making of the Modern House: A Social and Architectural History* (NY: Harry N. Abrams, Inc., 1998), 41.

30 In his autobiography *Miracle in the Evening*, Norman Bel Geddes described Frank Lloyd Wright's resistance to Barnsdall's request for a progressive theater. Wright insisted instead on developing a theater plan dating back to 400 B.C. Greece and refused to make provisions for modern lighting and scenery. Bel Geddes suggests that Wright, "by behaving as he did, was responsible in my eyes for thwarting what might well have been the greatest creative theater organization this country had ever seen, or will ever see." See Bel Geddes, *Miracle in the Evening*, 164, 167.

31 Frank Lloyd Wright, quoted in Friedman, *Women and the Making of the Modern House*, 42.

32 Norman Bel Geddes, *Miracle in the Evening*, 174.

33 Aline Barnsdall, quoted in Friedman, *Women and the Making of the Modern House*, 58.

34 Aline Barnsdall. Letter to Frank Lloyd Wright, 27 July 1916, quoted in Hoffman, *Frank Lloyd Wright's Hollyhock House*, 9.

35 Note that Wright's work of this genre was not only constructed in Southern California: other buildings were his A.D. German Warehouse (1915) in Richland Center, Wisconsin, and his Imperial Hotel in Japan (1913–1922). See Kathryn Smith, *Frank Lloyd Wright, Hollyhock House and Olive Hill, Buildings and Projects for Aline Barnsdall* (NY: Rizzoli International Publications, 1992), 41–43.

36 Between 1922 and 1932, Wright produced at least thirty projects around the U.S. that used a system of standardized concrete-block construction, five of which were built. The first proposed use was for the "Little Dipper" nursery school on Olive Hill, but he subsequently developed plans for projects in Lake Tahoe, Death Valley, Wisconsin, Phoenix, Tulsa, Buffalo, Hampton, VA., and Milwaukee that used this system. See Robert L. Sweeney, *Wright in Hollywood, Visions of a New Architecture* (NY: The Architectural History Foundation, Cambridge and London: The MIT Press, 1994), 1, 80.

37 Jeffrey Mark Chusid, "Freeman House," Historic Structure Report, 17, 22.

38 Rudolph Schindler. Letter to Harriet Freeman, 23 October 1951, Rudolph Schindler Papers, Architecture and Design Collection, University Art Museum, University of California, Santa Barbara.

39 Jeffrey Mark Chusid, "Freeman House," HSR, 121–26, 217–219.

40 Rudolph Schindler. Lecture at University of Southern California School of Architecture, 10 October 1949, Rudolph Schindler Papers.

41 Rudolph Schindler, "Furniture and the Modern House: A Theory of Interior Design," *Architect and Engineer*, vol. 123 (December 1935): 22–25, and vol. 124 (March 1936): 24–28, quoted in Sarnitz, *R.M. Schindler*, 52.

42 Rudolph Schindler's descriptions of his house quoted here and following are from "A Cooperative Dwelling," *T-Square* (February 1932): 20–21, quoted in Sarnitz, *R.M. Schindler*, 49.

43 Rudolph Schindler had met Gill through Lloyd Wright while both were working on Aline Barnsdall's project. Schindler's friend, Clyde Chace, had worked with Gill on the Horatio West Courts project in Santa Monica, before he helped Schindler construct his tilt-up concrete slab house.

44 Rudolph Schindler. Document, 18 February 1952, McCoy Papers.

45 Hamilton Harwell Harris, quoted in "Freeman House," HSR, 33.

46 Hamilton Harwell Harris, quoted in Esther McCoy, *Vienna to Los Angeles: Two Journeys* (Santa Monica: Arts + Architecture Press, 1979), 13.

47 Galka Scheyer. Letter to Rudolph Schindler, 12 April 1931, Esther McCoy Papers, Archives of American Art, Smithsonian Institution, Washington, D.C.

48 Philip Lovell, "Care of the Body," *Los Angeles Times Sunday Magazine*, 15 December 1929, p. 26, quoted in Thomas S. Hines, *Richard Neutra and the Search for Modern Architecture* (NY: Oxford University Press, 1982), 89.

49 Philip Lovell, quoted in Hines, *Search for Modern Architecture*, 89.

50 Rudolph Schindler, "Shelter or Playground" essay for "Care of the Body" column, *Los*

Angeles Times, 2 May 1926, quoted in Sarnitz, *R.M. Schindler*, 46–7.

[51] Richard Neutra, quoted in Hines, *Search for Modern Architecture*, 78.

[52] Henry Russell-Hitchcock, *Modern Architecture International Exhibition* catalogue (N.Y.: The Museum of Modern Art, 1932),158.

[53] Richard Neutra. Letter to Frances Toplitz, November 1929, *Richard Neutra, Promise and Fulfillment*, 179.

[54] "Talk with the Lovells," c.1958, interview transcript, McCoy Papers.

[55] Philip Lovell, quoted in Hines, *Search for Modern Architecture*, 89. According to Gregory Ain, Dr. Lovell ended up loathing their "Health House." He found the house "hot as hell" and poorly planned, citing the need to walk sideways in his 5 1/2' x 20' room to get around the bed and the lack of any overhangs in a room that faced west and south. See interview with Gregory Ain by Kathryn Smith, 2 July 1977, tape recording, McCoy Archives. Leah Lovell found living in the house "like a factory," with "no lilt, no happiness, no joy." See "Talk with the Lovells," c.1958, interview transcript, and tape recording of interview with Leah Lovell, n.d., McCoy Papers.

[56] Esther McCoy, *Richard Neutra* (NY: George Braziller, Inc., 1960), 7.

[57] Hamilton Harwell Harris. Letter to Esther McCoy, 8 April 1978, McCoy Papers.

[58] Rudolph Schindler, USC Lecture, 10 October 1949, Rudolph Schindler Papers.

[59] "Pity the Old-Fashioned Architect," *Hi-Hat Homes* (15 December 1927): 24–28.

[60] Philip Lovell, "Talk with the Lovells," c.1958, interview transcript, McCoy Papers.

[61] Richard Neutra. Letter to Dione Neutra, 1930, quoted in *Richard Neutra, Promise and Fulfillment*, 193.

[62] Dione Neutra. Letter to Vreneli, December 1931, quoted in *Richard Neutra, Promise and Fulfillment*, 219.

[63] Robert A. Brady. Letter to Richard Neutra, 25 February 1936, Richard J. Neutra Archive, Department of Special Collections, Charles E. Young Research Library, University of California, Los Angeles.

[64] William Beard, letter to Richard Neutra, 1 March 1935, quoted in Hines, *Search for Modern Architecture*, 329.

[65] Rudolph Schindler, "About Furniture" essay for "Care of the Body" column, *Los Angeles Times*, 18 April 1926, quoted in Sarnitz, *R.M. Schindler*, 46.

[66] Dione Neutra. Letter to Muetterli, March 1932, quoted in *Richard Neutra, Promise and Fulfillment*, 226.

[67] Dione Neutra. Letter to Frances Toplitz, July 1932; Richard Neutra. Letter to C.H. Van der Leeuw, July 1932; Dione Neutra, Letter to Muetterli, March 1932, quoted in *Richard Neutra, Promise and Fulfillment*, 226, 228.

[68] Peter Yates. Letter to Peyton Houston, c. 21 July 1934, quoted in Dorothy Lamb Crawford, *Evenings On and Off the Roof, Pioneering Concerts in Los Angeles, 1939–71* (Berkeley: University of California Press, 1995), 21.

[69] Bertha Mosk. Letter to Richard Neutra, January 1938, quoted in *Richard Neutra, Promise and Fulfillment*, 229.

[70] Mona Hofmann and the Barshas, quoted in Hines, *Search for Modern Architecture*, 143, 331.

[71] Thomas S. Hines, *Search for Modern Architecture*, 132.

[72] "Data on the Home of Anna Sten," from Lynn Farnol for Samuel Goldwyn Productions, Richard J. Neutra Archive.

[73] John Russell Taylor, *Strangers in Paradise, The Hollywood Emigres 1933–1950* (London: Faber and Faber, 1985), 82.

[74] "'Test tube School' in Bell, California (written down after a conversation with Mr. and Mrs. Neutra)," McCoy Papers.

[75] *Los Angeles Times*, quoted in Hines, *Search for Modern Architecture*, 164.

[76] Georgina D. Ritchie. Letter to Richard Neutra, 24 January 1950, Richard J. Neutra Archive.

[77] David C. Streatfield, *California Gardens: Creating a New Eden* (NY: Abbeville Press, 1994), 190.

[78] Eric Lloyd Wright, "Lloyd Wright's Studio, A Son's Reflections by Eric Lloyd Wright," in Alan Weintraub, *Lloyd Wright, The Architecture of Frank Lloyd Wright Jr.* (NY: Harry N. Abrams, Inc., 1998), 232.

[79] The slip-form method was also used by Schindler for the Pueblo Ribera Courts in La

Jolla, built between 1923 and 1925.

[80] Anais Nin, *The Diary of Anais Nin*, quoted in Thomas S. Hines, "The Blessing and the Curse," Weintraub, *Lloyd Wright*, 36.

[81] Lloyd Wright, quoted in David Gebhard and Harriette Von Breton, *Lloyd Wright Architect, Twentieth Century Architecture in an Organic Exhibition*, catalogue for an exhibition organized for the Art Galleries, University of California, Santa Barbara, reprint (Santa Monica, CA: Hennessey + Ingalls, 1998), 18–19.

[82] Jake Zeitlin, "Books and the Imagination: Fifty Years of Rare Books," interview by Joel Gardner c. 1977, compiled under the auspices of the Oral History Program (University of California, Los Angeles, 1980), 41.

[83] Jake Zeitlin, "Books and the Imagination," 118.

[84] Jake Zeitlin, "Books and the Imagination," 125.

[85] Anais Nin, *The Diary of Anais Nin*, quoted in Thomas S. Hines, "The Blessing and the Curse," Weintraub, *Lloyd Wright*, 36.

[86] Alice T. Friedman, *Women and the Making of the Modern House*, 57.

[87] Untitled document, possibly transcription of interview with Lloyd Wright by Esther McCoy, McCoy Papers.

[88] Lloyd Wright, quoted in *The Hollywood Bowl*, ed. by Michael Buckland and John Henken (L.A.: Balcony Press, n.d.), 41.

[89] Lloyd Wright, "Aliso Village Group Housing Project Result of Coordinated Planning," *Southwest Builder & Contractor*, vol. 101, no. 21 (21 May 1943):12–17.

[90] Hamilton Harwell Harris, Interview, 1985, Oral History Program (University of California, Los Angeles), quoted in Germany, *Hamilton Harwell Harris*, 11.

[91] Hamilton Harwell Harris. Interview by Judy Stonefield, 15, 22, 23 August 1985, under the auspices of the Oral History Program (University of California, Los Angeles), quoted in Lisa Germany, *Hamilton Harwell Harris* (Austin: University of Texas Press, published in association with University of Texas Center for Study of American Architecture, 1991), 22–3.

[92] Hamilton Harwell Harris. Letter to Lisa Germany, August 1988, quoted in Germany, *Hamilton Harwell Harris*, 24.

[93] Hamilton Harwell Harris, quoted in McCoy, *The Second Generation*, 41; quoted in Germany, *Hamilton Harwell Harris*, 25; letter to Pauline Schindler, 16 December 1974, McCoy Papers.

[94] Hamilton Harris, "AIA Gold Medal, First in Five Years, Awarded to Neutra," *North Carolina Architect* (June–July 1977): 8–11, quoted in Germany, *Hamilton Harwell Harris*, 34.

[95] "Houses by Hamilton Harwell Harris," *The Architectural Forum*, vol. 72, no. 3 (March 1940):171–186.

[96] Esther McCoy, *The Second Generation*, 44.

[97] "The House Unpretentious But Convenient," *Arts & Decoration*, vol. 48, no. 1 (March 1938): 27–9.

[98] Hamilton Harwell Harris. Interview by Esther McCoy, 12 June 1980, Raleigh, N.C.; McCoy Papers.

[99] "Modern Houses in America–House for George C. Bauer, Glendale, Calif.," *Architectural Forum*, vol. 71, no.1 (July 1030): 16 18.

[100] Gregory Ain, "Form Follows Fiction: Invitation to an Architecture Faculty to Re-examine and Question the Bases of Today's Architecture Training," quoted in David Gebhard, Harriette Von Breton, Lauren Weiss, *The Architecture of Gregory Ain, The Play Between the Rational and High Art*, exhibition catalogue (University of California, Santa Barbara Art Museum, 1980), 22.

[101] Gregory Ain. Letter to David Gebhard, 24 July 1973, quoted in Gebhard et al, *The Architecture of Gregory Ain*, 9.

[102] Julius Shulman, interview by author, 14 July 2001, Los Angeles.

[103] Esther McCoy, *The Second Generation*, 142.

[104] Julius Shulman, interview by author, 7 July 2001, Los Angeles.

[105] Raphael Soriano, "Substance and Function in Architecture," interview by Marlene L. Laskey c. 1985, completed under the auspices of the Oral History Program (University of California, Los Angeles, 1988), 78–9.

[106] Raphael Soriano, "Substance and Function in Architecture," 74.

[107] Raphael Soriano, "Substance and Function in Architecture," 144–5.

[108] Raphael Soriano, "Substance and Function in Architecture," 146.

[109] Raphael Soriano, "Substance and Function in Architecture," 125–127.

[110] Albert Frey. Letter to Le Corbusier, 10 November 1935, quoted in Rosa, *Albert Frey, Architect*, 79.

[111] Albert Frey, *In Search of a Living Architecture*, facsimile edition (Santa Monica: Hennessy + Ingalls, Art and Architecture Books, 1999), 38.

[112] "The Apartment Interior–Planning and Furnishing," *The Architectural Record*, vol. 80, no. 4 (October 1936): 308–319.

[113] Albert Frey. Letter to LeCorbusier, 22 April 1936, Rosa, *Albert Frey, Architect*, 79.

[114] Julius Shulman, interview by author, 14 July 2001, Los Angeles.

[115] Kem Weber, "The Shop," unpublished manuscript, c. 1930–32, Kem Weber Papers, Architecture and Design Collection, University Art Museum, University of California, Santa Barbara.

[116] All biographical information about Jock Peters is from an unpublished manuscript, "Jock Detlef Peters, Buildings and Projects," n.d., Jock Peters Papers.

[117] "Hi-Hat Homes," n.d. Jock Peters Papers.

[118] *The New York Times Magazine*, 22 May 1927.

[119] Pauline Gibling, "Modern California Architects," *Creative Art*, vol. 10 (February 1932): 111–115.

[120] David Gebhard and Harriette Von Breton, *Los Angeles in the Thirties 1931–1941*, 2nd ed. (L.A.: Hennessey & Ingalls, 1989), 37.

[121] Barker Brothers. Letter, 22 November 1926, Kem Weber Papers.

[122] Kem Weber, "Shall We in the Home Furnishing Business Wait for a Building Program?" unpublished manuscript, n.d., Kem Weber Papers.

[123] Nathan George Horwitt, "Reasoned Design," *Creative Art*, vol. 8, (May 1931): 377–379.

[124] Horwitt, "Reasoned Design," *Creative Art*: 377–379.

[125] Kem Weber, "Industrial Design," unpublished manuscript, n.d., Kem Weber Papers.

[126] The scope of Weber's role in the design of Disney Studios is not fully understood. According to David Gebhard and Harriette Von Breton's exhibition catalogue for *Kem Weber, The Moderne in Southern California, 1920 Through 1941*, Weber was responsible for the site plan and all buildings and furnishings. Drawings and renderings of furniture and interiors, as well as several exteriors, are included in Weber's papers at UCSB. Drawings of several building exteriors in the Disney Studios archives have Weber's name on them. However, while it seems that Weber provided overall design direction for most of the buildings and their furnishings, it has not been confirmed that he oversaw the construction documents or the design of building systems. Also, his role in the planning of the site has not been confirmed. See David Gebhard and Harriette Von Breton's exhibition catalogue for *Kem Weber, The Moderne in Southern California, 1920 Through 1941*, catalog for exhibition at The Art Galleries, University of Southern California, Santa Barbara, 2nd ed. (Regents of the University of California, 1976), 44.

[127] Hamilton Harwell Harris, quoted in Germany, *Harwell Hamilton Harris*, 95.

[128] Esther McCoy, "Arts and Architecture Case Study Houses," *Blueprints of Modern Living: History and Legacy of the Case Study Houses*, ed. Howard Singerman (Cambridge and London: The MIT Press, 1989), 16.

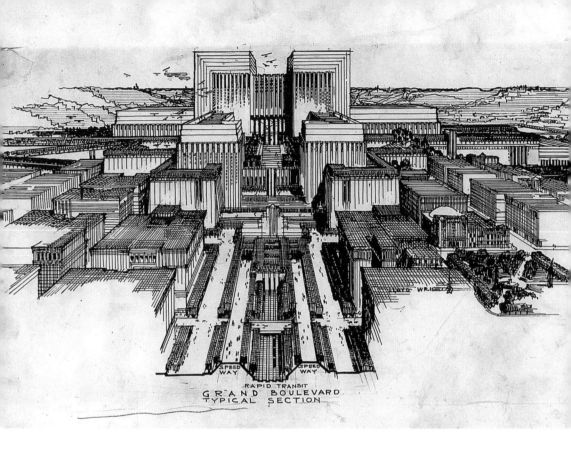

SPEED
WAY   RAPID TRANSIT   SPEED
WAY

GRAND BOULEVARD
TYPICAL SECTION

Project, *Civic Center for Los Angeles,* 1925; architect: Lloyd Wright.

Lloyd Wright's conceptual project for a Civic Center for Los Angeles proposed a composition of modern high-rises and terraced gardens interwoven with multi-level transportation systems that linked the city to the harbor, railroad, airports, and truck lines. (Department of Special Collections, Charles E. Young Research Library, University of California, Los Angeles)

Yucca-Vine Market, Hollywood, 1928; architect: Lloyd Wright.

For the Yucca-Vine Market, Lloyd Wright treated the façade as a giant billboard, with a striking geometric tower, cantilevered canopies, large areas of glass, and corrugated metal surfaces sprayed with aluminum paint to create a distinctive modern identity. The photograph was taken by Wright's modernist colleague, Will Connell. (Department of Special Collections, Charles E. Young Research Library, University of California, Los Angeles)

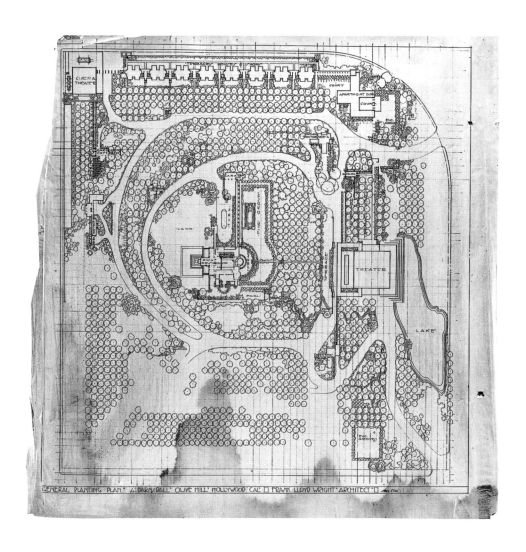

GENERAL PLANTING PLAN · A BARNSDALL · OLIVE HILL · HOLLYWOOD CAL · □ · FRANK LLOYD WRIGHT · ARCHITECT · □

General Planting Plan, *Olive Hill*,
Hollywood, c. 1920; architect:
Frank Lloyd Wright.

Aline Barnsdall hired Frank Lloyd
Wright to develop an "art park" on
a 36-acre knoll in Hollywood. The
plan comprised theaters, including
one for movies, performance spaces,
artists' studios and residences, and
her own house to be sited within
the existing olive grove. (Copyright
1992, 2002 The Frank Lloyd Wright
Foundation, Scottsdale, AZ)

Project, *Driv-in-curb-market,* Los Angeles, 1931; architect: J.R. Davidson.

Davidson's prototype for a driv-in-curb-market treated the building as a giant display window unimpeded by doors or columns. The tower, graphics, and lighting were scaled to attract people driving by. (Architecture and Design Collection, University Art Museum, University of California, Santa Barbara)

MEAT& FISH. VEGETABLES. DRUGS& FRUITS. BAKERY. CREAMERY FOUNTAIN. FLOWRS. TOWER. MEAT& VEGETABLES. GROCERY. DELICATESSEN

SUPER-MARKET

...market
...excluding of front display 17 feet deep
...obstructed by pillars or clerks
...designed by J.R. DAVIDSON   the architectural department of HITE-BILICKE LTD

Wilshire Boulevard Store facades,
Los Angeles, 1927-29; architect:
J.R. Davidson.

Davidson remodeled an existing
commercial building façade to create
storefronts that featured new materials
used in innovative ways: cadmium-
plated steel and copper for the Hite-
Bilike shops, copper and redwood in
the Satyr Bookshop, and a ceiling of
leaf copper for the Hi-Hat restaurant.
(Esther McCoy Files on Architects
1945–1989, Archives of American Art,
Smithsonian Institution)

KEM WEBER
1933

Interior furnishing designs for *"Tempo"*
Shop, Barker Brothers Store, Los Angeles,
1933/1934-9; designer: Kem Weber.

Kem Weber launched Barker Brothers'
efforts to develop contemporary design
for home furnishings. The "Tempo"
shop, created in 1934, included 12
display rooms and 22 settings for
modern furniture and accessories.
(Architecture and Design Collection,
University Art Museum, University of
California, Santa Barbara)

Exterior perspective, *Walt Disney Studios*, Burbank, 1939–40; designer: Kem Weber.

The Walt Disney Studios was one of the largest and most comprehensive modern architectural projects built in Southern California before World War II. Kem Weber developed designs for buildings, interiors, furniture, and signage. (Architecture and Design Collection, University Art Museum, University of California, Santa Barbara)

Case Study House #20, Altadena, 1958;
architect: Conrad Buff III, Calvin Straub,
and Donald Hensman.

Southern California's post-War modern
houses continued architectural themes
developed between the world wars.
As Schindler had predicted in the 1920s,
rooms would be at ground level and the
garden would become an integral part
of the house; the distinction between
indoors and outdoors would disappear;
rooms would become part of an organic
whole rather than separate boxes; and
walls would be few, thin, and removable.
(Photograph by Julius Shulman)

3

Photography

SOUTH OF POINT LOBOS

by Michael Dawson

Contents:

Foreword

I have had an obsession with Southern California history and photography for most of my adult life. Working on this essay afforded me the opportunity to indulge both passions simultaneously. The landscape of Southern California provided me with certain indelible images as a young child in the late 1950s. I can recall the magic of tall pepper trees with their languid branches touching the sidewalk as we walked to my grandmother's house in Sierra Madre on a hot summer day. I remember running down an endless sand dune somewhere in the Mojave desert almost before I was able to walk. I can still smell the cool, lemon scent of the seemingly ancient eucalyptus trees planted in scattered groves near my childhood home in Silverlake.

All of these memories of place were awakened in me when I began to locate and collect photographs of Southern California from the late nineteenth- and early-twentieth centuries. As I began to study the history of fine art photography in the United States, I realized that although there had been a consistent pattern of development and evolution in fine art photography produced in Southern California between 1890 and 1950, it was overlooked by the first wave of photographic historians of the 1950s, 60s, and 70s. Viewed as too commercial in approach or subject matter or conversely, following the "backward" traditions of pictorialism, a number of important archives of individual photographers and photographic organizations vanished as the creators passed away in the 1950s and 60s.

When I began this essay, my goal was to establish the existence of a creative photographic activity within Southern California between 1890 and 1950. This production embraced the profound shift from the soft-focused symbolism of the late-nineteenth century to the hard-edge clarity of the 1930s. There were several important landmarks to guide me on my journey but for much of the time I felt like I was travelling in uncharted territory.

Along the way I came across a number of important photographers whose work has received scant attention until this moment. Charles Lummis' photographs taken in the Southwest have received some critical attention but his extensive body of work done in Southern California has not been seriously considered. Only a brief mention has been made of Alvin Langdon Coburn's work in Southern California produced during a pivotal moment in his important career. Edward Weston's career in photography is widely studied and appreciated, yet little mention is made of his formative years in Southern California between 1906 and 1920.

The transformation of Hollywood from a quiet community of Methodists to the home of the most profound medium of the twentieth century tilted the balance of fine art photography towards the spirit of modernism. Photographers such as Karl Struss moved to California to work in the motion picture industry and brought their traditions of experimentation and innovation with them. Photographs produced by Fred Archer, Bertram Longworth, and Will Connell were profoundly influenced by their involvement in the film industry both within and without the studio gates.

The geographic boundaries of the Los Angeles basin frame the narrative of this essay. Like my own experience, the environmental and cultural resources of Southern California provided a critical reference point for all the photographer's discussed in this essay. I have tried to provide a detailed outline of all the photographers who are critical to an understanding of the development of fine art photography in Southern California during the first half of the twentieth century. It is my hope that this essay leaves the reader with new knowledge about Southern California as a geographic and cultural environment where creative expression in photography flourished, inspiring and motivating many national and international photographers.

"At present the most active focus of
pictorial activity in the country seems to be
in California. Perhaps it's in the climate, with
its great percentage of sunshine days which
call one into the great out-of-doors; perhaps
it's because of the helpful inspiration afforded
by the wonderful and varied scenery of this
great state. But whatever the reason, it is
here that the fire of photographic enthusiasm
seems to be now burning brightest."

−John Paul Edwards, 1919[1]

1

Sunshine Days

When noted photographer John Paul Edwards described the state of California photography in 1919, the concept of photography as a fine art was barely two decades old. In less than twenty years, California had become a leading center of a newly defined field: fine art photography. California, whose presence in the art world had been little noted prior to 1915, quickly began to emerge as a place to be reckoned with in the arts, and photographers were among those receiving the most notice. As Edwards remarked, and as with most accomplishments in the Golden State, sunshine and scenery were given credit for the successes made within the state's borders. Fine art photographers had found a congenial back-drop for their artistic ideals on the West Coast.

The ideals of fine art were formulated in the late 1890s, when American photographer Alfred Stieglitz ignited the passions of a small but energetic group of American and European amateur photographers who believed that photography was a valid medium for artistic expression. Stieglitz brought together a small but influential group of artists working in photography under the banner of the Photo-Secession. At his small gallery in New York, Stieglitz organized solo and group exhibitions featuring photographs by Edward Steichen, Paul Strand, Gertrude Käsebier, and Alvin Langdon Coburn, among others. By insisting on rigorous standards of quality and artistic vision, Stieglitz and the members of the Photo-Secession became the aesthetic and philosophical leaders of the fine art photography movement between 1898 and 1915.

The work Stieglitz and his colleagues produced came to be known as pictorialism, the goal of which was to create a symbolic impression of a person or scene, not a literal one. Pictorialism thereby freed photography from its previously understood role as a tool of scientific observation; at the turn of the century, this was a radical concept. Artists had always been defined as painters or sculptors; anyone using a mechanical device to create art, such as a camera, was not considered an artist, thus nothing produced by a machine was considered art. The debate concerning photography's status as an art raged.[2] Fine art photographers, who were generally affluent, professional men, or women of independent means, insisted that photography could indeed be an art. They redefined photography's place in the arts and elevated the status of the photographer as fine artist. Communities of fine art photographers throughout the United States and Europe soon organized into regional salons and camera clubs, communicating though magazines and journals including *The American Annual of Photography, Photo Era, Camera Notes, and Camera Work.* These journals kept photographers in touch with critical debates on photography as a fine art, provided reviews of exhibitions, and printed reproductions of photographic art.

The San Francisco Bay area was the first center for pictorial photography on the West Coast. During the first decade of the twentieth century, several international salons were organized in San Francisco under the auspices of the California Camera Club featuring the work of the leading pictorialists in California, the East Coast, and Europe. In 1901, *Camera Craft* magazine was founded as an extension of the activities of the club. The magazine ran independently until the early 1940s and was a critical link between fine art photographers throughout the western states.

Southern California did not immediately share in the intensity of pictorialist activity as experienced in Northern California. There was, however, a strong photographic tradition dating back to the late 1850s, when there was a demand for documentation of the region's developing infrastructure. By the mid-1880s, the wonders of Southern California's climate and scenery were the subject of commercial photographers whose images of orange orchards, verdant gardens and luxurious resorts were used to entice new residents into the towns and subdivisions springing up from Santa Barbara to San Diego.

Arriving in 1854, William M. Godfrey is acknowledged as the first resident photographer of Los Angeles.[3] His earliest views of Southern California include the dusty streets and buildings of downtown Los Angeles, portraits of the powerful Mexican and Anglo families, as well as coastal views around Santa Monica and San Pedro.

While Godfrey recorded the fledgling transformations of a developing economy, Carleton Watkins, one of the premier landscape photographers of the nineteenth century, traveled through Southern California in the late 1870s and early 1880s recording the triumphs of railroad construction linking San Francisco and Los Angeles via the Tehachapi Pass. He also documented the rapidly developing network of towns, farms, and civic improvements throughout the region. Other photographers also recorded the changing landscape, from rural to urban to suburban in Southern

Figure 1.
Herve Friend. (Attributed).
Long Beach. From the publication *Art Work on Southern California.* 1900.

Friend produced some of the first artistic photographs in Southern California when much contemporary photography was perfunctory at best, with little or no thought given to composition, the interplay of light and shadow, or overall aesthetic impact. (Private Collection)

California, but their work was of a commercial, not artistic, nature. By the dawn of the twentieth century, it was San Francisco which had developed into a major urban center with museums, a knowledgeable group of art patrons and a thriving art community spread throughout the Bay Area.[4] In contrast, Southern California was still a provincial backwater, lacking a patronage system supporting the arts. Most of the artists in Southern California, while enjoying the beauties of their surroundings, endured their isolation and cultural anonymity.

Southern California's commercial photographers specialized in landscapes for the tourist trade as well as portraits and documentation of capital improvement projects for local residents and business interests. Initial attempts to produce artistic photography in the region were stimulated by a small group of amateur photographers working within the genre of landscape photography. While amateur photography in the Bay Area was influenced by Stieglitz and the local Arts and Crafts movement, in Southern California photographers were influenced by the work of two local writers-photographers, Charles Lummis and George Wharton James. Both Lummis and James wrote and photographed widely, and both emphasized the inspirational value of the local landscape. They urged Southern California photographers to roam freely throughout valleys, mountains, and beaches and to ignore imported aesthetic theories or idealized notions of beauty. Recognizing the unique charms of Southern California, they extolled the beauty and singular character of the local landscape. A regional branch of pictorialism, distinct from that of the Bay Area, began to emerge, with its northern geographical boundary located at Point Lobos, the scenic spit of land reaching into the ocean at Carmel. More than a geographic boundary, Point Lobos became an aesthetic one, for it was here that the greatest of the Southern California photographers, Edward Weston, eventually settled, producing a major portion of his artistic work during the last three decades of his life. Weston became inextricably linked with the place through his book *My Camera on Point Lobos*, published by Virginia Adams and Houghton Mifflin in 1950.

Southern California pictorialism became noted for images of the crumbling Spanish missions, local landscape views and still-life compositions during the first fifteen years of the twentieth century, maturing during the late pictorialist period, between 1910 and 1930.[5] Late pictorialism developed

when Stieglitz renounced the movement he had initiated and began to focus his attention on the promotion of modern European artists including Pablo Picasso and Georges Braque, as well as American artists such as John Marin and Arthur Dove. By 1910, the practice of pictorialism had spread to a large group of amateur photographers who were not bound by a profound aesthetic or philosophical passion for photography, as were its founders. Rather, they were content to continue in previously explored genres and subject matter. In general, this second wave of amateur photographers joined the camera clubs and salon societies for their recreation and social activities, not from a burning passion to push photography beyond its contemporary artistic boundaries.

The Camera Pictorialists of Los Angeles was one of several organizations in the United States that continued to further the pictorialist discourse. Founded in 1914 by a small group of dedicated Southern California photographers, the Camera Pictorialists of Los Angeles organized over thirty international exhibitions of photography between 1918 and 1950. The majority of these exhibitions were held at the Los Angeles County Museum of Art, where they engaged the interest of local art critics and attracted a substantial audience interested in fine art photography. Admission to membership in the Camera Pictorialists was by invitation only, with the list of active members never exceeding fifteen individuals at the height of the club's activities. This policy insured that the club sustained its focus on the art and craft of fine art photography. Initially, the membership rested with a small group of nationally known pictorial photographers, including Louis Fleckenstein, who had moved to Los Angeles before 1910. Fleckenstein had been active in the salons during the early years of the pictorialist movement and brought a sense of knowledge and experience to the early organizational efforts of the Camera Pictorialists. By the mid-1920s, the club's strength had shifted to a younger group of photographers employed in the motion picture industry and the emerging field of advertising photography.

The Camera Pictorialist exhibitions revealed several distinct trends in Southern California photography by the late 1920s. An active community of Japanese-American photographers based in Los Angeles began to exhibit a series of landscape and still-life photographs as early as 1926. Their work revolutionized the world of fine art photography with an emphasis on unusual camera angles and flattened perspective, and as such, they were among the first modernist photographers in Southern California. Pictorialism was developing into modernism and, by 1932, the Camera Pictorialist salons included the work of California photographers Imogen Cunningham and Edward Weston, who practiced a distinct form of modernism emphasizing a pure and unmediated vision of everyday objects reproduced in the sharpest detail that the camera could provide.

Southern California fine art photography between 1910 and 1930 is inextricably linked to the artistic development of Edward Weston. Soon after his arrival in Los Angeles in 1906, Weston made the decision to pursue a career as a professional photographer. Moving quickly through the realm of commercial photography, he adopted the prevailing fine art aesthetics of pictorialism to attract wealthy clients to his portrait studio. He quickly became absorbed in the pursuit of photography as a fine art and dedicated his life to the exploration of a personal artistic vision through the medium of photography. Weston achieved a singular international reputation unmatched by any other photographer working in Southern California during the first half of the twentieth century. He was a founding member of the Camera Pictorialists of Los Angeles and was instrumental in establishing the rigorous artistic standards that became the hallmark of the organization.

While Weston was never actively engaged as a still photographer in the developing Hollywood film industry, many of the active members of the Camera Pictorialists earned their living in the motion picture business. Photographers such as Fred Archer and Karl Struss enjoyed international reputations as fine art photographers in the salon movement but failed to produce an extended body of work reflecting a mature and coherent artistic vision. Unlike Weston, Archer and Struss embraced the notion that their "personal" or "artistic" photography was primarily recreational in nature. This attitude reflects a pragmatic quality typical of many Southern California photographers whose professional commitments came before artistic innovation.

The rising tide of modernist photography in the late 1920s blurred the lines between commercial and fine art photography that had been carefully constructed during the pictorialist movement. The continued growth of the tourist industry in Southern California and the rapid development of industry and manufacturing led to the rise of a talented group of young photographers who were willing to blend their artistic vision with the commercial needs of an expanding client base eager to sell goods and services through photographic advertisements. Will Connell represents this type of new artist/commercial photographer. As early as 1926, Connell exhibited soft-focused landscapes of the region in leading salon shows while supplying these same images to tourist magazines and brochures that promoted the wonders of Southern California. Connell was one of the few photographers whose work experienced a rapid shift from pictorialism to modernism, through his contact with a group of writers, artists, and architects associated with Jake Zeitlin's bookshop in downtown Los Angeles, some of whom were part of the Hollywood film community.

A testament to the growth of Southern California was the establishment of the first full-time photography department on the West Coast associated with an art school. Organized in 1930, the Art Center School signaled that Los Angeles had become an important artistic and commercial center. Modeled on the Bauhaus school of design in Germany founded by Lazlo Maholy-Nagy, Art Center featured a rigorous program in painting and photography, as well as architecture and graphic design. Students studied their chosen art medium while gaining exposure to recent approaches in modern art and commercial design. An art gallery on the campus exposed the students to varied styles of art and design including the work of Stanton MacDonald-Wright, Edward Steichen, and Man Ray.

Thus, in the thirty years between 1900 and 1930, fine art photography in Southern California had evolved from a nascent form of pictorialism to a rigorous modernism. Yet despite the differences in style, the subject matter was often the same: the landscape of California. Whether in Herve Friend's views of Los Angeles County in the 1880s or in Edward Weston's dramatic images of trees, dunes, or desert in the 1920s and 1930s, California's landscape dominated the imagery. As John Paul Edwards had observed, the fire of photographic enthusiasm burned brightly in California, and nowhere more intensely than south of Point Lobos.

Figure 2.
Herve Friend. (Attributed).
Scene Near Hollywood. From the
publication *Art Work on Southern
California.* 1900.

Friend's photographs appeared in several
publications produced between 1887
and 1900 utilizing the elaborate and
expensive photogravure process. These
books promoted the Southern California
region to wealthy residents of the
Midwest and East Coast. Friend intuitively understood the rhetorical rules
of pictorial landscape photography as
articulated and disseminated through
books and magazines of the period.
(Private Collection)

2

Herve Friend: Early Fine Art Photography

Herve Friend produced some of the first artistic photographs in Southern California at a time when much contemporary photography was perfunctory at best, with little or no thought given to composition, the interplay of light and shadow or overall aesthetic impact. By 1887, Friend had compiled a series of finely composed landscapes in a publication titled *Picturesque Los Angeles County, California: Illustrative and Descriptive*, an album produced in the expensive photogravure process. This elaborate publication was singular in the genre of booster literature designed to increase the flow of tourists to the region throughout the year, a genre that increasingly relied on photography to sell the landscape and climate of Southern California.[6] Friend hoped that the high quality of his production and the careful composition of his photographs would "familiarize the tourist and resident with localities as will excite an interest in them, and cause them to seek out and enjoy with the author the many gems of natural scenery far away among the mountains and canons."[7] Friend was careful to note that the photogravure process was "extensively used in this country and in Europe for artistic reproductions, giving pictures with all the fineness of detail shown in the photograph, also possessing the delicate coloring and softness of the highly finished steel engraving."[8]

Another interesting portfolio of meditative landscape photographs, most likely made by Friend, is the publication *Art Work on Southern California* published in 1900. Issued in twelve separate parts with text by Lon Chapin, it was produced in the large format of a magazine and bound in red paper whose texture simulated alligator skin. Two examples from *Art Work on Southern California* are the images *Long Beach* (Fig.1) and *Scene Near Hollywood*. (Fig.2) Both are views of Southern California scenery and employ carefully composed elements of line, tonality, and mass that emphasize the meditative power of photographic landscape work. Friend intuitively understood the rhetorical rules of pictorial landscape photography as articulated and disseminated through books and magazines of the period.

The two publications containing Friend's photographs reveal some of the conflicts that were at the heart of the photographic profession in the late nineteenth century. In an attempt to recapture a share of the business that had been lost to the amateur market, professional photographers recast themselves as artists and craftsman, each as a unique visionary. In most regions of the country, professional photographers rejected the genre of landscape photography as too easy and un-sophisticated for their talents. Their notion of the artistic rested with their ability to construct and photograph elaborate tableaux recreating scenes from important works of literature and poetry. Unlike Friend, many photographers did not have access to the range of landscape that was available in Southern California, nor did they have clients rich enough to pay for the production of an extensive body of landscape photographs. In Southern California, real estate developers and promoters of the tourist trade understood that beautiful pictures of the local landscape would do more to entice wealthy customers to the region than pages of inflated rhetoric touting the climate and healthy atmosphere of the region. Thus in Southern California, the landscape photograph developed an artfulness based on commercial needs, with Friend as one of the first to exploit this unlikely mix.

Quinn
playing
human fly

3

Charles Lummis: Visual Iconoclast

Another individual who influenced the direction of fine art photography in Southern California but who remained outside the rhetoric of aesthetic debates, was Charles Fletcher Lummis; Lummis' arrival in Southern California in 1885 was a heralded event. He had walked the entire distance from Cincinnati to Los Angeles. While traveling across the continent, he wrote a weekly column for the *Los Angeles Times* describing his adventures. Lummis became friends with the irascible publisher of the *Times*, Harrison Gray Otis who gave Lummis the job of City Editor at the paper. Lummis came to know and love the Spanish and Mexican traditions of Southern California that were rapidly disappearing under successive waves of real estate booms and Anglo immigration from the Midwest and Northeast. Lummis enjoyed many careers as a journalist, ethnographer, magazine editor, and city librarian.[9]

Lummis began his work in photography soon after his arrival in 1885. He produced most of his photographs using the cyanotype process, which, translated from the Greek, means "dark blue impression." The process appealed to Lummis, which, because of its relative simplicity, a darkroom was not needed to develop the prints. The sensitized paper was printed in contact with the negative in direct sunlight and washed in a solution of distilled water. The cyanotype process was very popular among amateur photographers of the late-nineteenth and early-twentieth century and produced an image with a broad tonal range within the spectrum of the blue tint. For Lummis, photography had both a practical and expressive application, but above all, it was a medium of preservation. Lummis used photography to record the people and places he wanted to share with others, but he also used the medium to record a series of self-portraits during the last thirty years of his life in Southern California. These portraits reveal Lummis as a man of varied personas: historian, ethnographer, aristocrat in the Spanish and Mexican traditions of the original Southern California land grant families, and ardent proponent of outdoor life and physical culture.

Lummis' first major impact on the direction of fine art photography came when he assumed editorship of the magazine *The Land of Sunshine* in 1895. The magazine was closely allied with the Los Angeles Chamber of Commerce and Lummis was keenly aware of the stakes involved in promoting Southern California to the right class of people. *The Land of Sunshine* began publication

Figure 6.
Charles Lummis. *Quimu Playing Human Fly*.

Lummis photographed his son at play at his distinctive residence, El Alisal. His direct yet informal approach to photography defied the prevailing conventions of fine art photography. (1910 A.24.28 Courtesy Southwest Museum)

in June 1894 and immediately exhibited a sophisticated sense of design.

Under Lummis' direction, the magazine sponsored the first amateur photography contest in Southern California and the winning photographs were reproduced in it beginning with the January 1895 issue. Discussing the results of the photography contest, Lummis proclaimed that the landscape and atmosphere of Southern California were almost beyond the comprehension of the Eastern artist or photographer. He noted that Southern California has "the characteristic atmosphere of the arid lands, that ineffable clarity, that luminousness, which makes a photographic light to be matched in no other civilized country." [10] Always the booster, Lummis noted the practicality of living in such an artistic paradise: "And this inspiring sky is not something a thousand miles off, to which he can go only at great expense and in a hurry which permits no thoughtful work. It is the sky that he lives under and studies and employs at leisure." [11]

By eliminating professional photographers from participating in the contests, Lummis revealed his affinity with those who believed that true artistic inspiration was tainted by the professional photographers' attention to the commercial demands of the market. Although The Land of Sunshine never sponsored another photo contest, Lummis continued to sprinkle the magazine with artistic amateur achievements throughout his tenure as editor.

While Lummis believed that a photograph could be a work of art, he had difficulty embracing the pictorialist notion of artistic expression in photography. The practice of photography appealed to Lummis in its most straightforward and uncomplicated form. The pictorialist movement elevated the photographic print to a rarefied realm of intricate and time-consuming processes that often involved both darkroom and small-scale lithographic printing techniques. It is very likely that the soft-focused photographs and delicate renderings of light and shadow did not appeal to Lummis' "macho" sensibilities. Lummis valued artwork that expressed a "vigorous" individuality, particularly if the work depicted a vision of the land and people of the Southwest that corresponded with his own. An example of Lummis' unique brand of art criticism can found in an article written for The Land of Sunshine under the title "The Artist's Paradise"

"One of the strangest things about artists of palette or lens (for only a pervert can nowadays deny the capacity of the camera for genuine art work) is their sheeply habit of jumping the same old fence, one after the other… While they huddle like indeterminate sheep, the richest art-quarry in the world… is disintegrating. The frontier has gone, with all its rough but manly picturesqueness and they have caught hardly a gesture of it." [12]

One of Lummis' greatest successes was the attention he focused on the deteriorating architecture of the California missions. The Landmarks Club, founded by Lummis in 1894, raised public awareness concerning the perilous condition of these important sites of California's Hispanic heritage. During the first seven years of the club's existence, Lummis made a substantial contribution to the preservation of missions at San Diego, San Juan Capistrano, San Fernando and the Asistencia of Pala. Lummis took many photographs of the missions to convey the serious plight of these important structures. The notion of these sites as remnants of a by-gone era in California's romantic past appealed to the sensibilities of local pictorialist photographers. While Lummis had little interest in the pictorialist tradition, he worked tirelessly to promote the concept that California's Hispanic traditions were rooted in a misty haze of simplicity and beauty. He also believed that the promotion of this ideal past was a great tool for the continued development of the tourist industry in California.

Lummis was clearly aware that his tireless promotion of California's mission heritage stimulated a romantic fascination with California's Spanish and Mexican past among residents and tourists in Southern California. This fascination stimulated an interest in soft-focused photographs of the decaying mission architecture. A letter written in November, 1917 to the Los Angeles photographers Putnam & Valentine succinctly states Lummis' perspective:

"I've been waiting a long time before paying this bill hoping you would contribute these two prints of San Fernando to the Landmarks Club which has furnished $7700 worth of work in saving that old church; this considerable sum being donated by people of Public Spirit, to preserve a noble landmark of California History. So far as I know, photographers and artists are the only ones to whom the Missions have been a source of Revenue…" [13]

Lummis' association with Mrs. A.S.C. Forbes is an interesting example of the overlapping interests of promotion, preservation, and artistic activity that was common in the small circle of fine art photographers active in Southern California during the first two decades of the twentieth century. Married to a successful commercial printer in Los Angeles, Forbes was an amateur photographer associated with the El Camino Real Committee that lobbied successfully to establish a state highway along the original route linking the missions of Northern and Southern California. At Lummis' urging, Forbes became active in the Landmarks Club. She was also the main organizer of the First Los Angeles Photographic Salon held in 1902. Over 550 photographs were hung in the galleries of the Los Angeles Camera Club. This exhibition provided the members of the club and interested Los Angeles residents an opportunity to view photographs from around the country produced by amateurs in such varied genres as landscape, marine, portraiture, still-life, animal studies, architecture and interiors. Owing to Mrs. Forbes' close association with the exhibition and the prevailing interest of the pictorialists, it is not surprising that the elaborate catalogue for the exhibition used the image of the California mission on its cover. (Fig.3) Two small doors incised into the front cover reveal, when opened, a priest standing in the doorway. The image of the priest is framed within the margins of an ad for a Santa Fe Railroad excursion to the Southern California missions. The artist and the booster occupied one and the same mind at this time in Southern California, a seamless juncture of the ideals of art merging with the economic necessities of the region. This mingling occurs in many brochures and pamphlets produced by the Los Angeles Chamber of Commerce and other organizations which combined text with images from paintings in the popular plein-air style of the period as well as soft-focus photographs emphasizing the ideal beauty of the Southern California landscape.

Between 1910 and 1922 Lummis assembled a number of informal gift albums which consisted of plain sheets of rag paper, folded and then stitched at the spine. Photographs are generally pasted one to a sheet, with commentary and inscriptions in Lummis' hand. The photographs consist of self-portraits, portraits of his children, and views of El Alisal. The albums were sent to family members and close friends, including Joseph Munk, anthropologist and founder of the Southwest Museum, and Idah Meacham Strobridge, writer, publisher, and fellow Arroyo Seco resident. The juxtaposition of images was always carefully composed, allowing the albums to be read as expansive visual diaries. The photographs that appeared in these albums contain some of the most challenging and inventive imagery that Lummis created. Without the benefit or necessity of belonging to a specific movement or aesthetic philosophy, Lummis blended the symbolic imperatives of pictorialist practice with the unmediated and direct approach to portraiture and objects favored by the modernists.

Lummis photographed many of the guests who visited El Alisal: conservationist John Muir, painter Maynard Dixon, and poets Charles and Louise Keeler. Lummis was a thoughtful and attentive portrait artist as demonstrated in a pensive photograph of his secretary, Lillian Gildersleeve, made in 1911. (Fig.4) This sensitivity is particularly evident in his use of natural light to both illuminate and obscure details of the sitter's head and upper body.

One of Lummis' highly regarded accomplishments was the design and construction of his home on the banks of the Arroyo Seco. In much the same way that Lummis lavished time and attention on each detail of his house, he never seemed to lose interest in photographing the building and the life that his family lived within it. In a self-portrait made in 1904, Lummis pauses from the rigorous labor of home construction to celebrate the freedom of outdoor living and creative independence that embodied the Southern California lifestyle he cherished. (Fig.5) The joy of these photographs lies in the calm rendition of the intimate and the ordinary. Lummis' photograph of his son Quimu at play is at once both a document and an abstraction. (Fig.6)

Also appearing in the album format are several intriguing and introspective self-portraits that Lummis produced while visiting the Camulos Rancho in 1922. Located in the Santa Clara River Valley region of Ventura County, the rancho was Lummis' direct link to California's Spanish past. Lummis visited Camulos soon after his arrival in Southern California in 1885 and commenced a long-lasting friendship with its owners, Don José and Doña Ysabel del Valle and their children. Lummis was always welcome at the Camulos Rancho and often visited when he was in need of rest and relaxation. As the rapid economic progress of the 1920s began to radically alter the rural character of the Southern California landscape, Lummis retreated even further into his cherished dream of the Spanish past. Dressed in his distinctive corduroy suit, Lummis framed himself as a small diminutive figure supported by the giant base of a California oak tree resting quietly in the landscape of the aging rancho. (Fig.7) In their staged simplicity and their urgency, these images are examples of the most poetic work Lummis created.

Perhaps the greatest enigma of Lummis' photographic activity is a small series of images Lummis created while looking down the spiral staircase in the newly constructed tower of the Southwest Museum in 1914. (Fig.8) Lummis' motivation for taking this series is impossible to determine, but he must have been pleased with the images because he included them in a number of gift albums during this period. These images and several other of Lummis' personal photographs, suggest a lack of concern for the aesthetic principles of fine art photography in Southern California during the early twentieth century. His treatment of the stairs was uninformed by the Armory exhibition of modern art in New York, Alfred Stieglitz's landmark series of exhibitions at his 291 Gallery, or by similar photographic experiments begun by Paul Strand and others during this period. Lummis' unusual photographs of the Southwest Museum are strikingly modern and amazingly abstract. This uncharacteristic work is evidence of Lummis' desire to defy categorization.

Figure 9.
Alvin Langdon Coburn. *From
A California Hilltop*. Circa 1911.

Coburn was the first photographer
of international stature to reside in
Southern California. Under the influence of his friend and colleague, Arthur
Wesley Dow, Coburn took up the
challenge of interpreting the California
landscape through Dow's theories of
line, pattern, and tonal differentiation.
(Courtesy George Eastman House)

4

Alvin Langdon Coburn: Photographic Artist In The Southland

The first photographer to reside in Southern California for an extended period with definite ties to the national and international circles of fine art photography was Alvin Langdon Coburn. He first came to Los Angeles from Boston as an eight-year-old boy after his father's death in 1890. Coburn's maternal grandfather, Joseph Howe, had come to California from Ohio in 1849 seeking wealth and prosperity as a gold miner, and while gold did not become his salvation, Southern California real estate did. Howe purchased property in the area that later became downtown Los Angeles in the 1870s and 80s.[14] Coburn remembered that one of his uncles had given him his first camera when he first arrived in Los Angeles.

Coburn returned to Boston in 1891. His passion for photography continued to blossom and received further impetus after meeting the influential F. Holland Day in 1898. Although Day was asked to join as an original member of the Photo-Secession, his rivalry with Stieglitz led him to turn down the invitation.[15] A photographer of inter-national reputation, Day was never included in a single issue of *Camera Work*.

Day and Coburn were actually distant cousins. Day took an interest in his young relative's budding talent as a photographer and brought him into his circle of photographers.[16] By the time Coburn returned to Southern California in the summer of 1902, he had met the leading American photographers including Alfred Stieglitz, Edward Steichen, and Frank Eugene as well the Europeans Frederick Evans and Robert Demachy. Coburn's talent and his personal connections to the leading fine art photographers in America and Europe were aided by the money he inherited after his father's premature death. This independence gave Coburn the opportunity to pursue his passion for photography unhindered by the need to earn a living.

While other artists may have balked at the intellectual and social isolation of Southern California during this period, Coburn was stimulated by the pictorial possibilities of the regional architecture and landscape. Coburn took advantage of the well-appointed darkrooms of the Los Angeles Camera Club and in August and September of 1902, he wrote two articles on printing techniques that were published in the *Los Angeles Camera Club News*.[17] While no original prints appear to exist from this period, several articles published by Coburn in *Photo Era* magazine indicate that he was actively photographing the architecture of the

Figure 10.
Alvin Langdon Coburn. *Giant Palm
Trees, California Mission*. 1911.

———————

Coburn photographed the missions of
Southern California during an extended
visit in 1902 and again in 1911. Coburn
was most likely introduced to the
missions through acquaintances in the
Los Angeles Camera Club such as Mrs.
A.S.C. Forbes. (Courtesy George
Eastman House)

Figure 11.
Alvin Langdon Coburn. *Mount Wilson.*
1911.

Much of Coburn's landscape work from
1911 utilizes a flattened perspective
created by the use of a telephoto lens
and an abstraction achieved by concentrating on simple compositional
elements without the aid of extensive
manipulation of the photographic print.
Coburn's photographs represented a
novel approach to the medium then
practiced in Southern California.
(Courtesy George Eastman House)

Southern California missions.[18] Coburn was most likely introduced to the missions through acquaintances in the Los Angeles Camera Club such as Mrs. Forbes.

Coburn was the first photographer of international stature to incorporate Southern California regional iconography into his aesthetic vocabulary. His article and accompanying photographs on the San Juan Capistrano mission is a case in point:

"Nearly seventy years have since passed away, and San Juan Capistrano is still beautiful, even in its ruin. A glance at the pictures accompanying this article will show that it was built by artists in an age when Art was not only the beautiful way of doing things, but also the expression of man's joy in his work. The soul of the artist photographer will recognize a kindred spirit in these ruins and his pictures cannot fail to reflect this peculiar charm and beauty." [19]

By the time Coburn returned to Boston in late 1902, he had produced a substantial body of work from Southern California that he began to exhibit in such prestigious venues as the New York Camera Club and the Philadelphia Photographic Society. At his 1903 exhibition organized by the New York Camera Club, Coburn exhibited fifty-six photographs of which twenty-one were Southern California views, including Mount Lowe, Riverside, and the missions of San Gabriel, San Fernando, and Santa Barbara.[20] By the end of 1903, Coburn had been elected to membership in the prestigious ranks of the Photo-Secession as well as the England-based Fraternity of the Linked Ring. The Photo-Secession and the Linked Ring were both elite associations of artists who believed that photography was a valid tool of artistic expression. Like Coburn, most of the photographers were free from the necessity of making a living through photography and rejected all commercial aspects of the medium. At the age of twenty, Coburn was the youngest member of these important photographic societies.[21] At this point, the majority of Coburn's artistic work had been completed in California.

When Coburn again returned to Southern California for over a year between 1911 and 1912, he had completed a substantial portion of his important photographic work in New York and Europe including the publication of his New York and London books. Coburn had met, photographed, and been influenced by an array of English and American writers and intellectuals including

George Bernard Shaw, Edward Carpenter, Henry James, and Mark Twain. At the age of twenty-nine, Coburn took up residence in California with a substantial resume of European and American exhibitions, published books and articles, and an established reputation as a photographic artist on intimate terms with the individuals and the ideas that were shaping the direction of fine art photography.

Coburn returned to California with a renewed interest in landscape photography. Under the influence of his friend and colleague, Arthur Wesley Dow, Coburn took up the challenge of interpreting the California landscape through photography using Dow's theories of line, pattern and tonal differentiation. In collaboration with Ernest Fenollosa of the Boston Museum of Fine Arts, Dow began teaching a class in drawing and composition around 1890, which was the first formal introduction of Japanese artistic principles to American art students.[22] Creating photographs such as From A California Hilltop (Fig.9), Coburn successfully manipulated the photographic apparatus thereby flattening perspective and creating compositions with simple arrangements of line and pattern, in harmony with the Japanese concept of tonal variation or "notan."

Much of Coburn's landscape work from 1911 and 1912 utilized a flattened perspective achieved by the use of a telephoto lens and an abstraction achieved by concentrating on simple compositional elements without the aid of extensive manipulation of the photographic print. (Fig.10, 11, 12) Coburn's photographs represented a novel approach to the medium then practiced in Southern California and his work, combined with his international reputation, attracted interest in the local press. Alma May Cook, writing for the Los Angeles Herald Express in April 1911 noted that:

"In the West perhaps, we have been all too used to the 'artistic' photographs that depend almost solely on a camera out of focus and a deep-toned, sometimes heavy, carbon print. To those who have become accustomed to this work, the studies by Mr. Coburn will come as no less than a revelation." [23]

Coburn also contributed articles to East Coast photography magazines where he shared his excitement at the new direction his work had taken.

"Los Angeles is hemmed in by mountains on three sides, and on the fourth is the sea. There are, therefore, subjects innumerable for the knight of the lens. Peculiar hills, Japanese in outline, punctuate the landscape; orange groves and tropical trees of decorative aspect linger in the valleys; the Eucalyptus tree, which was brought there from Australia, has added a great beauty to the country, and everywhere you meet its graceful form. Silhouetted against a moonlit sky it is a leafy sonnet."[24]

Coburn also exhibited his photographs in two closely bracketed shows occurring during the end of 1911 and the early months of 1912. His first show at the Friday Morning Club displayed work from his *New York* and *London* publications as well as a broad sampling of his portraits of British and American literary figures. At the opening of the exhibition, Dow gave a speech highlighting the innovative nature of Coburn's photographic work. Dow and Coburn had just returned from a visit to the Grand Canyon with Dow coming to the West Coast because of Coburn's persistent urging. The organizers of the exhibition knew that an artist of international stature was in their midst and they attempted to reach out to various organizations in Southern California. A special reception was held for members of the Ruskin Art Club, the California Art Club, as well as a select group of individual artists from Long Beach, Pasadena, and Los Angeles.[25]

Coburn's second exhibition of photographs at the Blanchard Gallery contained almost thirty new photographs taken around Los Angeles, Yosemite, and the Grand Canyon. *Los Angeles Times* critic Antony Anderson, unaccustomed to looking at photographs as fine art, was admittedly perplexed: "They're utterly beyond my comprehension. When photography goes as far as that—well, it's uncanny. It makes me feel uncomfortable." [26]

As further evidence that this was an extremely fertile period in Coburn's career, he also managed to produce a book with six original platinum prints, *The Cloud* by Percy Bysshe Shelley with photographs by Alvin Langdon Coburn. The Los Angeles antiquarian book dealer C.C. Parker published the book in a limited edition with simple paper covers and a cloth spine. Coburn produced all of the platinum prints sometime before leaving Los Angeles in the late summer or early fall of 1912. All of the images were taken in the Grand Canyon or Yosemite with the exception of one photograph taken in Germany. The book was inspired by eighteen months of outdoor life in the

west. Writing to his fellow photographer and member of the Photo-Secession, Karl Struss, in early 1912, Coburn summed up the satisfaction he felt with his time in California; "There is a wealth of fine dramatic material out here, and I feel that I have struck an entirely new note in the things that I have done." [27]

It is interesting to note that Coburn was in Southern California during a particularly quiet period for fine art photography in the region. Between 1900 and 1910, San Francisco was the acknowledged center for artistic photography in California where under the auspices of the California Camera Club, a number of International and American salons were organized. In addition, they hosted traveling exhibits of Photo-Secession work as well as lectures by visiting artists and critics from the East Coast. Prior to 1914, Southern California did not have a similar group of fine art photographers well informed about pictorialist ideas and activities taking place on the East Coast and in Europe. Coburn was in contact with leading pictorialist photographers of Northern California including William Dassonville, but had little contact with local photographers while residing in Southern California. Coburn appears to have enjoyed the isolation of the region and reached a new level of sophistication in his photographic work.

By 1910 some of the creative fervor surrounding photography had begun to wane among the professional members of the California Camera Club. The situation was far worse in Southern California as the Los Angeles Camera Club began to falter soon after the organization of its elaborate salon in 1902.

In 1914, the most innovative activity in fine art photography shifted to Southern California with the formation of the Camera Pictorialists of Los Angeles, an organization that provided a vital forum for national and international fine art photography with consistency and vigor from its inception through the late 1930s. The formation of the Camera Pictorialists of Los Angeles was the brainchild of the most important photographer to live and work in Southern California during the first three decades of the twentieth century: Edward Henry Weston.[28]

Figure 12.
Alvin Langdon Coburn. *Venice,
California*. Circa 1911.

Coburn exhibited his photographs in
two closely bracketed shows held in
Southern California in 1911 and 1912.
(Courtesy George Eastman House)

5

Edward Weston: The Transformation of Fine Art Photography

"This is the place for you without an atom of a doubt. Every year you spend backeast is so much loss to you. This is the country you have been longing for." —Mary Weston Seaman writing to her brother Edward Weston from Southern California, 1905 [29]

So much has been written about the life and photography of Edward Weston that a thorough examination of his artistic contribution to the field of American photography is unnecessary here.[30] Photographic historian Mike Weaver has articulated a formula to evaluate the qualities a photographer must possess in order to advance the art of photography. Weaver states that the photographer must have a philosophical, aesthetic, technical, and craftsmanly approach to his art and these faculties must function in harmony at a particular creative moment. Weaver notes that most photographers have only one moment of artistic momentum that creates a work of lasting importance. It is safe to say Edward Weston was the only photographer in Southern California to grasp all of these qualities at a particular moment and then re-invent himself to meet the challenge all over again.[31]

Much of Weston's well-known and artistically mature work of the late 1920s and through the 1930s was influenced by the years he spent in Southern California between 1906 and 1924.[32] Unfortunately for the photographic historian, all of Weston's diaries and many of his photographic prints from this period were destroyed by the photographer in a moment of personal crisis and despair in the mid-1920s. The archival fragments that exist in several research institutions and private collections have begun to receive critical attention in the last several years and the scope of Weston's achievements during these years are beginning to be re evaluated.

Weston arrived in Southern California from Chicago in 1906 after repeated requests from his older sister May Weston Seaman who had moved with her husband to Tropico (now Glendale) around 1900. After a brief period of doing surveying work for the San Pedro, Los Angeles, and Salt Lake Railroad, Weston decided to work toward a career in photography, an occupation that had absorbed his interest since his father had given him his first camera in 1902.[33] Some of the earliest photographs by Weston from Southern California exist as a body of work known as *The Rincon Courtship Album* (Fig.13). This album documents a trip that Weston took with his future wife, Flora Chandler, and another friend to the headwaters of the San Gabriel River during the summer of 1907.

The album appears to be a collaborative project, with Weston taking the photographs and Flora supplying the descriptive captions. The album represents Weston's earliest attempt to use photography as a tool to express his personal thoughts and emotions. Weston's creative impulses led him through a varied terrain of aesthetic currents and personal identities between 1906 and 1923. *The Rincon Album* serves as a starting point in his career as photographic artist. As Weston matured as an artist, he became embarrassed by the photographs of his earlier years and made a determined attempt to obscure the roots of his creative development within the cultural climate of Southern California. This was accomplished through the use of selective memory in his later years as he recounted this period of his life to his first biographers, Nancy and Beaumont Newhall. As previously mentioned, Weston destroyed many of his photographs and diaries dated before 1921 which left the Newhalls with the task of exploring the collective memory of Weston's few remaining friends from the Southern California years who were still alive in the early 1950s.

The youthful and romantic Edward Weston seen in *The Rincon Album* seems to have jumped from the pages of the many articles appearing in local magazines promoting bucolic Southern California landscape of the first decade of the twentieth century. Rural in character but possessing economic opportunity, Southern California was the perfect environment for a young man like Weston whose ideals of healthy outdoor living were derived from the pages of *Physical Culture* magazine and whose prime motivation consisted of providing a livelihood for his new wife and family as a commercial photographer among the growing ranks of Midwestern expatriates like himself.

Determined to begin his career as a commercial photographer, Weston left California for a brief period in 1908 to study technique at the Illinois School of Photography. When he returned to Los Angeles he spent the next several years working under the direction of Louis Mojonier, one of the leading portrait photographers in Southern California at the time (Fig.14). An interesting and little-known series of photographs, taken in 1909 before the opening of his own photography studio, shows Weston and a neighborhood friend, Nell

Figure 13.
Edward Weston. *In Maiden and Manly Meditation Fancy Free*. 1907.

Some of the earliest photographs by Weston from Southern California exist in an album documenting a trip that he took with his future wife, Flora Chandler, to the headwaters of the San Gabriel River during the summer of 1907. (The J. Paul Getty Museum, Los Angeles. ©1981 Center for Creative Photography, Arizona Board of Regents)

Figure 14.
Group Portrait, Mojonier Studio Staff. Circa 1908. (Edward Weston at second row on left).

Determined to begin his career as a commercial photographer, Weston spent several years working under the direction of Louis Mojonier, one of he leading portrait photographers in Southern California at the time. (The J. Paul Getty Museum, Los Angeles)

Cole, during a photographic sojourn through the unspoiled hills of Griffith Park near Weston's home in Tropico. These two photographs and a small series of related images show Weston's earliest attempts at advertising photography (Fig.14, 15). In this instance, the ease of handling the lightweight Kodak camera posed a contrast to the bulky equipment and glass plate negatives he shouldered as a young amateur photographer and allowed photographic access to rugged terrain. An integral part of this simple narrative is the inviting scenery of Southern California that awaited the hiker at every turn.

Weston continued to explore commercial photography between 1909 and 1914. The summation of this brief period of Weston's work can be found in a promotional booklet titled, *Tropico, the City Beautiful*. All of the photographs in the booklet were provided by Weston and include a panorama of the city from a local hilltop, views of Weston's studio, as well as other prominent buildings. The most interesting view is a still-life composition taken in his studio showing a group of ripe peaches positioned next to a ruler to authenticate the size and fullness of the fruit from the local orchards (Fig.17). More than any others in the booklet, this image demonstrates Weston's full mastery of promotional photography.

Soon after the establishment of his Tropico studio in 1911, Weston realized that his talents and interests lay in the field of studio portrait photography. This genre provided Weston with both commercial and artistic success as early as 1913.[34] This success led to conflicts between his commercial and artistic inclinations that he would battle for the rest of his career, more often choosing poverty than accepting money for work he had no interest in producing. Before his first trip to Mexico in 1923, however, Weston continued to do commercial portrait work to supplement the family income derived from Flora's job as an elementary school teacher.

In a series of articles written between 1912 and 1922, a clear shift in Weston's professional and artistic intentions can be seen as his compositional strategies continued to evolve and mature. Two articles appearing in *American Photography* magazine in 1912 and 1913 articulate Weston's profound feeling that craft and technique were the hallmarks of any successful photographer. Weston mastered the technical aspects of photography through education, apprenticeship, and many hours spent in the darkroom. While the importance

of a sound technical base in photography remains a constant in Weston's essays, his philosophical outlook changes radically in this ten-year period.

In the early essays of 1912 and 1913, Weston's aesthetic is based on the prevailing ideas of pictorialism. Weston hoped to improve his reputation among the wealthier citizens of Southern California who were aware of the fine art photography movement and would be willing to pay a high price for portraits taken by a sophisticated camera artist. Weston rejected the assembly line quality typical of large portrait studios by insisting on paying close personal attention to all aspects of his work. This set Weston apart from most commercial portrait photographers and aligned him with the Arts and Crafts traditions in other applied arts practiced in Southern California, such as printmaking, ceramics, and book design. His comments regarding photographic salons and competitions sponsored by a number of camera clubs and photography magazines are especially revealing. "I am a great believer in the value of competitions and exhibitions, both as an education and as a business getter. By giving support you aid the magazines, salons, and exhibits, and in return receive splendid advertising upon winning a prize..."[35]

Between 1914 and 1924, Weston's great artistic growth was stimulated by a close circle of friends who introduced him to a variety of cultural and intellectual concepts that were rapidly translated into photographic compositions. Throughout his life Weston was unsure of his intellectual abilities and relied on his revolving circle to nurture and educate him. Margrethe Mather was one of Weston's earliest mentors and collaborators during his years in Southern California. Mather had taken up photography under the encouragement of her friend Elmer Ellsworth as early as 1912. One Sunday afternoon in 1913, Ellsworth and Mather were on a camera club excursion in Griffith Park and, bored with the company, Ellsworth suggested a visit to Weston's studio across the river in Tropico. Soon after they met, a passionate relationship developed between Weston and Mather and she soon became an assistant in his studio.[36]

While Weston was engaged with his early explorations as a photographic artist he appears to have promoted his work through a variety of channels. In May 1914, *Camera Craft* magazine, the major journal chronicling the activity of West Coast photographers, announced the formation of the Camera Pictorialists of Los Angeles. Along with Margrethe Mather, Weston was one of the catalytic members whom the magazine described as "pictorially ambitious" and, banding together, they expressed a need for "competent criticism and association".[37] Until the end of 1916, Weston appears to have devoted a fair amount of energy promoting the work of the Camera Pictorialists. Concurrently Weston continued to enjoy notoriety through the display of his work at a number of the prominent East Coast salons as well as his regular inclusion in the most prestigious annual exhibition of pictorialist work at this time, the London salon. Weston first received attention in the Los Angeles press in October 1915 when critic Antony Anderson declared that Weston's photography had awakened his interest in the artistic potential of the medium:

> "All this I have gleaned, not through personal experiments with dry plates and acid baths, but from careful scrutiny of the photographs shown by acknowledged masters of the craft. One such master is Edward Henry Weston of Tropico, who has many honors and medals in international exhibitions…. Each is truly a work of art for each has been touched with the artist's imagination, his powers of synthesis and arrangement so that their subtle chemistry seems to have obliterated almost every sign of the chemistry of the camera."[38]

Figure 17.
Edward Weston. *Peaches in Two Pyramid-Shaped Piles, One with Ruler.* Circa 1915.

This photograph was published in a promotional booklet for the city of Tropico with all of the photographs supplied by Weston. More than any other photograph reproduced, this image demonstrates Weston's full mastery of the genre of Southern California booster/promotional photography of the late 19th and early 20th century. (The J. Paul Getty Museum, Los Angeles. ©1981 Center for Creative Photography, Arizona Board of Regents)

It was undoubtedly Weston's growing reputation as an international artist among the Southern California art community that provided the opportunity for the Camera Pictorialists to exhibit at the First Annual Arts and Crafts Salon held at the Los Angeles County Museum of Art in Exposition Park in February 1916. The photographic exhibition was curated by Weston and included work by all the current members of the Camera Pictorialists of Los Angeles. Weston also curated the invitational section of the exhibit that gave the Los Angeles audience their first exposure to such important photographers as Karl Struss, Clarence White, Gertrude Käsebier, and Rudolf Eickemeyer. The exhibition catalogue also provides important insights to the liaisons Weston had made with important veterans of the Photo-Secession movement. In addition, Weston had already developed a relationships with West Coast photographers Anne Brigman and Imogen Cunningham Partridge.[39]

Figure 15.
Edward Weston. *Edward Weston with Nell Cole at Griffith Park in Vacation Time*. 1909.

These two photographs show Weston's earliest attempts at advertising photography. In this instance, the ease and facility of handling the lightweight Kodak camera posed a contrast to the bulky tripod, large camera, and suitcase of glass plate negatives shouldered by the young amateur photographer in the form of Edward Weston. (The J. Paul Getty Museum, Los Angeles. ©1981 Center for Creative Photography, Arizona Board of Regents)

Figure 16.
Edward Weston. *Edward Weston with Nell Cole*. 1909. (The J. Paul Getty Museum, Los Angeles. ©1981 Center for Creative Photography, Arizona Board of Regents)

Soon after the conclusion of the Arts and Crafts exhibition, Weston extended an invitation to Antony Anderson to attend a meeting of the Camera Pictorialists to engage the membership in a critique of their photographic work. Anderson had favorably reviewed the exhibition and the membership wanted to continue a dialogue with the foremost art critic in Southern California.[40] Anderson's article describing his meeting with the Camera Pictorialists provides important insight into the early membership of the organization, which represented the first viable association of fine art photographers assembled in Southern California. Having never engaged in a critical debate involving photographic art, Anderson had some trepidation in accepting the invitation. Upon arriving at the clubroom, Anderson was impressed by the brilliantly illuminated walls filled with new work from all fifteen members of the organization. Anderson and the photographers jumped into an active and engaged discussion considering composition, tonal values, and the construction of emotional impact in photography. Anderson concluded that all of these debates were focused on attaining the high ideals of "truth to nature and truth to art." Anderson sensed a focus and commitment on the part of the Camera Pictorialists that heralded a new beginning for fine art photography in Southern California.

"It seeks the radical and unaccustomed viewpoint, the new idea, the fresh impression.
It wants to break the trammels of tradition,
those strong bars to progress."[41]

By 1916, Weston had absorbed the philosophical and compositional strategies of pictorial photography and began to push the boundaries beyond conventional limits of the time. It was during this period that Weston appears to set himself apart from most of his colleagues in the Camera Pictorialist community, to begin a closer photographic collaboration with Margrethe Mather, and to look for inspiration from a small but advanced group of artists and writers who were engaged in a search for new modes of expression in the broadly defined area of modernist practice.[42] The inspiration for the Southern California modernists included Japanese and Chinese art, particularly the Japanese Ukiyo-E woodblock prints of the late 18th century, the poetry of Max Eastman and Carl Sandburg, the choreography of Ted Shawn and Ruth St. Denis and the political philosophy of Emma Goldman. By the time Weston delivered a lecture titled "Photography As A Means of Artistic Expression" to the College Women's Club in Los Angeles in October of 1916, he had firmly articulated that his primary involvement with photography was for artistic, not for commercial purposes. He began to visualize the concept of the straight photograph that was to become more strictly defined in the next several years. He notes that straight photographs "are without handwork, shading or manipulation of any kind. This does not mean that I never retouch, nor object to it if confined to an irreducible minimum."[43] By 1916, Weston had changed his attitudes towards the prominent salons and competitions and believed that they did not accurately reflect the new spirit of artistic photography. He noted that "Many a so-called photographic salon is entirely undeserving of such a title and the standard in them is so low that an award means next to nothing."[44]

Between 1914 and 1922, Weston and Mather collaborated on a number of photographic compositions and occasionally signed both of their names to an image. Mather had a number of contacts in the small but active community of Japanese artists living in Los Angeles at the time. Weston's 1918 portrait of Mather, *Epilogue* (Fig.18), is an intricate composition of light and shadow influenced by Japanese artistic sensibilities and most likely was influenced by the paintings and wood block prints that Weston and Mather observed on their visits to the studios of their Japanese friends.

Another major influence on Weston during this period was his friendship with Ramiel McGehee with whom Weston became acquainted in 1919, most likely through their mutual association with the dancer Ruth St. Denis.[45] MeGehee was extremely well educated, particularly in the area of Asian art. He translated Chinese poetry and had spent a number of years living in China and Japan. He had a large collection of Japanese and Chinese art which he loved to share and discuss with his friends.[46] Weston's relationship with MeGehee undoubtedly stimulated Weston to begin a bold series of portraits which experimented with shifting patterns of light and shadow to give a greater sense of depth and movement to the picture plane. Experiments such as *Ramiel in His Attic*, 1920, are unique within the spectrum of fine art photography in Southern California and indeed presage an interest in Japanese-inspired compositions which began to be produced by other leading photographers on the East Coast and in Europe beginning in the mid-1920s. (Fig.19)

By 1922, the seeds of Weston's mature vision were planted. He was close to a complete rejection of pictorialist aesthetics and actively searching for the approach to photography which would most clearly articulate the "supreme instants" that he felt were the complete province of the photograph, particularly in the genre of portraiture and still-life.[47] His unstinting practice of and devotion to photography for more than ten years, combined with a nurturing of his intellect through a close association with McGehee, Mather, and others led Weston to conclude that photography was the primary language of modernity. In a lecture delivered to the Southern California Camera Club in June 1922, there is a sense that Weston was on the verge of major life changes. By the fall of 1922 he would visit Alfred Stieglitz in New York and in August, 1923 he would depart on the first of two extended trips to Mexico which would clarify and extend his photographic explorations. In this lecture, Weston articulates the problematic tenets of pictorialist practice that he absorbed and finally rejected by 1922:

"Photography is a medium destroyed in value through manual interference—a medium so subtle that providing one is equally keen—the most profound instants—the finest nuances of light and shade may be captured in the magic silver, and at the very instant desired—not when memory has to rebuild—perhaps crudely—the past."[48]

When Weston returned to Southern California from his first trip to Mexico late in 1924, he immediately felt a profound sense of dislocation.[49] This was due in part to his unsettled relationship with his wife Flora but also due to the profound changes that were occurring in the Southern California landscape. Weston notes with disdain the amount of cheaply constructed homes that were popping up around his studio in Tropico, a by-product of the real estate boom of the mid-1920s. Southern California was a far different place from the one he had begun to call home in 1906. The rapid industrialization of Southern California during the 1920s also contributed to Weston's increasing disdain for the region. Typical of his comments are those from a letter written in 1946.

"Los Angeles would kill any one. The real-estate boys raped the southland, heavy industry killed

it. The Mexicans would have done much better. They at least understood living."[50]

Weston lamented the passing of the sparsely populated and pre-industrial Southern California of his youth. He brought his camera in 1925 to several industrial sites around Los Angeles to record the formal qualities of structures that he felt represented "the whirl of our seething maelstrom of commercialism."[51] It is not hard to observe the ironic contradiction in his photograph taken at the factory operated by Pacific Ready Cut Homes, a fabricator of instant homes that could be purchased by mail order, which had sprung up around Southern California (Fig.20). Another industrial composition taken at a plaster factory in 1925 shows Weston's increased visual sophistication in the handling of large industrial structures. He had learned to create formal yet abstract compositions from the study of small objects, vegetables, and details of the human form within the confines of the studio (Fig.21).

During Weston's years of experimentation and search for new directions in photography, the Japanese-American community in Los Angeles consistently demonstrated a longstanding support and appreciation of his photography.[52] Weston showed his photographs in the Japanese-American community on three occasions between 1921 and 1931.[53] Perhaps the most important exhibition occurred in 1927 at a pivotal transition in Weston's aesthetic development. All of Weston's exhibits were organized by a group of young artists and intellectuals who gathered together in an organization known as Shakudo-Sha. The name refers to a special bronze alloy of copper and gold which symbolically represents maturity and a respect for traditional artistic practice.[54] The main tenets adhered to by members of the Shakudo-Sha were a respect for their Japanese heritage and a simultaneous attempt to achieve artistic maturity through a passionate embrace of the philosophy of modernism. In photography, this embrace included an appreciation of simplified compositions utilizing line, pattern, and tone which formed the basis of Japanese art. The members of Shakudo-Sha absorbed the traditions of Japanese painting and woodblock printing while also sharing the American and European modernist fascination with the forms of contemporary machines as well as commercial and domestic products.

Japanese-American photographer Toyo Miyatake was the main link between Shakudo-Sha and

Weston. Miyatake and Weston became acquainted by 1920 and Weston informally became Miyatake's teacher on both an aesthetic and technical level.[55] The 1927 exhibition allowed Weston to exhibit a refined selection of his work completed over the previous four years that included images from his extended visits to Mexico. On the gallery wall, Weston placed a brief text that succinctly delineated his photographic and philosophic transitions.

"The prints in this exhibition are an approach to the medium of photography definitely opposed to the "impressionism" of the so-called "pictorialists." Impressionism is skepticism. It puts what one notices above what one knows. It means the monstrous heresy that seeing is believing. My desire has been to present with photographic beauty the thing itself rather than a weak interpretation. My finished print is visioned on the camera's ground glass at the time of exposure. To not feel completely then is to fail."[56]

Arthur Millier, art critic for the *Los Angeles Times* during the late 1920s, immediately recognized the impact of Weston's photography on modernist art practice.[57] He understood Weston's photographs of shells, details of the human figure, and industrial architecture as finely detailed representations of commonplace objects and images imbued with a rhythm and movement that illuminates their mystery and beauty. Thus Millier discussed the idea that photography pursued to its logical conclusion as a valid medium of artistic expression offered the potential to free painting from representation, allowing painters to seek symbols for their emotions which were parallel to but unlike the forms of the visible world. Weston passionately believed in the roll of photography articulated by Millier. He was an early champion of the idea that artistic photography required both a clarity and a philosophy of vision combined with a thorough knowledge of the mechanics of the medium. Weston's understanding of these elements led him to the logical conclusion that artistic photography was concerned with a continued search to refine and expand this clarity of vision. This led Weston to a strict approach to photography whereby he produced only contact prints from his 8 x 10 inch negatives and refrained from retouching either the negative or the final exhibition print.

Figure 19.
Edward Weston. *Ramiel in His Attic.* 1920.

Ramiel McGehee became a close friend of Weston soon after their acquaintance in 1919. McGehee was extremely well educated, particularly in the area of Asian art. Weston's relationship with McGehee undoubtedly stimulated Weston to begin a bold series of portraits which experimented with shifting patterns of light and shadow to give a greater sense of movement to the picture plane. (Center for Creative Photography, The University of Arizona. ©1981 Center for Creative Photography, Arizona Board of Regents)

6

Edward Weston and Merle Armitage

Although Weston moved to Carmel and Southern California lost its force as his artistic center, several important ties continued to bind Weston to the region throughout the 1930s. One of the most important was his association with Merle Armitage which culminated in the production of the 1932 monograph simply titled *Edward Weston*. Arriving in Los Angeles in the early 1920s, Armitage had a profound influence on the art and culture of Southern California throughout the modernist period (Fig.23).

Thanks to Arthur Millier, Armitage was first introduced to Weston around 1922. Millier invited Armitage to a party celebrating Weston's imminent departure to Mexico. Armitage immediately took a liking to the soft-spoken Weston. Weston discussed his evolving ideas on photography with Armitage and his estrangement from the photographic community in Southern California. Weston spoke glowingly of the artists he knew in Mexico, which reminded Armitage that he had recently received a group of etchings by Picasso. He invited Weston to view them. Acting spontaneously, Weston and Armitage left the party and as Armitage recalled:

> "Edward and I went to my gallery, and he for the first time saw original etchings and drawings by Picasso, notably the King Herod and Salome series. He was absolutely fascinated. Going and coming from the party to the gallery gave me a chance to sense his quality, and I asked him to write or get in touch with me immediately when he got back from Mexico. But during the balance of the evening, Weston and I managed a good deal of talk. I encouraged lavishly his conviction that the camera could be the great modern medium, IN THE HANDS OF AN ARTIST. Knowing of my painting collection, and my interests, he seemed encouraged to meet someone that had faith in something other than paint and brushes, the etching needle or the lithographic crayon."[58]

After returning from his second trip to Mexico in 1927, Weston renewed his friendship with Armitage. Both men recalled that their friendship was solidified during this period and became a bond that would be maintained until Weston's death in 1958. With Armitage's connections to the small but energetic group of art patrons interested in modernism, Weston's photographs attracted the attention of such collectors as Walter

Figure 23.
Edward Weston. *Portrait of Merle Armitage*. 1938.

Several important ties continued to bind Weston to the Southern California region throughout the 1930s. One of the most important was his association with Merle Armitage. Arriving in Los Angeles in the early 1920s, Armitage had a profound influence on the art and culture of Southern California throughout the modernist period. (Private Collection. ©1981 Center for Creative Photography, Arizona Board of Regents)

Arensberg, Philip Lovell, Cedric Gibbon, and Galka Scheyer. Soon after their reunion in 1927, Armitage became convinced that Weston's work deserved a monograph that would accurately convey the strength of his photographs to a wider audience. Simply titled, *Edward Weston*, the book became the first American photographic monograph of this early modern period. It is especially significant to the history of Southern California photography that this magnificent project was conceived, designed, and printed in Los Angeles.[59]

By 1932 the monograph was ready to begin production. For some time Armitage and Weston had been working on a selection of prints, but Weston feared that the reproduction quality would not be adequate to impart a sense of the original photograph. Although Weston knew that the cost and labor would be prohibitive, he insisted that the book could be accomplished with original photographs tipped into each copy. In a letter to Armitage, Weston noted that: "Much as I would like a book, I cannot accept the results. Every vestige of photographic quality is gone, they look nothing like my work – harsh, coarse. Sorry. Maybe sometime we can work out a plan to use original prints as discussed."[60]

For Armitage to attempt the production of such an elaborate book in Los Angeles was a daring feat in itself. At this time, very few high quality books were produced on a commercial scale anywhere in the United States outside of New York, the center of American book publishing. Armitage had previously engaged the printing services of Lynton Kistler for a number of quality programs and promotional brochures advertising Armitage's opera and concert events. He believed that Kistler could accomplish the job but he was making a leap of faith. Kistler had never attempted a book of this scale and quality. Armitage once remarked that the Weston book went through the presses, "just ahead of labels for tomato cans, and was followed by circulars for a burlesque show."[61]

Armitage worked closely with Kistler while the book was in production and they suffered through one challenge after another. Armitage had selected a thick glossy paper stock imported from Germany and it presented an enormous problem for Kistler: the black ink would not adhere to the slick surface. Armitage recounted that the problem was solved by a journeyman printer whom Kistler had recently hired. After carefully inspecting the press, the printer poured gasoline on the printing plates and

Figure 20.
Edward Weston. *Ready-Cut Homes, Inc.* Negative: 1925, Print:1954. Gift of Jon. B. Lovelace.

When Weston returned to Southern California from his second trip to Mexico late in 1924, he immediately felt a profound sense of dislocation. Weston detested the number of cheaply constructed homes that were being built around his studio in Tropico. It is not heard to observe the ironic contradiction in his photograph taken at the factory operated by Pacific Ready Cut Homes, a fabricator of instant homes which could be purchased by mail order. (The J. Paul Getty Museum, Los Angeles. ©1981 Center for Creative Photography, Arizona Board of Regents)

lit a match. This act sent Armitage and Kistler running for the fire exits but the printer was unfazed and calmly started the press. After the plates had been warmed by the fire, the ink spread smoothly over the plates and adhered to the paper.[62]

Aside from the design and supervision of the production of Weston's book, Armitage undertook the fundraising for the project. He began this project in the depths of the Depression and even wealthy patrons needed to bc coaxcd into the project. Armitage managed to sell forty copies of the book on a subscription basis of $10 per copy. His greatest triumph was a $500 payment from Southern California art patron Alice Rohrer. Because of this contribution, Armitage wisely determined that the book should be dedicated to Rohrer. Armitage also prevailed on the noted New York bookseller and publisher Erhard Weyhe to put his name on the title page and to purchase fifty copies when the book was printed. Although Weyhe ostensibly appears as the publisher of the book, this was more promotional fiction than economic reality.[63]

Although the Weston monograph of 1932 is acknowledged as a landmark of photographic literature, the market for the book at the time was rather thin. Armitage recalled that he and Weston managed to sell one hundred copies of the five hundred printed, and after a short period, were forced to remainder almost two hundred copies at less than the cost of printing. For many years Weston would sell copies at his studio and Weyhe slowly dispersed copies from his New York bookshop. For Armitage, the project was a labor of love from start to finish and was a concrete example of his respect and admiration for Weston's achievements in modern photography. Armitage vividly remembered delivering the first copies to Weston at his home in Carmel. Weston carefully examined each page of the book, and getting more and more excited as he reached the end, stood up quickly and kissed Armitage on both cheeks.[64]

Promoting Weston's work satisfied an emotional and creative need for Armitage that was stifled by his own self doubts as a creative talent.[65] Weston understood that Armitage was a special person in his life and was the first individual to successfully promote Weston's work on a scale commensurate with the importance of his artwork. Armitage's admiration for both Edward and his son Brett Weston was demonstrated by two additional book projects: 50 Photographs: Edward Weston published in 1947 and Brett Weston published in

1956. Armitage had known Brett since he began to photograph in the late 1920s, and Brett Weston became a celebrated photographer in his own right.

Soon after the publication of the Weston monograph in 1932, Weston acknowledged the important role that Merle Armitage played in his life. Weston wrote to Armitage in 1933:

"You may not be aware, Merle, that you have been a real stimulus in my life. How? Through your response to, your understanding of, my work; which in turn has stimulated me to greater effort,—knowing I have functioned, fulfilled my destiny. No one on my horizon could have done this book as you have done it, Merle; you had vision, initiative, and daring! Others talked about an E.W. book,—but you acted!— and have my gratitude."[66]

EDWARD
WESTON

19 32
NEW YORK E.WEYHE

Figure 22.
Frontispiece illustration and title
page of the first monograph on
Edward Weston. 1932.

Printed, designed, and financed in
Los Angeles in the early 1930s, this
publication is recognized as one of the
first monographs on photography of
the modern era produced in the United
States. The entire project was conceived
and completed due to the diligent effort
of Merle Armitage. (Private Collection)

7

Louis Fleckenstein: The Pictorial Tradition

While the artistic progression of Edward Weston's photography between 1909 and 1927 in Southern California is clearly the major event of these two decades, other photographers influenced and contributed to the development of fine art photography in the region. Chief among the influential photographers from this early period was Louis Fleckenstein. Fleckenstein moved to Los Angeles from Minnesota around 1910 and was the first photographer with established international credentials as a pictorialist to reside in Southern California.[67]

In 1903 Fleckenstein and a fellow photographer from the Midwest, Carl Rau, organized the Salon Club of America, a national network of fine art photographers with the express purpose of distributing and sharing work among photographers throughout the United States. The Salon Club was established to provide a forum for younger pictorialists to share their work among a group of peers and to elicit criticism that would advance their work. Fleckenstein also prevailed upon Curtis Bell of the Metropolitan Camera Club in New York to organize a group of the most active clubs into a new organization known as the American Federation of Photographic Societies.

The fervor for fine art photography which had stimulated Fleckenstein to action resulted in the organization of the First American Photographic Salon held in New York City in December of 1904. This exhibition traveled to a number of cities in the United States and was responsible for an enormous growth in camera clubs and salon exhibitions in the United States during the first decade of the twentieth century. Another important development influenced by the First American Salon was the establishment of Alfred Stieglitz's first gallery in New York to show work produced by his chosen circle of photographers organized under the group known as the Photo-Secession. Stieglitz objected to the broad selection of work in the First American Salon and strove for a more refined definition of fine art photography demonstrated by the members of the Photo-Secession.[68]

Photographers such as Edward Weston, Margrethe Mather and a handful of others must have viewed Fleckenstein's arrival in Los Angeles as a watershed event. While documents and events suggest that Edward Weston was the initial driving force behind the organization of the Camera Pictorialists of Los Angeles in 1914, Fleckenstein's arrival in Southern California most certainly stimulated a small but active group of

Figure 24.
Louis Fleckenstein. *Mountain Ranges.*
Circa 1915.

Fleckenstein's most influential Southern
California photography was accomplished while an active member in the
Camera Pictorialists of Los Angeles
between 1914 and 1922. This compressed view of the undulating curves
of the San Gabriel Mountain range suggest the influence of the compositional
philosophy of Arthur Wesley Dow
which had been evident in the work
produced by Alvin Langdon Coburn
several years earlier. (The J. Paul Getty
Museum, Los Angeles)

Figure 25.
Louis Fleckenstein. *The Castaways*.
Circa 1915.

———————

Fleckenstein combined four different
negatives to produce this evocative
image of three figures enveloped in
a dreamlike California landscape. The
intersecting lines and curves of the
photograph draws the viewer into the
composition creating both a representation and an abstraction of the
landscape depicted. (The J. Paul Getty
Museum, Los Angeles)

photographers to come together and reach for a higher level of achievement and recognition than the work exhibited in the First Los Angeles Photographic Salon of 1902. Fleckenstein is listed as the head of the Camera Pictorialists at the time the group organized its First International Photographic Salon in 1918. Fleckenstein most likely assumed control of the organization when Edward Weston and Margrethe Mather resigned from active participation in the club sometime in 1916 or 1917. Fleckenstein remained as chairman of the club until the end of 1922 and oversaw the organization of annual salons. Fleckenstein's involvement in the club seems to have waned after 1922 but he returned to exhibiting and serving as a juror in the salons in the late 1920s through the early 1930s.[69]

Fleckenstein's most influential Southern California photography was accomplished while he was an active member in the Camera Pictorialists of Los Angeles between 1914 and 1922. Shortly after his arrival in Los Angeles around 1910, Fleckenstein established a portrait studio in downtown Los Angeles. Existing photographs suggest that Fleckenstein enjoyed some success photographing children, Los Angeles socialites, and performing artists who desired a photograph stamped with the distinctive logo, "Portrayed by Fleckenstein." In 1924 Fleckenstein accepted the position as the first Arts Commissioner of Long Beach, prompting a move to that city and a decrease in his involvement in the Southern California community of fine art photographers.

While Fleckenstein's photography never exhibited a radical departure from his roots in pictorialism, the California landscape pushed his photography away from overworked allegorical narratives to a level of subtle abstraction. An interesting example of this transformation is evident in the photograph *Mountain Ranges*, produced around 1915 (Fig.24). This compressed view of the undulating curves of the San Gabriel Mountain range suggest the influence of the compositional philosophy of Arthur Wesley Dow. The photograph shows no evidence of handwork or manipulation during the printing process. This abstract composition of flattened perspective is constructed through the use of a telephoto lens and the smoothly graded tonalities produced by light, shadow, and atmospheric distance. Dow's philosophy of composition emphasized the expression of form over allegorical content in the search for a profound aesthetic experience. Fleckenstein's experiments with this

strategy of representation moved his photography away from the deeply sentimental and allegorical compositions of his early years towards a more modernist vision.

Somewhat more complex in terms of its construction is the photograph *The Castaways*, 1918 (Fig.25). Fleckenstein combined four different negatives to produce this evocative image of three figures enveloped in a dreamlike Southern California landscape. The figures are dressed in the traditional hiking costume of the period and suggest the evocative openness of the Southern California landscape that was a consistent subject of fine art photographers of this period. The intersecting lines and curves of Fleckenstein's photograph draw us deeper into the composition creating both a recognizable representation and an abstraction of the landscape depicted.

Fleckenstein also appears to be one of the few fine art photographers in Southern California who found affinity with Charles Lummis as a photographer. Fleckenstein's photograph of Lummis and an unidentified friend taken in the living room of Lummis' home in the Arroyo Seco around 1918 articulates Fleckenstein's fascination with Western artifacts as well as the relaxed demeanor of Lummis himself (Fig.26). Fleckenstein created an exciting pattern of rhythmic fragmentation through the incorporation of a series of Navajo rugs laid on the floor and through the asymmetrical view he composed using the walls of the home and the placement of the figures. Fleckenstein's arrival in Southern California stimulated him to produce photographs that were more progressive and experimental in nature. Conversely, his stature as a pictorialist photographer stimulated a small community of Southern California workers to refine their vision as fine art photographers.

Figure 26.
Louis Fleckenstein. *Charles Lummis Playing a Guitar*. Circa 1915.

Fleckenstein appears to be one of the few fine art photographers in Southern California who interacted with Charles Lummis as a fellow photographer. Fleckenstein's image of Lummis taken in the living room of Lummis' home in the Arroyo Seco articulates Fleckenstein's fascination with western artifacts and the relaxed dress and demeanor of the man himself. (The J. Paul Getty Museum, Los Angeles)

8

Fred Archer: A Southern California Innovator

Fred Archer was representative of fine art photographers in Southern California and was without a doubt the individual with the longest history of participation in the Southern California Salon movement (Fig.27). Raised in Los Angeles, Archer was the youngest member of the Camera Pictorialists of Los Angeles at its founding in 1914. Archer participated in the Arts and Crafts exhibition organized by Edward Weston in 1916 and exhibited work in twenty-eight of the thirty-one salons organized by the club between 1918 and 1950. Archer was also only individual to maintain membership in the organization during its entire thirty-six years of existence.

Archer's dedication to photography can be explained in part by the fact that he grew up in the photography business. His father originally had a commercial studio and later started a camera manufacturing and repair shop. It was in this environment that Archer developed his technical expertise with camera, lens, and darkroom techniques that he would continue to refine throughout his career. After military service as an aerial photographer in World War I, Archer returned to Southern California in 1919 and obtained a job with Universal Pictures in the art title department. Archer soon became head of the department and is credited with pioneering the use of photographic backgrounds for motion picture titles as well as the use of animation in title sequences.

Archer left Universal in 1924 to work with Cecil B. DeMille's production company where he became head of the art title, still photography, and portrait departments. Archer departed from the film industry in 1935 to become a faculty member of the Art Center School in Los Angeles during the late 1930s. In 1948, Archer's only book, *Fred Archer On Portraiture*, was published. This popular text remained in print for a number of years. By the mid 1940s, Archer had established his own school of photography near downtown Los Angeles that he ran successfully until his retirement in the late1950s.[70]

Like many professional photographers of his generation, Archer viewed his artistic practice as a passionate hobby that helped him relax from the pressure and routine of his commercial life. Archer's earliest photographs are finely crafted, soft-focused landscapes of Southern California which were admired in many international salons of the period, including the prestigious London Salon where Archer exhibited his first photographs as early as 1914.[71] During the 1920s, Archer

Figure 27.
Edward Weston. *Portrait of Fred Archer.*
Circa 1919.

————————

Fred Archer was a well-known fine art
photographer in Southern California
with a long history of participation in
the regional salon movement. (Special
Collections, Frances Howard Goldwyn
Hollywood Regional Branch Library.
©1981 Center for Creative Photography,
Arizona Board of Regents)

exhibited a number of compositions utilizing small-
scale models built for motion pictures. Archer
used these models and combined them with
photographs of actors and actresses dressed in
costumes to create dramatic narrative photographs
which were well received in the salon exhibitions
of the period. He became particularly well known
for a sequence of photographs based on stories
from *The Arabian Nights*.

Archer's most lasting contribution to American
fine art photography was a series of light abstractions made without a camera that he produced in
the late 1920s (Fig.28).[72] Archer apparently utilized
a small pane of glass that reflected light directly
onto a sheet of unexposed photographic paper.
As Archer moved the glass in various angles and
directions, the reflected light created striking compositions. As these images were made without the
use of photographic negatives, each print is a
unique and distinctive image. Sometime in the late
1930s, Archer again utilized his skills of model
making and multiple printing to create a futuristic
composition describing the mechanics of photography (Fig.29). Archer created a dense juxtaposion
of laboratory equipment, mannequins, and photographs illustrating the various stages of the
photographic process from the exposure of the
negative to the development of the print. This
unusual composition may have been used as an
early advertisement for his photography school.

These two examples of Archer's work demonstrate his intellectual and technical range, but
unfortunately, he never returned to these techniques with any consistency or commitment. Like
other talented photographers who were his
colleagues in the Camera Pictorialists of Los
Angeles, the range of his artistic vision was
hampered by his view of this activity as primarily
recreational. While Archer and his colleagues continued to refine their technical skills as professional
photographers, their intellectual and artistic development were restrained by the lack of a sustained
approach to the medium which was personal and
non-commercial in nature. This pragmatic view
of artistic practice as a form of recreation and
relaxation was particularly dominant among the
membership of the Camera Pictorialists from the
late 1930s until the club's demise in 1950.

9

Anne Brigman: Member of the Photo-Secession

Anne Brigman, a photographer who maintained a consistent artistic vision throughout her lifetime, was one of the most famous pictorialist photographers living in California. During the first decades of the twentieth century, Brigman resided in Northern California. In 1902, she first began exhibiting Sierra Nevada landscapes of human figures intertwined with stark, windblown trees. The emotional impact and mysterious quality of her photographs created an immediate impact at the Second San Francisco Photographic Salon in January of 1902, and by 1903 Brigman was included in the elite membership of Alfred Stieglitz's Photo-Secession group. Stieglitz included Brigman's work in all of the Photo-Secession exhibitions organized at his New York gallery through 1908 after which his attention shifted towards the promotion of modern European painting and sculpture.[73] This inclusion as a Photo-Secession member was a unique status for a California photographer.

With few variations, Brigman's aesthetic vision and subject matter remained consistent until she moved to Southern California in 1929. After settling in the Long Beach area, Brigman began a series of photographs of the shifting sands along the ocean shore. By 1931 she had developed a small group of these images that possess a stark, poetic abstraction of a natural form. These photographs differ from her Sierra Nevada images through a concentrated focus on the tones and patterns of eroded sand and a specific lack of symbolic or allegorical narrative (Fig.30).

In a revealing article that Brigman wrote for the California magazine *Camera Craft*, she documented the debates taking place during the judging of the Camera Pictorialists' International Salon of 1930. Although her own work had shifted from pictorialist symbolism to more modernist modes of representation, Brigman found it disconcerting that the jury preferred modernist studies of pattern and form at the expense of narrative compositions.

"I believe on my soul that I have been guilty of very little 'sweet stuff' in my twenty-five years as a worker with the camera in the high mountain wilds; I dare to call the gentlest of them 'Hardy romances'—but this Jury—and they were an up and coming, clean cut, intelligent bunch, had their six shooters out. I turned and looked at Karl Struss in the semi-darkness, after a vote of three 'no's' had swept away some lovely landscapes. Karl Struss smiled his good old boyish smile and said slowly, 'The no's have it, Anne'"[74]

Figure 30.
Anne Brigman. *Sand Erosion*. 1931.

After settling in the Long Beach area
to be closer to her sisters and her ailing
mother, Brigman began a series of
photographs in the shifting sands
along the ocean shore. By 1931 she
had developed a small group of these
images which possess a stark, poetic
abstraction of a natural form. (The
Wilson Center for Photography)

Figure 31.
Anne Brigman. *Intaglio*. 1931.

Brigman's Long Beach photographs
differ from her Sierra Nevada images
through a concentrated focus on the
tones and patterns of eroded sand and
a specific lack of symbollic or allegorical narrative. (Courtesy George Eastman
House)

The divergence between Brigman's latter work
and her Sierra Nevada compositions, done
between 1905 and 1925, was successfully
resolved in her 1949 publication *Songs of a
Pagan*. After moving to Southern California,
Brigman began writing poetry under the tutelage
of Helen Mathews.[75] After taking up the craft of
poetry, Brigman's photographs lost much of the
symbolic and allegorical content that typified the
work of her early and middle years. Brigman
adopted a sparse and more resolutely abstract
approach to photography both in terms of subject
matter and composition. *Songs of a Pagan* articulated Brigman's realization that her photographs
were at last most clearly defined and made more
profoundly resonant through a marriage of text and
image. Paired with one of her abstract compositions of water and sand taken near her home in
Long Beach, Brigman writes:

> I dimly dream of the time to come
> When I shall stand free
> In a world of forgotten glories…
> Enfolded in garments
> As soft as the breath of the wind from the south
> Woven of light and mist…
> And lovely in line as a broken wave's smooth flow.[76]

Brigman's sense of loneliness, loss, and resolution
finally reached a conclusive form in this partnership
of word and image. Like the photographs of Louis
Fleckenstein, Brigman's work never embraced the
full impact of modernist photography. Nevertheless,
in her later years in Southern California, her photographs formulated a level of subtle abstraction free
of allegorical narrative, suggesting that her work
continued to be influenced by contemporary
debates concerning fine art photography. Brigman's
closest links to these debates were her friends in
the Camera Pictorialists of Los Angeles.

10

The Camera Pictorialists of Los Angeles: Linking Pictorialist and Modernist Practice in Photography

While it is possible to trace the individual creative direction of a few photographers like Louis Fleckenstein, Fred Archer and Anne Brigman, the development of fine art photography produced in Southern California between 1916 and 1940 must be viewed though the ongoing activities of the Camera Pictorialists of Los Angeles. Between 1918 and 1950 the Camera Pictorialists organized thirty-one international exhibitions of photography.

The success and longevity of the Los Angeles salons are due in large part to the enthusiastic leadership and diligent efforts of a revolving core of active members. Critical to this success however, was the longstanding support of the curatorial and administrative staff of the Los Angeles County Museum of Art that hosted and promoted all of the salon exhibitions between 1918 and 1947.

This continuity of venue provided a consistent audience for the exhibitions and established a high level of credibility among the photographers who sent their work for inclusion in the exhibitions. In 1922, the museum provided an additional level of support for the salons through the annual purchase of a small number of prints shown.[77] These acquisitions were both a farsighted recognition that photography had entered the realm of fine art and that a group of Los Angeles photographers were aware of and in touch with the finest practitioners in the medium. The majority of acquisitions were European photographers well established in the pictorialist tradition, but in 1932, the museum purchased works by Imogen Cunningham, Edward Weston and a small group of Japanese-American photographers.[78]

The antecedents of the annual salons began with the first exhibition of the Camera Pictorialists organized by Edward Weston in conjunction with the First Annual Arts and Crafts Salon in 1916. The membership of the club had a substantial turnover between 1916 and 1918, with only six of the original fifteen members still active when the First International Salon opened in January 1918. Edward Weston and Margrethe Mather may have left due to philosophical and aesthetic differences, while other photographers may not have shared the enthusiasm for the amount of work involved in annual exhibitions. The success of the first exhibition ensured that the salons would become an annual event.[79]

By the time of the Fifth International Salon in December 1921, the Camera Pictorialists had captured the attention of the leading photographers on both a national and international level. The Los Angeles salons established a consistently high standard of quality and were keenly attuned to the tension between the philosophy of pictorialism and a growing impulse to define art photography within the tenets of modernism. The rigor of this exhibition was established with the inclusion of Edward Weston and Karl Struss as jurors. The exhibition included work by Weston's compatriots Johan Hagemayer and Margrethe Mather. Weston also made a rare contribution of four prints to the salon, including a portrait of Italian photographer, Tina Modotti as well as one of his cubist abstractions, *The Ascent of Attic Angles.*[80]

While most of the salons up to this date had received favorable press coverage, the Fifth International Salon transmitted the idea that photography was indeed an art form to reckon with and was a visual language that spoke to its audience in a direct and visceral manner. Typical of the press coverage of this exhibition was the enthusiastic support of R.W. Borough writing for the *Los Angeles Record:*

> "If you want to hold onto your preconceived notions about the inflexibility of the camera, stay away from the exhibit. What these photographers are doing will shock and thrill you to the core."[81]

The Fifth International Salon marked a maturity in philosophy and organization for the group. While this exhibition was a high point of innovation for the club, and indeed for fine art photography on a national level, the Camera Pictorialists continued to organize juried exhibitions that balanced tradition and innovation with a consistent attention to professionalism in the design and promotion of the annual events. This attention to detail earned respect among photographers because the salons were the only venue for photographers to exhibit their work during the 1920s and 1930s (with the exception of several galleries that dared to exhibit photography as art.)[82]

Much of the vision demonstrated by the Camera Pictorialists in the 1920s can be attributed to the energy of John Stick. Typical of the fine art photographer of the period, Stick earned a living outside the realm of commercial photography. Stick was a practicing attorney, yet he devoted a tremendous amount of energy towards the promotion of fine art photography. In addition to his involvement in the annual salons, Stick was responsible for the design and printing of a small journal known as

Figure 32.
John Stick. *The Bathers.* Circa 1920.

Typical of the fine art photographer of the pictorialist era, Stick earned a living outside the realm of commercial photography. His photography is representative of a transitional period in fine art photography which had moved away from the heavily mani-pulated print popular during the first two decades of the twentieth century. Stick, like many of his contemporaries, continued to value a softness of image created by the use of a camera lens designed to diffuse the optical precision of the scene depicted. (Dennis and Amy Reed Collection)

The Pictorialist. Begun in 1924 and running for at least several issues, the magazine developed a dialogue among photographers who exhibited at the annual salons but who lived at distances which precluded their involvement in local Camera Pictorialist meetings and events.

The few examples remaining of Stick's own photographic work are representative of a transitional period in fine art photography which had moved away from the heavily manipulated gum print or retouched negative, popular during the first two decades of the twentieth century. Like Stick, many photographers continued to value a softness of image created by the use of a camera lens designed to diffuse the optical precision of the scene depicted. Stick's photograph from the early 1920s, *The Bathers*, uses a softness of focus to concentrate the viewer's attention on the formal qualities of the image created by the movement of the surf and the shifting sensation of tone and mass created by a sense of flattened perspective (Fig.32). This genre of landscape work was especially prevalent in California photography of this period. The subtlety of Stick's composition as a representative California landscape is enhanced by a dreamlike abstraction of its formal qualities. By carefully balancing this tension between literalness and abstraction, Stick creates multiple avenues of approach to this photograph.

By 1930, a distinctly modernist approach began to dominate the scope and direction of the International Salons organized by the Camera Pictorialists. Under the steady influence of Will Connell, Karl Struss, Fred Dapprich, and James Doolittle, the club made a conscious effort to embrace the impulse toward sharp focus compositions, radical camera angles, and still-life photographs of manufactured or organic objects highlighted by new approaches to lighting and design. Typical of these new approaches is Lynton Vinette's still-life *Trilogy* (Fig.33). In this composition, Vinette explores compositional possibilities by using small gourds positioned against a cone-shaped background. The photograph is lit from a sharp angle to create multiple patterns of light and shadow. This photograph was created around 1932 when Vinette became active in the Camera Pictorialists.

By 1930, the driving force behind the Camera Pictorialists was no longer the sophisticated amateur typified by John Stick, but commercial photographers like Connell, Dapprich, and Doolittle. Doolittle's introduction to the Thirteenth International Salon of Photography held in 1930 makes clear that the Camera Pictorialists wanted to move the dialogue on fine art photography to a new register:

"If, in this year's offering, the organization seems to have shown fewer of what may be termed 'pretty pictures,' it is due to no lack of the appreciation of the beauty which well reflected the point of view of other years but by a recognition of beauty in things seldom pictured or by a newer treatment of conventional subject matter. This year are shown fewer prints than in previous salons notwithstanding the constancy in number of entries but this is merely the working out of a determination to present photography which shall reflect the point of view of today. No avenue of progress is open along the well-traveled road of yesterday."[83]

The Camera Pictorialists strident approach to new visions in the medium spread quickly among California's modernist photographers. The Fourteenth International Salon contained work by Imogen Cunningham, Sonya Noskowiak, Willard Van Dyke, as well as Brett and Edward Weston. This period of advanced modernist practice in California within the "salon" environment suggested a brief but fruitful interaction between the artistically inclined photographers of Northern California and the commercially based practitioners from Southern California. A letter from Edward Weston to Will Connell discussing the 1931 salon catalogue suggests ongoing differences between the regional approaches to photography, but acknowledges a shared goal in moving the photographic discourse towards a new horizon.

"The presentation of work is ahead of the American annuals I have known… I can't agree with all selections but I know your answer. I would never have ordered the book from prospectus sent out: awful selections-though Doolittle's 'ad' clever. You have gone a step ahead…"[84]

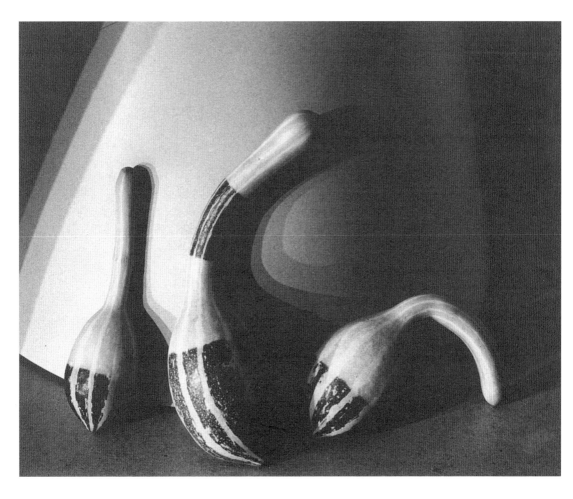

Figure 33.
Lynton Vinette. *Trilogy*. Circa 1932.

By 1930, a distinctly modernist
approach began to dominate the scope
and direction of the International
Salons organized by the Camera
Pictorialists of Los Angeles. The club
made a conscious effort to embrace the
impulse toward sharp focus compositions, radical camera angles, and still
life photographs of manufactured or
organic objects highlighted by new
approaches to lighting and design.
(Dennis and Amy Reed Collection)

11

Karl Struss: Hollywood Cinematographer and Fine Art Photographer

Karl Struss' reputation as a fine art photographer and successful cinematographer in Hollywood added prestige and influence to the Camera Pictorialists reputation during this period of change and innovation between 1928 and 1932. Struss' involvement with fine art photography began in 1908 when he was a student of New York photographer Clarence White.[85] By 1910, Struss' somber, mysterious landscapes and finely composed portraits attracted the attention of Alfred Stieglitz, who included Struss' work in the juried section of the International Exhibition of Pictorial Photography at the Albright Art Gallery in Buffalo, New York.[86] Between 1910 and 1912, Struss associated with the elite group of photographers in Stieglitz's Photo-Secession group, including Alvin Langdon Coburn and Gertrude Käsebier. In 1912, Struss became the last photographer admitted to the Photo-Secession and in April of the same year, a selection of his photographs was featured in *Camera Work*.[87]

Karl Struss arrived in Southern California in 1919 determined to break into the thriving Hollywood motion picture industry. His knowledge of the technical aspects of photography combined with a refined aesthetic sense of the medium soon propelled him from still photographer to leading cinematographer with Cecil D. De Mille. In 1929 Struss and Charles Rosher shared the first Academy Award in Cinematography for their work on F.W. Murnau's film *Sunrise—A Song of Two Humans*. For over forty years, Struss continued to work as a cinematographer, completing one hundred forty six films over the course of his career.[88]

Despite his hectic schedule as a cinematographer, Struss continued to exhibit regularly in the European and American pictorialist salons of the 1920s and 1930s. Struss' work during this period generally lacks the innovation and rigor of his New York period but there are some distinct exceptions. His composition *Sails: En Route to Catalina* taken in 1929, was widely exhibited and reflects much of the innovative style championed by the Camera Pictorialists of this period (Fig.34). Struss' disruptive use of the mast, rigging, and sails bisecting the broad horizon of the ocean creates a taut and lively composition.

This experimental composition reflects Struss' close attention to his still photography during the late 1920s and early 1930s, when he was also an active participant in the salon exhibitions co-ordinated by the Camera Pictorialists. Struss was a firm believer in the pictorialist ideals of

Figure 34.
Karl Struss. *Sails Enroute To Catalina*. 1929.

Despite his hectic schedule as a cinematographer, Struss continued to exhibit regularly in the European and American pictorialist salons of the 1920s and 1930s. This experimental composition reflects Struss' close attention to his still photography during this period when he was also an active participant in the salon exhibitions co-ordinated by the Camera Pictorialists. (Courtesy Paul Kopeikin Gallery*)*

photography. He rejected the notion of "pure photography" championed by Ansel Adams, Edward Weston and other adherents of the Northern California f/64 movement.[89] The f/64 movement was a direct reaction to the continued strength of pictorial photography in California. Adherents to the f/64 philosophy believed that fine art photographs should reflect an unmediated approach between the subject/object photographed and the optical precision inherent in the medium of photography. It was their belief that manipulation of the negative or print destroyed the true impact of artistic photography.[90]

Struss, however, was no stranger to innovations in photography. Struss brought an important sense of balance to the Camera Pictorialists who were moving rapidly towards an embrace of modern photography championed primarily by Will Connell, James Doolitte, and Fred Dapprich. Struss was almost twenty years older than the other directors of the club and was the only member to exhibit at the highest levels of the photography salons in America and Europe before coming to Hollywood. He had personally observed the aesthetic shifts in fine art photography since the early twentieth century. While not opposed to new approaches to photography, Struss was not as influenced by the modernist excess for unusual camera angles and dramatic lighting as were other members of the Camera Pictorialists. His participation added refinement to the quality of modernist work that was included in the important salons of the early 1930s. The delicate balance between innovation and tradition is the hallmark of the Camera Pictorialist salons of the early 1930s, a distinction that brought the Club international attention and influence during this period.

The innovations championed by the Camera Pictorialists in this era were the last substantive contributions the club made to the changing discourse of fine art photography and indeed may have been the last salon exhibitions of critical importance held in the United States.[91] The success of the 1932 Los Angeles salon may have precipitated an invitation by Lloyd LaPage Rollins to exhibit the 1933 salon at the DeYoung Museum in San Francisco.[92] Rollins, as director of the museum, was responsible for showing photography produced by members of the f/64 group during this same period.

By 1932, only Fred Archer remained active in the Camera Pictorialists from the original founding members of 1914. The dynamic shift of influence

in the Club, which changed from sophisticated amateur to multi-talented commercial photographer, was the last major development the club was to undergo. While the Camera Pictorialists were able to organize innovative and dynamic exhibitions during the Depression in the early 1930s, the effects of the economic crisis drained the energy and variety from photography shown in the Los Angeles salons by the mid-1930s. The outbreak of conflicts in Europe by the late 1930s further drained the salons of European work and only a few sporadic salons were held during the years of World War II. By the late 1940s, the small but energetic discourse of fine art photography had shifted to private art schools and university art departments stimulated by the unprecedented enrollment of students pursuing their education through the G.I. Bill. The main tenet of post-war fine art photography was an emphasis on personal expression and a rejection of commercialism in the medium.[93]

In his insightful introduction to the last Salon of Photography organized by the Camera Pictorialists in January of 1950, Will Connell highlights the crucial contribution the Camera Pictorialists made to the medium while simultaneously imparting the sad recognition that the salon tradition had outlived its importance.

"For almost the whole of the first quarter of the century, the Salon was the one great tool by which the insurgent photographer could exert leverage on both the public and the photographic mind, in his effort to prove that here was a medium by which an artist could speak. By the mid-twenties this fight had been pretty much won. It not only was all right for a photograph to look like a photograph, but it had been proven that an individual could express himself through the medium with all the artistry of approach and clearness of statement that would be afforded by any of the arts... But to some people the Salon has now become, apparently, a grading ground on which the tyro seeks a mark: A, B, C, or F minus."[94]

12

Japanese-American Photographers: A New Direction for Fine Art Photography

Will Connell noted that by the mid-1920s, photography achieved some respect as a fine art among art critics and the general public. One of the most profound transitions, which occurred during photography's shift from a pictorialist to modernist aesthetic, was stimulated by a group of Japanese-American photographers based in the Pacific Coast cities of Seattle, San Francisco, and Los Angeles. These photographers led the pictorialist movement away from the stifling confines of sentimental, symbolic, and allegorical formulas in portrait and landscape photography towards what was phrased at the time as "abstract pictorialism." [95]

The Japanese-American photographers replaced the sentimental aesthetics of pictorialist practice yet worked within the similar genres of still-life compositions, landscape photographs, and portrait work. The Japanese-American aesthetic differed tremendously from pictorialist representation in that it was highly influenced by the sumi-e tradition in painting composed in shades of black and gray using varying dilutions of ink. This tradition, embraced by photographers, placed an emphasis on simple compositions of line and tonality that encouraged a quiet emotive response to the atmosphere suggested by the image. [96]

Los Angeles, more than San Francisco and Seattle, was viewed as the center of activity for Japanese-Americans both in terms of the number of photographers and the innovative nature of the work produced. [97] The Japanese Camera Pictorialists of California was formed in 1923 but became more active as an organization several years later. Although the title of the organization suggested a broad base of membership throughout the state, all of the members lived and worked in the Los Angeles area. Almost all of the twenty-six charter members of the club were immigrants from Japan, however, many of the photographers returned to their homeland before the outbreak of World War II.

Unlike many of the Anglo photographers active in the Camera Pictorialists of Los Angeles, very few of the Japanese photographers earned a living in commercial photography. The economic and cultural barriers made if more difficult, if not impossible, for the Japanese-American photographer to enter the commercial arena. Conversely, the time they spent with photography was devoted to refining their artistic vision free from commercialism. The founder and undisputed leader of the Japanese Camera Pictorialists was Kaye Shimojima, who insisted that each member of the club have a thorough understanding of photography and be able to make all of his own photographic prints. Club members engaged in lengthy critiques of each other's work and would often experiment with similar compositions to explore subtle differences in approach and technique.

While not all Japanese-American photographers working in Los Angeles were associated with the Japanese Camera Pictorialists, most of the active photographers knew each other and contributed work to the various salon exhibitions sponsored in the Japanese community. Typical of the range of work produced in Southern California during the late 1920s and early 1930s are the photographs by Hiromu Kira, A. Kono, and T. K. Shindo. These photographs share an experimental vision combined with a thorough knowledge of the craft of photography (Fig.35, 36). By 1928, the work of Japanese-American photographers from Los Angeles had reached the salons of the East Coast and Europe and was reproduced in such prestigious publications as Photograms of the Year and Pictorial Photography in America.

Leading photographers of the period such as F. J. Mortimer acknowledged the powerful rupture that the Japanese-Americans had created in the world of pictorial photography. Initially, photographers such as Mortimer referred to the new camera angles, subtle tonal gradations, and repetitive compositional patterns as "stunt pictures" although they ultimately recognized that the Japanese-American influence had helped to reinvigorate the pictorialist movement. Mortimer acknowledged in 1928:

"A greater appreciation of the value of design and decorative pattern, as well as a better feeling for placing, may also be attributed to this influence. It may be conceded that most of these eccentricities did possess a vitality and force that was peculiarly compelling in its intensity, and, while other features may have been repellent to worshippers of beauty or the champions of traditional form, the true pictorialist was quick to analyze their appeal..."[98]

The outbreak of war with Japan in 1941 put a definitive end to the photographic activities of the Japanese-American photographers. War hysteria forced the internment of all people of Japanese ancestry living on the Pacific Coast. This had a catastrophic impact on these communities and, in particular, they suffered the loss of most of the original photographs produced by this innovative group of photographers. While a few of the photographs were preserved in institutional collections and small holdings were safely stored for the duration of World War II, the majority of the photographs exist only as reproductions in various photographic publications of the period.

Figure 35.
Hiromu Kira. *Curves*. Circa 1930.

One of the most profound transitions which occurred during photography's shift from a pictorialist to a modernist aesthetic was stimulated by a group of Japanese-American photographers based in the Pacific Coast cities of Seattle, San Francisco, and Los Angeles. These photographers led the pictorialist movement away from the stifling confines of sentimental, symbolic, and allegorical formulas in portrait and landscape photography towards what was phrased at the time as "abstract pictorialism". Los Angeles photographer Hiromo Kira was at the vanguard of this movement. (Dennis Reed Collection)

13

Will Connell: Photography and the Gentle Art of Thinking

"Los Angeles is a city that has conquered the impossible, done the inconceivable, produced the remarkable and, she has been proud, justly and without restraint. Take photography for instance. Here are Will Connell and a host of other artists who have tied pictorial to commercial and mechanical to art. Are not these names worthy of a city that chooses not to hide its light under a bushel?" Sigismund Blumann, 1931[99]

Aside from Edward Weston, only Will Connell was involved in a highly varied group of intellectual and artistic circles. Connell's work not only bridges the shift of fine art photography from pictorialism to modernism, but also makes a transition from the intellectual communities of the art world to the practice of commercial photography.

Will Connell was born in 1898 in McPherson, Kansas where his father was a cowboy and his mother was a school teacher. The family moved to the Oklahoma Territory when Connell was a small child. Several years later they moved to Oregon where Connell's father abandoned his wife and young son. His mother moved to Los Angeles in 1914 where Connell attended high school during World War I. In 1918, Connell dropped out of school with the intention of joining the recently formed U.S. Army Air Service of the Signal Corp. He had a strong desire to be a pilot but before he could complete his training, the war was over and his squadron was never sent to Europe. After his discharge from the Army, Connell went to work at a drugstore where he held a variety of jobs which included helping the pharmacist. He soon knew enough about chemistry to pass the state exams for a pharmacist's license. A man of quirky sensibilities, Connell kept his certification as a pharmacist up to date even though he never worked in the profession.[100]

Connell's interest in photography dates back to 1910 when his grandmother gave him a Brownie camera. Soon after his flirtation with pharmacology, Connell went to work in a camera and photographic supply store. Combining his existing knowledge of chemistry with an awareness of lenses, cameras and other equipment, Connell began to consider a career as a professional photographer. At this time he was deeply influenced by the soft-focused landscapes and portraits he observed in the exhibitions held by the Southern California Camera Club and the Camera Pictorialists of Los Angeles, and he studied such publications as *Camera Craft*, *Photo-Era*, *American Annual of Photography and*

Camera Work. Connell began to immerse himself in photography, taking long excursions by motorcycle or car to various scenic locations in the desert, mountain and beach areas of Southern California.

Much of Connell's early photography was either lost or destroyed over the years. A few surviving lists indicate that by 1926 Connell was successfully exhibiting his photographs in several of the most prestigious East Coast and Canadian salons.[101] Concurrent with his drive to achieve recognition in the arena of fine art photography, Connell had committed himself to succeeding as a commercial photographer by quitting his job in the photographic supply business. Many years later Connell confirmed his happiness with his career choice when he stated in his typical deadpan style: "I am a photographer because for me photography is the most satisfactory way of talking to people. It's commercial photography because I also like to eat."[102]

One of Connell's earliest clients was the Los Angeles booster organization known as The All Year Club funded by the Los Angeles Chamber of Commerce. The All Year Club was created to entice tourists to Southern California during every season of the year. Connell's soft-focused views of the mountains, deserts and beaches of Southern California appeared in many of the brochures and magazines published under the All Year Club's imprint. These photographs are also strong examples of fine art photography in a pictorialist vein that exhibited a distinctive California style. This style is characterized by a lack of extensive manipulation or reworking of the negative or print in favor of simple compositions of light and shadow with wide vistas emphasizing the gentle contours of the California landscape. Such photographs as *Coast at the Foot of Topanga Canyon*, and *San Jacinto* could function successfully as fine art photographs in the world of the pictorialist salon and as successful commercial products on the pages of an All Year Club brochure (Fig.37, 38).

Connell's association with Phil Townsend Hanna provides an insight into the varied activities of Southern California's small circle of intellectuals and artists who seamlessly interchanged their commercial and artistic goals. Hanna was editor of *Touring Topics* magazine and something of a serious photographer himself. A regular feature of the monthly magazine was a rotogravure section touting a mountain, desert or coastal vista in California from the camera of a photographer of note. *Touring Topics* was a publication of the

Figure 37.
Will Connell. *Coast at the Foot of Topanga Canyon*. 1926. Department of Special Collections, Charles E. Young Research Library, UCLA.

By 1920, Connell began to immerse himself in photography, taking long excursions by motorcycle or car to various scenic locations in Southern California. At this time he was deeply influenced by the landscape and portraits he observed in the exhibitions held by the Camera Pictorialists of Los Angeles as well as the careful study of such publications as *Camera Craft*, *Photo-Era*, *American Annual of Photography* and *Camera Work*.

Figure 38.
Will Connell. *San Jacinto*. 1928.

Connell's soft focused views of the
mountains, deserts, and beaches of
Southern California functioned successfully as fine art photographs in the
world of the pictorialist salons and as
successful commercial products on the
pages of magazines and brochures
promoting the scenic wonders of the
region to potential tourists and residents
from the mid-west and east coast.
(Department of Special Collections,
Charles E. Young Research Library, UCLA)

Automobile Club of Southern California; thus every effort was made to get the reader into his car and out on the road. Connell became a regular contributor to *Touring Topics* by 1928 and appears to have solidified a strong friendship with Hanna. Hanna was also a member of the Camera Pictorialists of Los Angeles and no doubt become aware of the strength of Connell's photographic work through this association.

Phil Hanna can also be credited with introducing Will Connell to Los Angeles book dealer Jake Zeitlin. Hanna first met Zeitlin in the rare book department at the Bullock's Department Store sometime in 1926. Because of a noticeable lack of gathering places for a small but emerging arts community, Zeitlin's shop immediately became a focal point for local writers, painters, photographers, graphic designers and architects.

Sometime during his early association with Zeitlin, Connell began an informal series of portrait studies that he termed "Swell Photographs" (Fig.39). These early portraits were generally taken in Connell's studio, where the sitter was provided with an assortment of props and positioned against a backdrop depicting fragments of an eighteenth century English landscape painting. The style and presentation of these portraits on Connell's custom-printed mounts is a direct parody of the nineteenth century cabinet card portrait easily obtainable from any commercial photographer of the period. The way in which Connell parodies the cabinet card while simultaneously reinventing its functionality as a sophisticated business card beautifully illuminates his dual interest in photography as artistic expression and commercial endeavor. These photographs also provide one of the few sources of visual documentation of this nascent group of Los Angeles intellectuals and artists who embraced the spirit of modernism in literature, painting, photography and the performing arts. Members of this community included Merle Armitage, writers Carey McWilliams, Louis Adamic, Paul Jordan Smith, and Jose Rodriguez, as well as the artist Grace Marion Brown, and architects Lloyd Wright and Kem Weber.

Connell's involvement with the Zeitlin group parallels increased experimentation in his work beginning in 1928, when he moved away from the soft-focused approach of his earlier photographs. Images such as *Gallantry* can be seen as breaking away from pictorialism through the use of high key lighting and a focus on several distinct compositional elements while still retaining a pictorialist affinity for evoking an idealized emotion or state of being (Fig.40). Compositions such as *Diffusers* demonstrate Connell's increased interest in the formal qualities of the objects depicted and a rejection of symbolic and allegorical narrative content (Fig.41). Connell's continued fascination with the visual language of modernism is seen through his experimentation with camera-less photography beginning in 1930. Also known as photograms, this technique involved putting objects on a sheet of sensitized photographic paper and exposing the paper to a light source of varying intensity.

In his 1981 essay on Will Connell, photographic historian Van Deren Coke argued that Edward Steichen's experimental approach to fashion photography, produced for *Vogue* and *Harper's Bazaar* around 1930, was the primary factor leading to Connell's embrace of modernism in the early 1930s.[103] Notwithstanding Steichen's influence on American commercial photography of the 1930s, it is likely that Connell had direct contact with European practitioners and it is certain that by 1928 he had direct access to European books and magazines through his association with Zeitlin. The material that Connell was able to purchase through Zeitlin's bookshop exposed him to modern trends in European advertising that combined a new emphasis on photographic illustration with radical innovations in typographic design.

By 1930 Connell's active involvement with the Zeitlin circle, his direct participation in the activities of the Camera Pictorialists of Los Angeles, and his career as a commercial photographer, left little time for the pursuit of purely creative projects. For Connell, the creative part of his personality regularly functioned as a tool to increase his competitive edge in the world of commerce. His lack of commercial projects during the Depression in 1932 resulted in his most fully realized artistic project, the Hollywood satire *In Pictures*. Connell describes the origins of this project in his 1949 publication *About Photography*:

"In [19]32, to keep from going bats, I took on a project of a picture series, which later was published as a satire of Hollywood. This started out to be a series of experimental shots for possible show use somewhere and was quite innocently and blithely undertaken. Actually it became a prolonged and agonizing lesson in the gentle art of thinking."[104]

In 1937 *In Pictures* was published by T. J. Maloney of New York consisting of forty-eight photographs pared with a text by Hollywood screenwriters Nunnally Johnson, Patterson McNutt, Gene Fowler, and Grover Jones. The text runs independently through the book, constructed as a story conference between four writers that digresses into wildly absurd dimensions. The photo series can be broken down into two clearly observed trajectories that are interwoven throughout the book. One dimension is a clear infatuation with and celebration of the technical aspects of filmmaking and the second is a critique of the Hollywood "studio system."

Like many artists of his generation, Connell had directly experienced the early years of cinema before the codes of narrative filmmaking were firmly established. Connell exploited his technical skills to impart a sense of excitement in relation to the possibilities the cinema offered for developing a completely new medium of visual communication as was rigorously explored in the work of Russian filmmakers Dziga Vertov and Sergei Eisenstein. This can be clearly seen in two of Connell's photographs from the series *Sound* and *Lights* (Fig.42, 43).

The second trajectory articulated in his photo essay is a clear disdain for the Hollywood style of filmmaking which was at its height during the 1930s. Connell's photographs explore the dehumanizing nature of the "studio system" which exploited the majority of its workers while selecting a few lucky people to live the life of royalty. This conception of Hollywood has much in common with the cynical and claustrophobic vision of writer Nathaniel West in such books as *Miss Lonelyhearts* and *Day of the Locust*. Connell's photograph *Extras* suggests the inverted world inhabited by those on the edge of the motion picture industry (Fig.44). The reversed lettering across the photograph situates the viewer in the position of the casting director gazing out from his office toward the hopeful, longing glances of the men and women waiting for their chance at fame and fortune.

By all accounts, *In Pictures* was not a commercially successful publication. However, it received critical attention in such photo magazines as *Camera Craft* and *U.S. Camera*.[105] A critical examination of the Hollywood film industry in picture format was not something that attracted a great deal of attention outside of the photographic community. Today, *In Pictures* is recognized as a landmark of photographic bookwork because of the fact that a complex, critical narrative is read visually through Connell's skillful sequencing of the images.

Through his work on the *In Pictures* project, Connell developed a strong interest in photomontage. This innovation found a direct application in a number of advertising campaigns throughout the 1930s. With the exception of Barbara Morgan, who produced a large body of montage work and wrote articles advocating the use of montage techniques, few American photographers engaged in a sustained exploration of this type of image making.[106] Connell was the only photographer on the West Coast to work with photomontage on a sustained basis and to incorporate montage in his commercial assignments. His earliest photomontage work applied to commercial photography appeared around 1932, utilizing a spare juxtaposition of several compositional elements.

Connell also worked with multiple exposures on a single sheet of photographic paper to suggest the flow of action within the confines of a single photograph. His use of the multiple exposure technique reached a high level of sophistication in a 1937 photograph for Rio Grande gasoline (Fig.45).

By 1937, Connell was constructing very dense compositions that required cutting and pasting a number of images together and re-photographing the entire montage. Connell's work in photomontage reached a high level of sophistication in an image depicting the excitement of Hollywood night life commissioned for one of the All-Year Club brochures in the late 1930s (Fig.46). In less than a decade, Connell's contributions to All-Year Club publications had moved from soft-focused landscapes to complex montages. Connell was a master technician with a innate sense for constructing complex, resonant images. One can only wonder what photographs Connell might have created if his work had traveled more frequently beyond the boundaries of the commercial world.

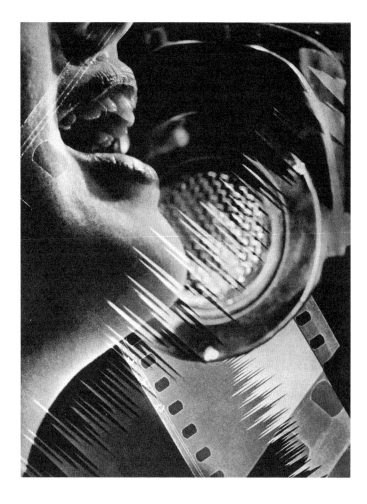

Figure 42.
Will Connell. *Sound*. From the book,
In Pictures. 1937.

Connell's satire of the Hollywood studio
system is a masterpiece of photographic
bookwork. Connell utilized his skills in
camera and negative manipulation to
impart a sense of excitement in relation
to the potential possibilities the cinema
possessed for developing a completely
new medium of visual communication.
(Private Collection)

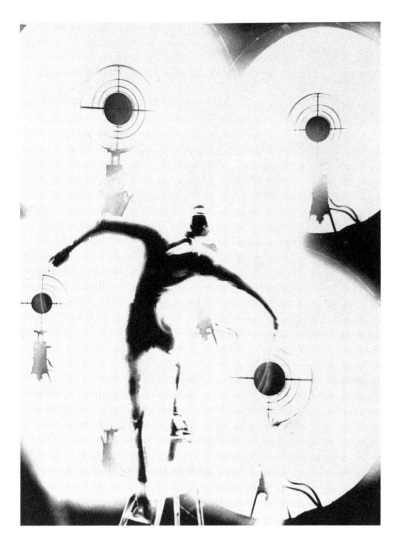

Figure 43.
Will Connell. *Lights*. From the book,
In Pictures. 1937.

Connell began work on the *In Pictures*
project during the depth of the
Depression in 1932 when there was
little commercial photography work
available. This series of photographs
was Connell's most fully realized
artistic work. (Private Collection)

Figure 44.
Will Connell. *Extras*. From the book,
In Pictures. 1937.

Connell's photo essay expresses a clear
disdain for the Hollywood "studio
system" which exploited the majority
of its workers while selecting a few
lucky people to live the life of royalty.
The reversed lettering across the photograph situates the viewer in the
position of the casting director gazing
out from his office toward the hopeful,
longing glances of the men and women
waiting for their one chance at fame
and fortune. (Private Collection)

14

Bertram Longworth: Inside the Studio Gates

A rare example of sophisticated photomontage work produced inside the studio gates can be seen in the work of veteran Warner Brothers still photographer Bertram Longworth. Little is known about Longworth's early years as a photographer before coming to Hollywood, and the only known examples of his experimental work are found in his 1937 publication *Hold Still Hollywood*. Patterned loosely after Will Connell's publication *In Pictures*, Longworth's book exhibits none of the conceptual strength of Connell's work. The best of his work has a dynamic quality that compares with other photomontage work produced in the 1920s and 1930s both on the East Coast and in Europe.

An article in the January 1938 issue of *International Photographer*, (a magazine devoted to the cinematographers and still photographers in Hollywood) suggests that Longworth's book was an attempt to raise the status of the studio still photographer by showing that the best workers in the profession knew how to create artistic images from the ordinary requirements of recording activities on the movie set.

Longworth's montage *Swing Kings* suggests the jumping rhythms of Cab Calloway's big band music by juxtaposing an image of the musician with the tense animation of a young woman enthralled by the music (Fig.47). This image suggests Longworth's sense of how film promotion could ideally be handled by a creative photographer.

A more arresting image that had no apparent publicity value is Longworth's composition, *No Man's Land* (Fig.48). This photograph juxtaposes a World War I battle scene, complete with a soldier running through a landscape of barbed wire and smoke-filled sky, with a naked woman holding a pistol clutched in both hands. Longworth's conceptual model is open for debate, but the sheer irrationality of the image would undoubtedly have engaged the interest of any Surrealist writer or painter. This image in one sense represents the cacophony of imagery that Hollywood was sending into the world to an eager audience waiting for the latest new style and sensation. It is curious that so little experimental work like Longworth's emerged from photographers working in the Hollywood studios in the 1920s and 1930s. While the Hollywood photographers may have had little interest in the philosophy of modernism and the political uses of photomontage, it seems that the technical challenges of the "New Vision" would have captured their imagination and challenged them to incorporate experimental techniques into their official capacity as publicists and promoters of Hollywood film production.[107]

Figure 47.
Bertram Longworth. *Swing Kings* from
the book, *Hold Still Hollywood*. 1937.

A rare example of sophisticated photomontage produced inside the studio
gates can be seen in the work of veteran Warner Brothers still photographer
Bertram Longworth. His montage of Cab
Calloway highlights Longworth's vision
of how film promotion could ideally
handled by a creative photographer.
(Private Collection)

No Man's Land

Figure 48.
Bertram Longworth. *No Man's Land*.
from the book, *Hold Still Hollywood*,
1937.

This photograph juxtaposes a World War
I battle scene with a naked woman holding a pistol clutched in both hands.
Longworth's conceptual model is open
for debate but the sheer irrationality
of the image would undoubtedly have
engaged the interest of any Surrealist
writer or painter. It is curious that so little work like Longworth's emerged from
photographers working in the Hollywood
studios in the 1920s and 1930s. (Private
Collection)

15

Art Center School: Photography Comes of Age

A momentous event in the development of modern photography in Southern California was the establishment of the Art Center School in 1930.[108] Located just west of downtown Los Angeles in the Westlake Park district, Art Center was the first art school in the United States to establish a full-time curriculum in photography. The impetus for establishing the photography department underscored Art Center's profound understanding that photography was "a legitimate modern medium."[109]

The establishment of a photography department in Southern California by 1930 underscored both the artistic and economic development that had taken place in the region over the previous twenty years. The founding faculty members were Will Connell and James Doolittle, the prime movers in introducing the Camera Pictorialists salons of the late 1920s and early 1930s to contemporary trends in modern photography. The establishment of the photography department by these pioneering individuals highlights the profound union that artistic and commercial photography had achieved by 1930. The ideal of the modernist photographer was the professional craftsman attuned to the business needs of advertising, journalism, and motion picture production, who simultaneously maintained a philosophical basis for artistic production. In many ways these goals were mirrored in the careers of photographers like Connell and Doolittle and were more firmly rooted in the culture of Southern California with the establishment of the Art Center School.

By 1941, the Art Center School had achieved an international reputation and the photography department had expanded to include Ansel Adams, Fred Archer and Clarence Sinclair Bull as faculty members. With many of the photography faculty born and raised in California, it is not surprising to see some of the original regional boosterism slip into the school's promotional literature:

"Brilliant California sunlight (original reason for the Motion Picture industry centering here) offers a dominant advantage over any other location in the world. Outdoor shooting in year-round sunlight provides unparalleled picture opportunities. Brilliant Pacific beaches, dunes, and deserts, harbor activities, mountains and ranches give endless variety to supervised classes on location."[110]

Art Center School was founded under the direction of Edward R. Adams and based on the philosophical model established by Lazlo Moholy-Nagy at the Bauhaus School in Germany. Faculty members were all practicing artists and designers, class enrollment was limited to promote maximum interaction between faculty and students, and no grades were assigned to evaluate class projects. Students graduated from the photography program in a time frame ranging from three to four years depending on the evaluations from faculty members and a final review by Edward Adams. No diplomas were issued to graduating students but a letter of referral was produced for the student upon completing Art Center training.

While the curriculum at Art Center has always been associated with commercial photography, there was a profound sense of modern aesthetics and philosophy that the students were expected to absorb and then demonstrate in their work. Art Center organized a regular lecture series for the students that included such distinguished speakers as Frank Lloyd Wright, Edward Steichen, and Edward Weston. The school gallery organized regular exhibitions of internationally known artists such as Stanton MacDonald-Wright, Man Ray, and Guy Pène Dubois. In addition, the Art Center Film Society presented over sixty American and European films a year ranging from documentary to non-representational color abstraction. Art Center also produced an annual student exhibition that occupied all of the gallery space and freely mixed the best work produced in the medium of painting, drawing, and photography.

Edward Kiminski was a painter and designer who had a strong impact on the photography students at Art Center. In his photocomposition class, students were encouraged to expand their conceptions about photography. Kaminski pushed students to explore movement and form through the use of lighting, camera angles, photomontage, and multiple exposures. Students were initially expected to explore their original compositions through charcoal drawings on paper and then interpret the sketch using photography. While other photographers instructed the students in technical aspects of the medium or shared the important requirements needed for specialized work as a professional photographer, Kaminski attempted to tap the creative potential of each photography student.

A few examples of student work from the late 1940s show the creative range Kaminski was able to coax from his students. One nude study displays a dynamic composition of movement and simultaneous vision achieved by the multiple exposure of a single negative (Fig.49). Another untitled photograph displays a striking juxtaposition of a mask and a detailed view of rock, water, and sand engaging the contemporary fascination with Abstract Surrealism that was seen in the marvelous paintings of Helen Lundeberg, Lorser Feitelson and other Southern California artists of the period (Fig.50).

The photography department at Art Center was a unique program in California through the 1930s and 1940s. The interdisciplinary nature of the program and the distinctly modern philosophy of the curriculum brought together the artistic and commercial impulses of Southern California photography that had been moving on parallel tracks with varying degrees of momentum since the 1890s.

Conclusion

Between 1890 and 1950, fine art photography in Southern California developed along a circuitous path, traveling from regional boosterism to pictorialism, and finally toward a modernism based in advertising and design. Southern California nurtured the talents and vision of Edward Weston during his formative years and he is now recognized as an artist of international stature. The Camera Pictorialists of Los Angeles forged an important link between pictorialism and modernism. The salon exhibitions organized in the 1920s through the mid-1930s were international forums for the expression of these shifting aesthetic approaches. Will Connell developed a number of innovative approaches to photography within the arena of advertising and commercial work.

At the beginning of the twentieth century, Southern California cultural activities were largely isolated from the artistic centers of the East Coast and Europe. Photographers who thrived in the region drew inspiration from the landscape and the climate and were attracted by the lack of stratified cultural institutions as well as the lure of the emerging motion picture industry. The subtle yet distinctive innovations of fine art photography in Southern California during the first five decades of the twentieth century are just beginning to come into focus as we explore the cultural and artistic roots of modern Los Angeles

Acknowledgements

Assembling a research project of this nature is truly a team effort. I would not have been able to complete this essay without the help of the following individuals to guide me through the maze of the institutional archive: James Davis and Simon Elliott, Department of Special Collections-Charles E. Young Research Library, UCLA; Gary Kurutz, California State Library; Weston Naef and Kate Weir, J. Paul Getty Museum; Amy Rule and Leslie Calmes, Center for Creative Photography; Dan Strehl, Los Angeles Public Library-Samuel Goldwyn Branch; Joseph Strubel, George Eastman House, Kim Walters, Southwest Museum; Jennifer Watts, Huntington Library; and Tara Wenger-Harry Ransom Humanities Research Center.

I am also grateful to the many collectors and dealers in the photographic and book world who patiently guided me to reference sources and individual images: Sid Avery, Joseph Bellows, Andrew Cahan, Susan Herzig, Paul Hertzmann, Dennis Reed, Stephen and Mus White and Michael Wilson.

At an early stage in my research, Will Connell Jr. generously shared his knowledge and resources with me. Gloria Gerace also provided invaluable support as this project came together. Stephen Callis patiently transported his camera equipment to a variety of locations in Southern California to copy photographs for reproduction.

A special thanks is owed to Tom Andrews, the Officers and Board of the Historical Society of Southern California, and the John Randolph Haynes and Dora Haynes Foundation. I was awarded a generous research grant enabling me to travel to Austin and Rochester in pursuit of information regarding Merle Armitage and Alvin Langdon Coburn.

Beth Gates Warren enthusiastically supported this project and provided me with several primary sources that greatly aided my research efforts. Her passion for photography and Southern California and her tenacity as a scholar are an inspiration to me.

Victoria Dailey provided crucial support at many stages of this project. Her keen sense of language and knowledge of Southern California history has substantially added to the quality and clarity of this essay. Ann Gray has patiently supported this project over a long period and I am grateful for her longstanding commitment.

I am grateful to Muir and Agnes Dawson, Francis DellaVecchia, Nathaniel Des Marais, Alex King Harris, David Reichert, and Andrew Wilson who patiently kept the home fire burning during the periods when I was off traveling or buried in some aspect of this research project.

A special note of appreciation is due to my son Miles who has patiently endured my absences and distractions over the long course of this project.

Finally, to my wife Andrea Liss, whose love, courage, and keen intellect are a constant source of inspiration to me. I would not have been able to complete this project without your guidance and support.

Footnotes

[1] John Paul Edwards, "The Sixth Pittsburgh Salon," Camera Craft, 26, no. 5, (May 1919); 177–185.

[2] The matter was made more complicated by the technological innovations that had occurred since the 1880s, including the invention of the portable hand-held camera and the rise of photo-finishing services. This combination encouraged millions of Americans to take up photography and to explore the joys of a process that had previously been the province of the professional. Thus amateurs were competing with professionals and the distinctions between them became blurred.

[3] See Ralph W. Andrews, *Picture Gallery Pioneers, 1850 to 1875.* (New York: Superior Publishing Co., 1964), p. 78.

[4] For an engaging discussion of the San Francisco art scene of the late nineteenth century see Brigitta Hjalmarson, *Artful Players: Artistic Life in Early San Francisco*, (Los Angeles: Balcony Press, 1999).

[5] For a detailed examination of this period in American fine art photography, see Christian A. Peterson, *After the Photo-Secession: American Pictorial Photography, 1910–1955*, (New York: WW Norton, 1997).

[6] Jennifer Watts, Curator of Photographs at the Huntington Library, has done an extensive amount of research on the genre of promotional photography in Southern California between 1870 and 1920. Publication of this research is eagerly awaited by scholars of California history and American photography.

[7] Herve Friend, *Picturesque Los Angeles County, California: Illustrative and Descriptive*, (Chicago: American Photogravure Co., 1887), p. 3.

[8] Ibid.

[9] For biographical details on Charles Lummis, see Keith Lummis and Turbese Lummis-Fiske, *Charles F. Lummis: The Man and His West*, (Norman: University of Oklahoma Press, 1975) and Dudley Gordon, Charles F. Lummis: Crusader in Corduroy, (Los Angeles: Cultural Assets Press, 1972)

[10] Charles Lummis, "Our Amateur Photographs," *Land of Sunshine* 2, no. 2, (January, 1895): 28.

[11] Ibid.

[12] Charles Lummis, "The Artist's Paradise," *Land of Sunshine* 6, no. 6, (May, 1897): 232.

[13] A copy of this letter is in the correspondence file of the Charles Lummis Archive, Southwest Museum, Los Angeles

[14] Alvin Langdon Coburn, *Alvin Langdon Coburn Photographer, An Autobiography*, ed. Helmut and Allison Gernsheim (New York: Frederick A. Praeger, 1966), p. 12.

[15] William Innes Homer, *Alfred Stieglitz and the American Avant-Garde.* (Boston: New York Graphic Society, 1977), pp. 27–28, 36.

[16] Coburn, *Alvin Langdon Coburn Photographer*, p.14.

[17] Copies of these articles can be found in the Alvin Langdon Coburn Scrapbook, 1901–1904 in the George Eastman House, Rochester, NY.

[18] In 1902, Coburn wrote four articles on Southern California missions illustrated with his photographs for *Photo Era* magazine. These articles appeared in the August, September, October, and November issues.

[19] Alvin Langdon Coburn, "The California Missions-San Juan Capistrano," *Photo-Era*, (October, 1902): 255.

[20] The Coburn Archive at the George Eastman House contains a set of manila cards listing the photographer's exhibitions and the prints exhibited. The cards are located in Box 12, Folder 24.

[21] Alvin Langdon Coburn Scrapbook, 1901–1904,

[22] Arthur Dow, *Composition: A Series of Exercises Selected from a New System of Art Education*, 5th ed., (New York: Baker and Taylor Co.,1903), p. 5.

[23] Alma May Cook, "Camera Wizard Develops Hitherto Unknown Fields," *Los Angeles Herald Express*, 15 April 1911.

[24] Alvin Langdon Coburn, "Coburn in California. A Characteristic Letter," *Photography*, (September 19, 1911). A copy of the article is in the Alvin Langdon Coburn Scrapbook, 1911–1917.

[25] An article from the *Los Angeles Evening Herald*, 8 December 1911, details these events.

[26] Antony Anderson, *Los Angeles Times*, 4 February 1912.

[27] Three page MLS from Coburn to Karl Struss dated January 24, 1912. Private Collection.

[28] On two separate occasions Antony Anderson named Edward Weston as the leader of the Camera Pictorialists of Los Angeles. The first occurrence is in a *Los Angeles Times* review of the Arts and Crafts exhibit on 13 February 1916, section III, p. 4. The second occurrence is a *Los Angeles Times* article from 16 June 1916, section 111, p. 2.

[29] Charis Wilson, "Family Portrait," in the exhibition catalogue *Edward Weston's Gifts to His Sister*, (Dayton: Dayton Art Institute, 1978), p. 17.

[30] A particularly cogent review of Weston's early years in Southern California and his aesthetic transformations can be found in Gilles Mora's essay, "Weston the Magnificent" published in *Edward Weston: Forms of Passion*, (New York: Henry N. Abrams Inc., 1995), pp. 9–25. See also the exhibition catalogue by Susan Danly and Weston J. Naef, *Edward Weston in Los Angeles*, (San Marino, CA: The Huntington Library and Art Gallery, 1986).

[31] Mike Weaver, *Alvin Langdon Coburn: Symbolist Photographer, 1882–1966*, (New York: Aperture, 1986), p. 9.

[32] The other major influence was two extended trips to Mexico in the mid-1920s. See Amy Conger, *Edward Weston in Mexico, 1923–1926*, (Albuquerque: San Francisco Museum of Modern Art/University of New Mexico Press, 1983).

[33] Substantial details relating to Weston's biography and exhibition history can be found in Amy Conger, *Edward Weston: Photographs from the Collection of the Center for Creative Photography*, (Tucson, Center for Creative Photography, 1992).

[34] Ibid. See "Appendix C, Exhibitions," pp. 59–64.

[35] Edward Weston. "In A One Man Studio" 1913. Published in Peter Bunnell, ed. *Edward Weston On Photography*, (Salt Lake City: Gibbs M. Smith Inc./Peregrine Smith Books, 1983), p. 13.

[36] See letter dated October 4, 1950 to Edward Weston from Margrethe Mather. Nancy Newhall was in the process of editing Weston's Daybooks and wanted him to contact many of his old friends to confirm details in the manuscript. File AG38: 3/4T, Edward Weston Archive, Center for Creative Photography, Tucson.

[37] *Camera Craft* 21, no. 5, (May 1914): 250.

[38] Antony Anderson. *Los Angeles Times*, 31 October 1915, section III, p. 21.

[39] A checklist of photographs for the exhibition can be found in the catalogue, *First Annual Arts and Crafts Salon*, (Los Angeles: Museum of History, Science and Art, 1916).

[40] Antony Anderson. *Los Angeles Times*, 13 February 1916, section III, p.4.

[41] Antony Anderson, *Los Angeles Times*, 11 June 1916, section III, p. 2.

[42] Terry Smith's book *Making the Modern, Industry, Art, and Design in America*, (Chicago: University of Chicago Press, 1993), is helpful in defining the hybrid forms of modernism within American art and culture between 1910 and 1940.

[43] Edward Weston, "Photography as a Mean of Artistic Expression" in Bunnell, *Edward Weston on Photography*, p. 19.

[44] Ibid.

[45] A letter from Edward Weston to Merle Armitage dated April 12, 1944 confirms this date: "I have just finished reading 20 years of correspondence with Ramiel; every letter written him from 'Dear Mr. McGehee' in 1919 to 'Ramiel Querido' in 1939. My hair stood on end when faced with letters which I had marked 'destroy at once.'" Merle Armitage Archive, Harry Ransom Humanities Research Center, Austin, Texas.

[46] Ibid. Biographical information on Ramiel MeGehee comes from a lengthy letter written to Nancy Newhall from Merle Armitage; undated, but probably from the late 1950s.

[47] Edward Weston. "Random Notes on Photography" in Bunnell, *Edward Weston on Photography*, p.29.

[48] Ibid.,p.30.

[49] See Nancy Newhall, editor. *The Daybooks of Edward Weston, Volume 1. Mexico.* Millerton, Aperture, 1973, pp.113–114.

[50] Letter to Merle Armitage dated October 28, 1946. Armitage Archive.

[51] Edward Weston. "Random Notes on Photography" in Bunnell, *Edward Weston on Photography*, p.32

[52] Edward Weston, *The Daybooks of Edward Weston. Volume 1. Mexico*, ed. Nancy

Newhall, (Millerton, N.Y.: 1973), pp. 121–122. Weston discusses the successful exhibition of his photographs in the Japanese-American community in 1925.

[53] Amy Conger. *Edward Weston: Photographs*, "Appendix C, Exhibitions," pp. 58–64.

[54] Dennis Reed. *Japanese Photography in America, 1920–1940*, (Los Angeles: Japanese-American Cultural & Community Center, 1985), p. 35.

[55] Ibid.

[56] Quoted in Arthur Millier's article "Photos by Weston in Japan Art Club," *Los Angeles Times*, September 1927.

[57] See previously mentioned article and another article by Millier titled "Some Photographs by Edward Weston," *Los Angeles Times*, 10 July 1927.

[58] Letter from Merle Armitage to Nancy Newhall titled "Early Notes on Edward for Nancy," April 13th, 1961, Armitage Archive. In addition to his duties as concert promoter, Armitage formed a partnership with Erwin Furman to open a small art gallery in the offices of the decorating firm of Cannel & Chaffin. Armitage hired Millier to run the gallery. When the *Los Angeles Times* art critic Anthony Anderson retired, Armitage used his influence with Harry Chandler to hire Millier for the job. Millier became an articulate spokesman for modern art in Southern California, continuing his position with the *Los Angeles Times* for over thirty years.

[59] Letter from Nancy Newhall to Merle Armitage dated February 20, 1961, "As far as Beau and I are aware, your first book on Edward was the first noble black-and-white job done in photography on this side of the ocean at that time." Armitage Archive.

[60] Letter from Edward Weston to Merle Armitage circa 1930: Armitage Archive. See also a series of letters from Armitage to Edward Weston in 1932 found in the Weston Archive at the Center for Creative Photography in Tucson detailing the progress of the Weston monograph. In several letters Armitage encouraged Weston to contact important writers whom Weston knew in Carmel who could make contributions to the book by giving important name recognition to the project. Weston did enlist the enthusiastic support of Lincoln Steffens, and Armitage secured the help of Ramiel MeGehee as editor of the project.

[61] Letter from Merle Armitage to Brett and Cole Weston, April 6, 1961, Armitage Archive.

[62] Ibid.

[63] Letter from Merle Armitage to Brett and Cole Weston, April 6, 1961. Armitage Archive.

[64] Letter from Merle Armitage to Brett and Cole Weston dated April 6, 1961. Armitage Archive.

[65] Letter from Merle Armitage to Edward Weston dated June 6, 1947: "I also was able to discern that my own abilities or talents were mediocre, in comparison with first class standards of ability or accomplishment. Perhaps that was one of the factors which led me to become finally an impresario…" Weston Archive, Center for Creative Photography, AG38:1/10.

[66] Letter from Edward Weston to Merle Armitage dated June 11, 1933. Armitage Archive.

[67] For biographical information on Fleckenstein, see the undated exhibition catalogue from the Stephen White Gallery with an essay by White.

[68] Sadakichi Hartmann, "The Salon Club and the First American Photographic Salon at New York" in Harry Lawton and George Knox, eds. *The Valiant Knights of Daguerre*, (Berkeley: University of California Press, 1978), pp. 118–126.

[69] Fleckenstein's activities with the Camera Pictorialists of Los Angeles can be traced through a review of the salon catalogues produced by the Club during these years.

[70] Biographical information on Archer can be found in Jack Wright. "PSA Personalities, Fred R. Archer, FPSA," *PSA Journal* (March 1946): 118–119 and "Obituaries," *PSA Journal* (June 1963).

[71] *PSA Journal* (March 1946): 118.

[72] Archer exhibited photographs he titled as "Design by Reflection" and "Design with Glass" in both the 11th and 12th International Salon of Photography organized by The Camera Pictorialists of Los Angeles in 1928 and 1929. The exhibition catalogues have a checklist of all photographs included in the salons.

[73] Susan Ehrens, *A Poetic Vision: The Photographs of Anne Brigman*, (Santa Barbara: Santa Barbara Museum of Art, 1995), p. 23.

[74] Anne Brigman, "A Jury and a Salon," *Camera Craft* 37, no. 3 (March 1930): 126–128.

[75] Ehrens, *A Poetic Vision*, p.35.

[76] Anne Brigman. *Songs of A Pagan*, (Caldwell: Caxton Printers, 1949). Excerpt from the poem, "Shining Raiment", p.74.

[77] The catalogue of the Sixth International Salon of Photography held in Los Angeles in November and December, 1922 notes that eight photographs had been purchased, "In recognition of the position which pictorial photography occupies today in the realm of art, the Los Angeles Museum has determined to establish a permanent collection of pictorial photographs."

[78] In 1998, LACMA curator Tim Wride organized an exhibition of these purchases titled "High Lights, Shadings, and Shadows: LACMA, Pictorialism, and the International Salons of Photography."

[79] Several large books containing newspaper clippings from the *Los Angeles Times*, the *Tribune*, and the *Herald* describe the impact of the First International Salon. The Los Angeles County Museum of Art Scrapbooks contain a variety of newspaper and magazine reviews of exhibitions held at the museum in the 1920s and early 1930s.

[80] See the checklist of prints published in the exhibition catalogue for the Fifth International Salon.

[81] *Los Angeles Record*, 17 December 1921.

[82] See the activities of the Julian Levy, Delphic, and Weyhe Galleries in New York, Increase Robinson in Chicago, and Jake Zeitlin in Los Angeles.

[83] Catalogue of the Thirteenth International Salon of Photography, 1930, p. 2.

[84] Letter from Edward Weston to Will Connell dated April 4, 1931. Private collection.

[85] See Barbara McCandless' essay, "A Commitment to Beauty" in *New York to Hollywood: The Photography of Karl Struss*. (Fort Worth: Amon Carter Museum,1995), p. 19.

[86] Ibid., p. 23.

[87] Ibid., p.25.

[88] See Richard Koszarski's essay "The Cinematographer" and his checklist of Struss' films in *New York to Hollywood: The Photography of Karl Struss*, pp. 167–206, 233–240.

[89] John and Susan Edwards Harvith. "The Man Behind the Camera" in *New York to Hollywood*, p. 209. Struss' "definition of 'pure photography' he told us, was using original negatives to make platinum prints; 'impure photography' he said, was the production of literal, wide-angle glossy bromide prints without any diffusion."

[90] For the most informative study of this movement, see Therese Heyman, *Seeing Straight: The f.64 Revolution in Photography*, (Oakland: The Oakland Museum, 1992).

[91] For a discussion of the direction that the salon exhibitions throughout the United States took after the mid-1930s, see Christian Petterson, *After the Photo-Secession*.

[92] See the exhibition catalogue for the Sixteenth Annual International Salon of Pictorial Photography, 1933.

[93] For a discussion of this issue relative to California see Louise Katzman, *Photography in California, 1945–1980*, (New York: Hudson Hills Press, 1984).

[94] See the exhibition catalogue for the Thirty-First International Salon of Photography, 1950, p.1.

[95] Sigismund Blumann, "Our Japanese Brother Artists," *Camera Craft* 32, no. 3 (March 1925): 109.

[96] Dr. K. Koike, "Japanese Art in Photography," *Camera Craft* 32, no. 3 (March 1925): 110–115.

[97] Dennis Reed's *Japanese Photography in America 1920–1940* is still the primary source for information on the activities of the Japanese-American photographers in Southern California.

[98] F.J. Mortimer, "Pictorial Photography in 1927," *Photograms of the Year* (1927): 9

[99] Sigismund Blumann, "Club Notes", *Camera Craft* 38, no. 7 (July 1931): 356.

[100] For biographical information on Will Connell, see Philippe Halsman's article "Will Connell" in *U.S. Camera International Annual 1963*, (New York 1962): 100–115; Van Deren Coke's catalogue essay in *Photographs by Will Connell: California Photographer and Teacher 1898–1961*, (San Francisco: San Francisco Museum of Modern Art, 1981); and Janet Tearnen's unpublished Master's Thesis, *The Photography of Will Connell: Reflections of Southern California, 1928–1950* completed in 1992.

[101] Collection 893. Box 59, Will Connell Archive, University Research Library, Dept. of

Special Collections, UCLA. A large collection of Will Connell's photographs as well as a random selection of notes and personal correspondence are in this collection. The Connell Archive contains a hand written scorecard listing all of the pictorialist salons that accepted Connell's work as well as the titles of the works that were exhibited between the years 1926 and 1930.

[102] Will Connell, *About Photography*, (New York: T.J. Maloney Co., 1949), p. 5.

[103] Van Deren Coke, *Photographs by Will Connell*, p.5.

[104] Will Connell, *About Photography*, p.6.

[105] Will Connell, "Depression Island," *Camera Craft* 44, no. 7 (July 1937): 309–316. See also book review on p. 355.

[106] See Sally Stein, "'Good fences make good neighbors': American Resistance to Photomontage Between the Wars" in *Montage and Modern Life: 1919–1942*, (Cambridge: MIT Press, 1992), pp. 129–189.

[107] Another Hollywood photographer to employ photomontage techniques on a sporadic basis was Ted Allen. I'm grateful to Sid Avery for showing me Allen's work in the Motion Picture & Television Archive, Van Nuys, California.

[108] From the booklet *The Art Center School*, 1941. "The Art Center School, founded eleven years ago by a group of practicing artists and designers, has established new high levels in modern art training."

[109] Ibid., p.45.

[110] From the booklet, *Photography, The Art Center School*, 1939, p. 5.

Figure 3.
Exhibition Catalogue for the First
Los Angeles Photographic Salon. 1902.

This exhibition highlights the first
group of fine art photographers in
Southern California. The subject matter
of many photographs in this exhibition
reflect the contemporary fascination
with the decaying architecture of the
California Missions. The interest in the
missions was stimulated by a regional
nostalgia for the Spanish/Mexican era
of the late 18th and early 19th century.
(Private Collection)

Figure 4.
Charles Lummis.
Portrait of *Lillian Gildersleeve*, 1911.

Lummis photographed many of the
guests who visited El Alisal: John Muir,
Maynard Dixon, and Charles and Louise
Keeler. This portrait of his secretary
demonstrates Lummis' skill as a
thoughtful and attentive portrait artist.
This sensitivity is particularly evident
in his use of natural light to illuminate
and obscure details of Gildersleeve's
head and upper body. (A.16.17
Courtesy Southwest Museum)

Figure 5.
Charles Lummis.
Self-Portrait at El Alisal. 1904.

Lummis took a break from building his
home in the Arroyo Seco to make this
self-portrait. Lummis is best known for
his photographs of Native Americans
in Arizona and New Mexico which
appeared frequently as illustrations in
his books. He also recorded the day to
day activities of family and friends in
Southern California beginning with his
arrival in Los Angeles in the late 1880s
and continuing into the 1920s. (P.32575
Courtesy Southwest Museum)

Figure 7.
Charles Lummis.
Self-Portrait at Camulos Rancho. 1922.

Lummis was a frequent visitor to the
Camulos Rancho which he discovered
soon after his arrival in Southern
California in 1885. Lummis was always
welcome at the Camulos Rancho and
often visited when he was in need of
rest and relaxation. In this photograph,
Lummis positioned himself as a small
diminutive figure supported by the
giant base of a California oak tree resting quietly in the landscape of the
aging rancho. (A.25.4 Courtesy
Southwest Museum)

Figure 8.
Charles Lummis. *Stairs in the Tower of
the Southwest Museum*. 1914.

Lummis created this photograph looking down the spiral staircase in the
newly constructed tower of the
Southwest Museum. This image, and
indeed a variety of Lummis' personal
photographs, suggests a general lack
of concern for the aesthetic principles
of fine art photography in Southern
California during the early years of the
20th century. (Hallmark Photographic
Collection, Hallmark Cards Inc., Kansas
City, Missouri)

Figure 18.
Edward Weston. *Epilogue*. 1919.

Between 1914 and 1922, Edward
Weston and Margrethe Mather collaborated on a number of photographic
compositions and occasionally signed
both of their names to an image.
Mather had a number of contacts in the
small but active community of Japanese
artists living in Los Angeles at the time.
Weston's 1919 portrait of Mather is an
intricate composition of light and shadow influenced by the paintings and
wood block prints that Weston and
Mather observed on their visits to the
studios of their Japanese friends.
(Center for Creative Photography, The
University of Arizona. ©1981 Center
for Creative Photography, Arizona
Board of Regents)

Figure 21.
Edward Weston. *PlasterWorks/Western
Plaster Mill, Los Angeles*. 1925.

This composition shows Weston's
increased visual sophistication in the
handling of large industrial structures.
He had learned to create these formal yet
abstract photographs from the study of
small objects, vegetables, and details of
the human form within the confines of
the studio. (The J. Paul Getty Museum,
Los Angeles. ©1981 Center for Creative
Photography, Arizona Board of Regents)

Figure 28.
Fred Archer. *Dancing Lady*. Circa 1928.

Archer's most lasting contribution to
American fine art photography was a
series of light abstractions produced in
the late 1920s. As Archer moved the
glass in various directions, the reflected
light created striking compositions.
(Dennis and Amy Reed Collection)

Figure 29.
Fred Archer. *Untitled*. Circa 1938.

Archer utilized his skills of model making
and multiple printing to create a futuristic composition describing the mechanics
of photography. The composition may
have been used as an early advertisement
for his photography school. (Center for
Creative Photography, The University of
Arizona)

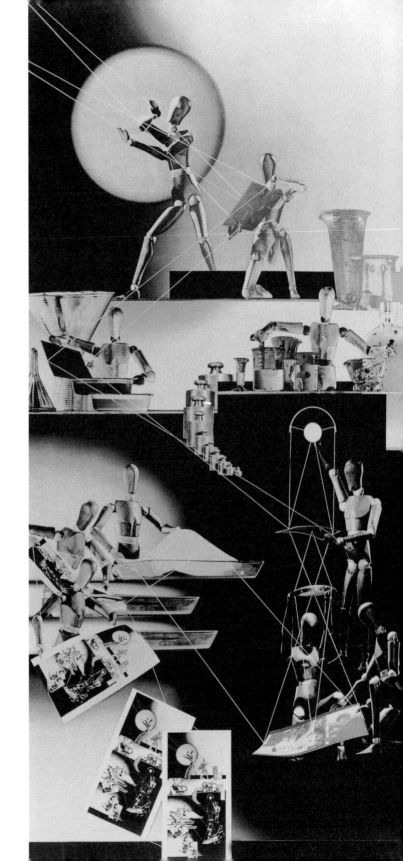

Figure 39.
Will Connell. *Portrait of Jake Zeitlin*.
Circa 1928.

Figure 36.
A. Kono. *Perpetual Motion*. Circa 1930.

Unlike many of the Caucasian photographers active in the Camera Pictorialists of Los Angeles, very few of the Japanese-American photographers earned a living in commercial photography. By 1928, the work of Japanese-American photographers from Los Angeles had reached the salons of the East Coast and Europe and were reproduced in such prestigious publications as *Photograms of the Year* and *Pictorial Photography in America*. (Dennis Reed Collection)

Connell was introduced to Los Angeles book dealer and poet Jake Zeitlin by the editor of *Touring Topics* magazine, Phil Townsend Hanna. During this period Connell began an informal series of portrait studies that he termed, "Swell Photographs". These photographs provide one of the few sources of visual documentation concerning a nascent group of Los Angeles intellectuals and artists who embraced the spirit of modernism in literature, painting, photography and the performing arts. (Department of Special Collections, Charles E. Young Research Library, UCLA)

Figure 41.
Will Connell. *Diffusers*. 1931.

This image highlights Connell's lifelong interest in industrial design and demonstrates his increased interest in the formal qualities of the object depicted, lacking any symbolic or allegorical narrative content. (Department of Special Collections, Charles E. Young Research Library, UCLA)

Figure 40.
Will Connell. *Gallantry*. 1928.

Connell's involvement with the Zeitlin group corresponds to a strong sense of experimentation in his work beginning in 1928 as he moves away from the soft focused approach of his earlier photographs. In this image, Connell begins to distance himself from the aesthetics of pictorialism while still retaining the pictorialist affinity for evoking an idealized emotion or state of being. (Department of Special Collections, Charles E. Young Research Library, UCLA)

Figure 46.
Will Connell. *Hollywood Night Life*. 1937.

By 1937, Connell was constructing very dense compositions which required cutting and pasting a number of images together and re-photographing the entire montage. Connell's work in photomontage reached a high level of sophistication in an image depicting the excitement of Hollywood night life commissioned for one of the All-Year Club brochures of the late 1930s. Connell's contributions to All-Year Club publications had traveled from soft focus landscapes to complex montages in less than a decade. (Department of Special Collections, Charles E. Young Research Library, UCLA)

Figure 45.
Will Connell. *Photomontage for Rio Grande Gasoline*. 1937.

Connell was the only photographer on the West Coast to work with photomontage on a sustained basis and to incorporate montage in his commercial assignments. Connell worked with multiple exposures on a single sheet of photographic paper to suggest the flow of action within the confines of a single photograph. (Department of Special Collections, Charles E. Young Research Library, UCLA)

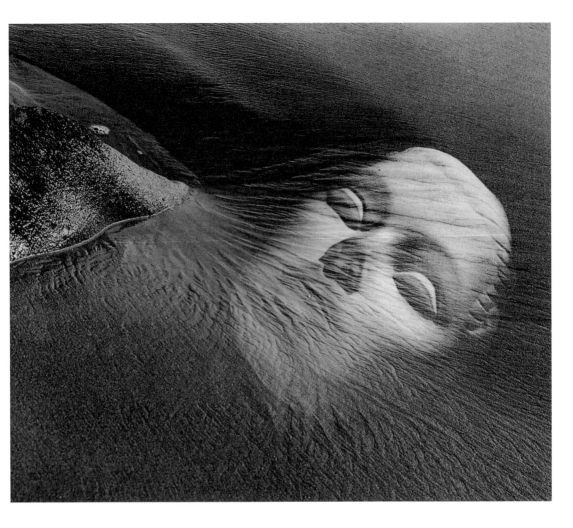

Figure 49.
Art Center Student Project. *Untitled*.
[Multiple Exposure Figure Study]. Circa
1948.

A momentous event in the development
of modern photography in Southern
California was the establishment of the
Art Center School in 1930. Art Center
was the first art school in the United
States to establish a full time curriculum
in photography. The establishment of a
photography department at this date in
Southern California underscored both the
artistic and economic development which
had taken place in the region over the
previous twenty years. (Courtesy Joseph
Bellows Gallery)

Figure 50.
Art Center Student Project. *Untitled*.
[Multiple Exposure with Mask and
Sand]. Circa 1948.

Edward Kiminski was a painter and
designer who had a strong impact on
the photography students at Art Center.
Kaminski pushed students to explore
movement and form through the use of
lighting, camera angles, photo montage
and multiple exposure. Students were
initially expected to explore their
original compositions through charcoal
drawings on paper and then interpret
the sketch using photography. (Private
Collection)

Index

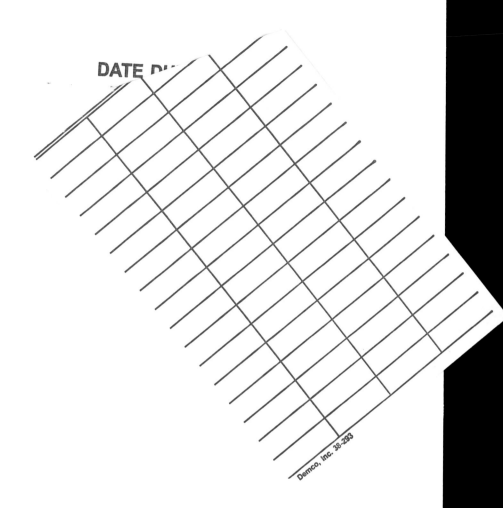

DATE DUE

Demco, Inc. 38-293